RALLY YEARBOOK

1999-2000

p

Toyota was one of the season's most consistent manufacturers with Carlos Sainz and Didier Auriol.Reigning champion Tommi Makinen has been the man to beat in 1999, the finn led the series from the start.
The chinese childrens discovered the world championship rallyes.

RALLY YEARBOOK

1999-2000

Pictures
Pascal Huit

Written by
Stefan L'Hermitte
Philippe Joubin

Translated by
Eric Silbermann

Statistics and results
Severine Huit

ISBN 0-75253-625-7

Jordils Park, Chemin des Jordils 40, CH-1025 St-Sulpice, Suisse. Tél. : (++41 21) 697 14 14. Fax : (++41 21) 697 14 16.

This is a Parragon Book

This edition publised in 2000

Parragon
Queen Street House, 4 Queen Street, Bath BA1 1HE, UK

ERICSSON
MITSUBISHI
OMP

FOREWORD

Hyvä lukija,

Monte Carlosta mieleeni muistuu suomalainen kannattaja, musiikin ja urheilun ystävä, joka oli ottamassa minua vastaan Lucéramin STOPilla soittaen Suomen kansallislaulua trumpetilla. Aivan kuten Colin McRaen säkkipillin soittaja, joka kannustaa meitä erikoiskokeiden lähdössä soitollaan.

Koskahan järjestettäislin muusikkofanien välinen kilpailu ?

Rallin MM-sarjassa on mukana entistä enemmän tiimejä ja sarja Kiinnostaa yhä suurempia katsojajoukkoja. Minua ilahduttaa nähdä enemmän ja enemmän Suomen lippuja reitin varrella eri kisoissa ; jopa toisella puolelia maapalloa.

Mitä siis teen nyt, voitettuani neljännen maailmanmestaruuteni? No mitä luulisitte - tietenkin lähden metsästämään viidettä!

Luotan täydellisesti Ristoon, nuotteihimme, itseeni ja tietenkin autoomme.

Mitsubishin tiimi on aivan poikkeuksellinen ja Mitsulla näette minut myös kaudella 2000.

Nyt edessäni on lyhyt, mutta ansaittu lepotauko, jonka aikana aion kerätä voimia tulevalle kaudelle, juhlin tätä neljättä maailmanmestaruuttani ja vuosisadan vaihtumista. Tehän voisitte käyttää tuon ajan vaikkapa näiden L'Année Rallyes -teoksen loistavien parissa.

Monte Carlo: I remember a Finish supporter, who was both a patriot and a music lover. He was playing the national anthem on a trumpet when I arrived at the final stop at the top of Luceram. It was like when Colin McRae's bagpipe player pipes up at the start of stages to give us a bit of encouragement.

When will we see a contest for musical supporters?

The world rally championship, with even more teams taking part now, attracts a huge crowd of enthusiastic supporters and I am happy to see more and more Finnish flags being waved along the way, even in the Antipodes.

Australia: what will I do now that I have won my fourth title? I will set out in search of a fifth no less!

Always flat out, I have total confidence in Risto, in my notes, in myself and in the way the car behaves.

The Mitsubishi team is really exceptional and I will be with them again for the 2000 season.

I plan on taking a well earned rest after 14 hard fought rallies, with a fourth title to celebrate and a new century to see in. Tiring work! As we wait for the fun to start up again, I would suggest you spend the time looking at the superb images to be found in the pages of the "Rally Yearbook."

See you soon,

Tommi Mäkinen

Valvoline
NESTE
7
MARTINI
Mc Rae
Grist
MICHELIN
45
CITROËN
V-RALLY
17
MICHELIN
20
10
SAFA
Marlboro
Marlboro
Marlboro Safari Rally Kenya WINNER
Marlboro Safari Rally Kenya WINNER
Marlboro Safari Rally Kenya
2
TOYOTA
Marlboro
SAFARI RALLY
24

RALLY YEARBOOK 1999-2000

18

26

SHAKEDOWN

I think I enjoyed this past season's rallying, but I am not absolutely sure. The special stages are more and more often lined with hideous plastic which is there supposedly to protect the public. While it is important to ensure the safety of the spectators, some organisers, like those in Finland for example, have proved it is possible to locate them so that they miss none of the spectacle, but without damaging the personality of the scenery.

It is vital to conserve the image and atmosphere of each rally. We should see the animals in Kenya, the sea and the villages in Greece and Corsica. The backdrop must remain in place.

The retirement of Ove Andersson's team will leave a big void. I will remember for a long time the spectacle of the mechanics in Australia as they desperately tried to revive the engine on Didier Auriol's Corolla. It was probably one of the last great moments of the end of this millennium.

Didier and Denis made us dream. I always hoped the title would come their way and that they would be the first to bring down the great Tommi Makinen. But on the other hand, what an incredible record Tommi has just established and indeed, I hope it will not end there.

After a year of looking and learning, in 2000, the Peugeot team should prove that it can be as good as the best, although it has to be admitted that it is becoming harder and harder to make a mark in rallying. Yet again, 1999 was a good year for the Finns. 2000 should produce some pleasant surprises.

Pascal HUIT

THE AUTHORS

Stefan L'HERMITTE
Chief reporter covering motorised sports for the French magazine, "L'Equipe Magazine." His first involvement was with the African tracks on the Paris-Dakar rally, before discovering the joys of the world rally championship and Formula 1.

Pascal HUIT
has been a rally specialist photographer for as long as he can remember. He could not bear to miss some of his favourites like the Safari or Finland. He always arrives several days before the start, not liking to turn up unprepared. His photographs are published in several magazines and are syndicated all over the world by the Presse Sports/L'Equipe agency.

Philippe JOUBIN
Born in le Mans, just a stone's throw away from one of the most famous tracks in the world. Enthusiastic about old cars and motor sport, he covers the entire world rally championship for the motoring pages of the French daily sports paper, "L'Equipe."

THANKS

The authors would like to thank everyone who has helped them in the production of this book. A special thanks to Tiina Lehmonen, the press offices at Citroën, Ford, Hyundaï, Mitsubishi, Peugeot, Seat, Skoda, Subaru and Toyota, at Castrol, Piero Sodano of the FIA, to Aime Chatard, Andy Pope and Chris Williams of Michelin, Guy Dassonville and all the Pro Canon service team, at the La Comete laboratories (Paris) and Picto (Lyon), as well as Bruno Jouanny of Asia (Lyon). Thanks also to Tommi Makinen for agreeing to write the foreword to this work.

All the pictures of this book were of Pascal Huit, except the pictures "1000 Lakes" 1975, 12.1 page12 and 13.1 page 13 of Reinhard Klein, the picture RAC 1992 page 19 of Les Kolczak.

Toyota, world champions. A giant says farewell

Nothing can stop Tommi Makinen. Even though the competition has never been tougher, the Finn took a fourth consecutive world championship title at the end of a season during which he was dominant, if not crushing. It was an amazing exploit which put in the shade Toyota's efforts in taking the constructors' crown, just before they quit rallying for pastures new. Luckily, Makinen has no such plans.

Punching the air with a gloved hand...

IT IS WELL KNOWN THAT THE FINN is not exactly an exuberant character. It is just coming up to midday in Australia when Tommi Makinen finally gives his car its head and points it towards the finish. A few happy words are exchanged over the radio and the driver "high fives" his co-driver before punching the air with a gloved hand. And that was pretty much it. Tommi Makinen and Risto Mannisenmaki have just taken another title; the fourth in a row for the driver and the second for the co-driver. They are happy, end of story. There are no pompous speeches, no unseemly explosions of misplaced joy. Later, at the Bunnings service area they would be generous in their praise of the Mitsubishi lads and lasses, especially Andrew Cowan and Bernard Lindauer. But it would go no further than that. It has to be said, they had time to see this one coming. When they came to Australia for the penultimate event of the season, the requirements were plain for all to see. To be champion, Makinen had to score four more points than Didier Auriol, the only opponent left in the running. If he did not succeed in this mission, then there would be everything to play for on the Rally of Great Britain, two weeks later. The Mitsubishi driver wanted to avoid this situation at all costs, given his awful past record in the mud and fog of the British Isles. With the Frenchman crashing out of the event, the Finn's task was made much simpler. Finishing third on the Antipodean event did not use up too much of his talent. "Cor! A fourth title. I find it hard to believe," he puffed, his eyes shining brightly at the end of the rally. "Anyway, of all my titles, this was the easiest win."

Juha Kankkunen - Juha Repo: 23 wins. An event

TRUE AND FALSE. This season was intense and chaotic at times. No less than six drivers and five different marques won rallies and there were several changes of fortune, with no one capable of dominating for long. None of that should hide the fact this was Makinen's year. Leading the championship thanks to a win in the opening round in Monte Carlo, he was never headed. Only Didier Auriol came close, matching his points tally on two occasions in the course of the year, after Argentina and China. No other driver seemed capable of posing a threat, even if Makinen was often shadowed by McRae in the early part of the year and then, on occasions, Kankkunen, Burns and only rarely by Sainz.Despite this, the champion did not have an easy time of it. Sure, he got off to a great start with success in Monaco and Sweden, but in Kenya, the winning machine ran off the rails. What with his exclusion for unwanted outside assistance and his teammate Freddy Loix's terrible accident, the equilibrium within the team with three diamonds took a knock. For a long time, too long after that, Makinen had to make do, while dealing with a host of niggles; dodgy brakes here, transmission worries there and so on. But he managed to hang on in there. As for Freddy, he was never really on the pace all season. Maybe he was a victim of circumstance, but if so there were too many circumstances. The young Belgian, who has no doubt lost none of his skill at the wheel which showed so much promise not that long ago, did not improve once he had recovered from his African accident. He began to collect crashes and poor stage times as though they were going out of fashion. It was hard to pinpoint the cause of Loix's woes, but certainly part of the fault lay with a car set up to suit Makinen's driving style. He was not much use to the team, unlike Burns who had played his part in Mitsubishi's first constructors' title in 1998. Loix is in luck however, as the team and especially Marlboro have decided to keep him on for 2000. Lady Luck will not pass the same way twice.

Makinen - Auriol: eternal adversaries

IN FACT, Mitsubishi came close to losing both its jocks. When

the spiral of disillusion and discontent prevented Makinen from shining, he started to make ever stronger contact with Ford on the one hand, Seat on the other and even Peugeot. But force of habit and a perfect understanding of the working of a team pretty much built around him, steered him towards signing on for another two years with the Reds. Then the wins started coming back at a gallop. Success in New Zealand and San Remo, ignoring for a moment the Finland fiasco, gave him renewed confidence. With two more years tied up he was on maximum attack once more.

THIS BAD PATCH for Mitsubishi allowed its rivals to come out to play, with Auriol first out of the blocks. Incredibly consistent, the Frenchman had one of his best seasons as you can judge for yourselves: before he retired on the Australian event, the bald headed wonder had retired just once in twelve rally starts, finishing all eleven events in the points, even picking up the extra bonus points for the final stage. In Corsica as in Finland, he was quickest on this novelty stage idea, snaffling up a handy six points in total. But strange as it may seem, he was the most outspoken opponent of this new system, cursing it even as he won! The only thing Auriol needed was a quicker Toyota. The same could be said for Carlos Sainz, who seemed resigned to his fate this year, not going as well as his team-mate. He could not be faulted for his reliability, but the incredible road holding problems encountered by both men were a constant handicap. Especially as the Corolla appeared to have reached the very limits of its development. One victory all the same and what a win it was, did eventually brighten up the lives of Auriol and Toyota thanks to a great drive in China. The Japanese giant is pulling out, called away by the siren song of Formula 1 and at least it left in style, taking the constructors' championship. The fact it did so, owed little to the intrinsic qualities of the car or to a team which appeared to lack motivation and was often confused and inconsistent. No, it owed it to the quite remarkable consistency and steadiness of its two drivers. Let us hope that, back in Japan, they appreciate the talents of these circus hoop artists.

FORD CERTAINLY had just cause to feel let down by its drivers. After two wins which were as surprising as they were ahead of their time - Kenya then Portugal -the brand new Ford Focus was never again in a position to fight for top honours. Not only did the American car company's baby run into numerous reliability problems, which is acceptable with a brand new car, but on top of that McRae and Radstrom were crashing out of events in ever more violent and spectacular fashion. The English rate McRae as the quickest driver and even that is not a given. However, he seemed to slip back into his crashing ways of old, racking up a spectacular consecutive triple, in China, Sanremo, Australia and Great Britain. Ford could have come out of the season on a much higher note, but McCrash saw to it that they did not! By comparison, Richard Burns can probably now lay claim to the title of quickest Brit. Safe, quick and now experienced too, the young Englishman was on sparkling form once he got used to working with his new team in the early part of the year. He should have won Argentina, but team-mate Kankkunen "nicked" it off him, but his wins in Greece and Australia and his total domination at home on the rally formerly known as RAC were extremely convincing. Perhaps even more remarkable was his second place in Finland. At the tender age of twenty eight he looks like rapidly eclipsing McRae. He will need to learn to harden himself to pressure, after Kankkunen occasionally used him to carve out a more than respectable season. At one point, after his win at home in Finland, the old stager could even have dreamed of an unheard of fifth world championship title. However, partly due to his dislike for tarmac, his performance graph looked a touch too much like the teeth of a saw.

The quite remarkable consistency and steadiness of its two drivers...

NEVERTHELESS, MR. K was one of the most entertaining performers of the year, as indeed were the French teams. First we had the Citroen effect. Guy Frequelin's outfit proved to be capable of achieving something that neither Peugeot nor Renault had managed up until then: namely to win rallies fair and square with a Kit Car. They notched up a memorable double on the roads of Catalunya and Corsica, with Bugalski's name to the fore, although unlucky Puras deserved to have taken victory on at least one occasion. The wins were greeted with gritted teeth by the championship regulars, who took consolation from the fact that brilliant though it was, the kit car's future was now all behind it. By the time of the San Remo, the once impressive Xsaras were no longer a match for the four wheel drive boys, who had made serious progress by then. On top of that, the kit cars would have to carry a heavy weight penalty in 2000 and then have their engine power restricted in 2001. Sadly, despite the success, Citroen's red army would not be allowed to move up the ranks to WRC, as had once been hoped. The remarkable Xsara WRC, which was launched on the day after the team's triumph in Corsica will not be allowed to show what it can do on the rally stages of the world. It is all down to politics apparently. Because the seats are all taken, and in style it has to be said, looking at what Peugeot did this year. Citroen's PSA cousin had an extraordinary half season, learning its way round the world championship. Every time the cars appeared they made progress: Delecour led briefly in Corsica on the tarmac at the car's maiden outing. Gronholm and Delecour then set fastest stage times on the loose in Greece. Gronholm won a leg in Finland. They did the triple at the end of one leg of the San Remo with Panizzi getting all the way to the podium. In 2000, there is little doubt that the 206 and the Ford Focus will be the cars to beat, while the men who will drive them - Delecour, Gronholm and Panizzi on the one hand and McRae and Sainz on the other, have the capability to blow the pack apart. If Auriol can raise Seat's game, if Mitsubishi manages to hold its own with its now "old" Lancer, it looks like a pretty safe bet that the last year of the twentieth century will also be the best year!

Renault "2 litre" world champions. Clever

TOYOTA
TEAM EUROPE
COROLLA
Castrol
MoviStar
MICHELIN
TOYOTA
swissair
Marlboro

the end

After twenty seven years of rallying, an adventure is coming to an end. Toyota will not be present in 2000. The decision to take early retirement was reached at the end of September. Ove Andersson, former Alpine driver, creator of Andersson Motorsport, which metamorphosed into Toyota Team Europe, effectively the competition arm of the Japanese constructor, has been the key figure in this saga. He has seen his creation take 43 wins, three constructors' world championships, the last being the latest 1999 edition and four drivers' titles.

Rallying is now a thing of the past for the team and in the next couple of years, Toyota will make its first tentative steps into the world of Formula 1. "We have the opportunity to take a crack at Formula 1, which is an incredible challenge," explained Andersson. "For all of us working at TTE it is a great once in a lifetime opportunity. In terms of the running and management of a company, I am very proud of this move. However, as a rallyman through and through, I am disappointed. So it is a case of combining joy and sadness."

What better reason therefore than to turn the pages of the photo album with this rallyman, as we look at the great moments of joy and sadness in Toyota's rallying history.

TOYOTA
THE END

12.1
With a Celica and a Corolla Levin in the 1973 RAC Rally, all the Toyota team members and the five service vehicles pose for the family photo.

1975

**Thousand Lakes Rally,
a win for Hannu Mikkola/Asto Aho (Corolla Levin)**

"I had tried to persuade Toyota to become involved in a little team based in Europe. I had in fact led the rally in Finland in a Toyota. My idea was to learn and to put together a team with the European importers. Toyota Finland had contacted me to run this car in the 1000 Lakes and of course I chose Hannu Mikkola. That was how it started. The first Toyota rally win in 1973 (in the USA with Canadian Jack Boyce) had nothing to do with my team."

1980

**Portuguese Rally,
Jean-Luc Therier/Michel Vial (Celica RA 40)**

"It was the start of picking up a few good results for us. In fact, I remember Jean- Luc more for the time we spent together in the Alpine team, a very happy team actually, than for his joining TTE. He was a great guy. One of the most talented I have ever met. In fact in 1980, I had not seen him for a long time. Once Renault stopped, Jean-Luc did not drive very much. We were contesting the French championship with the Toyota importer and as there was a spare seat for Portugal I decided to employ Jean-Luc."

1984

**Safari Rally,
a win for Bjorn Waldegard/Hans Torszelius
(Celica Twincam turbo)**

"It was fantastic, really incredible. It was one of the most important moments of my life. First of all, I had quite a fight with Toyota to persuade them to go to Kenya, as it was Datsun territory. But I knew that up against the four wheel drive cars, from Audi and Peugeot, Africa was the only place we could win. Finally we were given permission. We won in the Ivory Coast the previous year of course, but I really

13.1

13.1

For its rally debut, the Group 4 Celica RA63 finished in the top two places on the 1982 New Zealand Rally, in the hands of Waldegaard and Eklund.

13.2

At the end of 86, Toyota had a Group B car ready to roll when the class was banned. TTE therefore decided to enter the powerful but heavy 3 Liter Supra. Best result in World Championship : L-E Torph 3rd Safari 1987.

13.2

believed we could win the Safari only at our third attempt. Bjorn was remarkable, but it was a win for the entire team. We had a lot of problems. I can remember one mechanic changing the turbo and his arms were getting burnt and there was smoke. Incredible!"

1985

Safari Rally,
a win for Juha Kankkunen/Fred Gallagher
(Celica Twincam turbo)

"To be honest, nobody had expected the win in 1984. But I think our second win in '85 changed our destiny. At first I was a bit angry with Juha, because he was being beaten by Weber. I said to him, "attack" and he replied, "if I attack, I'll go off." He was right: Weber's engine broke and Juha won his first world championship rally. This time the factory realised what we could do. Toyota then gave us more money, more help and more confidence. It was also the making of Juha. We took him on and it helped him progress and that is why our relationship with Juha was so strong and friendly. He went to Peugeot at the end of '85. It was a big disappointment for me, but it was to be expected as Peugeot had so much more to offer him!"

1986

Olympus Rally, Henry Liddon and Björn Waldegard

"For a long time, Henry was like the father to the whole team. He was an artist really. Working out the pre-event plans was not his strong point, but when he was in the plane, directing everything from up there, he could control the whole team. It was incredible. When he had his fatal accident in the Ivory Coast in 1987, it really was a great loss. His replacement found it very difficult to integrate with the team because of Henry's personality and the confidence the guys had in him. We started working together when he was my co-driver in the seventies. When TTE started, he was my co-driver and the team manager as well. His loss was a terrible blow."

1989

Safari, Bjorn Waldegard, Lars Erik Torph and Erwin Weber

"For me, Bjorn was really the African specialist. He loves Africa so much! He did a lot for our team and those victories we got in Kenya. In 1984, at the time of our first win, I remember that, when I arrived in Kenya, I saw him straightaway. Immediately he said to me: "listen Ove, if the rally car is as good as the recce car, we can win!" I burst out laughing telling him not to be stupid. In the final analysis, 50% of what made a win over there was Bjorn. He had such a good understanding of what had to be done; how to stay calm, where to attack, how to manage the rally by being out in front or in the dust at the back."

1990

RAC Rally, a win for Carlos Sainz/Luis Moya (Celica GT-Four/ST165)

"Before the RAC, Carlos already had the championship in the bag after the San Remo rally. The previous year he retired with mechanical failure while in the lead. This time he won. Carlos is in fact the first "modern" driver we worked with. He joined the team and I remember that right from the first test session the mechanics were saying, "this guy is crazy!" He was so determined when he had a problem that he never stopped. The slightest difficulty and he would work like mad to solve it. Carlos helped us a lot to reach a very high level of professionalism with his will to win and his own professional standards. I have a lot of respect for him."

1992

Safari Rally, Markku Alen/Ilkka Kivimaki (Celica GT-Four/ST185)

At this time we had signed an agreement with Markku. In fact, the thing I remember most was his incredible character. He was totally unpredictable. We did the Safari with him and I remember this anecdote. It was the start of the final leg and we were waiting for him. Markku started and then, after a few minutes we heard him say: "the car is stopped." We immediately started asking ourselves what the problem was. Then the mechanics went into the stage with a Land Cruiser and at the very first corner they found Mr. Allen...on his roof! Also, he would never be able to tell us if the car was oversteering or understeering. "Ask my co-driver," he would reply. I swear it's true!"

14.1

On the 1988 Tour of Corsica, Kankkunen and Eriksson gave the first four wheel drive Toyota its debut.

15.1

Toyota at its peak: Kankkunen, Alen, Duncan and Iwase occupy the top four places in the 1993 Safari.

1993

Monte Carlo, a win for Didier Auriol/Bernard Occelli (Celica GT-Four/ST185)

"My most emotional moment with Didier was when he won the Monte Carlo shortly after he joined the team. The last night of the Monte that year, I had honestly never seen anyone drive like that. It was really incredible. His speed, his concentration, his whole manner of tackling the event. He was on another planet to be at that level. The way he caught Delecour was masterful! Exceptional!"

1993

Safari, the TTE

"It is just unbelievable. There were more than 100 people called in just for the Safari. Four cars...with hindsight, it was ridiculous. We had grown a lot at that point and we were still growing. The cost of all this was out of all proportion. We had about three or four helicopters. The way the rules changed to reduce the costs was actually a good thing. But for Japan, the Safari was so important. At the time, we did what a lot of other teams would have done in our position."

1993

Kankkunen/Juha Piironen (Celica GT-Four/ST185)

"Juha had left us at the end of 85 for Peugeot. When we got the four wheel drive Celica, he came back to us. And he was one of the key elements in 89, before he left at the end of 89. In Australia he took the Celica's first world championship win. I was very disappointed when he left and his departure made me very angry. It's true we were having a lot of problems as we were learning about the integral transmission. But the basis was good. Given the feelings I had towards him and what we did, I had expected more in return. He finally came back in 93 and we won the Constructors' championship. Which is why I still have a soft spot for Juha!"

1994

Corsica, a win for Didier Auriol/Bernard Occelli (Celica GT-Four/ST185)

Another magnificent win. Didier is a strange driver; fantastic and very honest. When everything is going well, he is unbeatable, as we saw back in 1994, or more recently in 1999 in fact. I have known him for such a long time and I really appreciate his talents. We enjoy an excellent relationship, even if we are not very close, as we are with Carlos. The team grew up with Carlos. With Didier it is different."

1995

Catalunya, Didier Auriol/Bernard Occelli (Celica GT-Four/ST205)

(NB. After this event, Toyota was excluded)

"This car is....I don't want to talk about it. Please...Then we came back with the Corolla WRC starting in mid 97. Of all the cars we have entered, it will always be my favourite. I always wanted to see a car like this used for rallying. I had asked Toyota since 1972 to rally the Corolla."

1998

Monte Carlo, a win for Carlos Sainz/Luis Moya (Corolla WRC)

"This win, coming after the scandal, not wishing to say any more on the subject, when it had been important to keep the team motivated and ensure that people did not leave, this win with Carlos back with us again, was very important for the entire team. It was very emotional. It was important to have Carlos back at the heart of TTE, but I also think that Carlos wanted to come back. In the end, it was very unfortunate to have missed out on the drivers' crown because of a mistake. He so much wanted an evolution engine, that we fitted it without putting it through sufficient testing. We had done a lot, but honestly not enough. We should have won. It was a big disappointment, especially for Carlos."

16.1
Ove Andersson congratulates Carlos Sainz after his first Toyota win on the 1990 Acropolis.

16.2
Didier Auriol' first visit to Safari put up an impressive performance - 3rd place on the podium -.

16.1

16.2

1999

1999-China, a win for Didier Auriol/Denis Giraudet (Corolla WRC)

"I think we have performed as well as the other teams this year. As I have often said before, I feel we also won in Catalunya and Corsica (NB. Citroen won, but on both occasions, the best WRC car behind the Xsara was a Toyota.) Our win in China was historic. I knew Toyota was on the point of deciding to pull out of rallying, but I felt that this result might help produce a positive decision as to our future in rallying. The relationship between China and the announcement that we were quitting which came one week later, was very emotional. Because I myself was confident. In my mind, the question was whether or not we could continue after the end of 2000, not to stop at the end of 99. I was not expecting that at all."

17.1

17.1

The entire team formed a guard of honour to congratulate Auriol and Giraudet, winners of the first Rally of China.

17.2

The end of the rally programme has left all the members of TTE and its boss in a state of expectation.

17.2

TTE Digest

Toyota was officially entered in rallies since 1972, thanks to the Andersson Motorsport team, which became Toyota Team Europe in 1975. This team, based in Cologne, Germany was bought by Toyota Motor Corporation in 1994. It employs around 300 people of 17 different nationalities.

Since 1972, Toyota has achieved:

43 World Championship wins (the first in the USA in 1973, but not as TTE to the last in China 1999.)

Three Constructors' World Championships: 1993, then 1994 with the Celica GT-Four/ST185 and 1999 with the Corolla WRC.

Four Drivers' World Championships: Sainz (1990 and 1992, Celica GT-Four/ST165) Kankkunen (1993, Celica GT-Four/ST185) and Auriol (1994, Celica GT-Four/ST185)

Toyota also won two European Drivers' Championships with Enrico Bertone (1995) and Armin Schwarz (1996;) an Asia Pacific title (Sainz, 1990) and six Middle East championships (Mohammed Bin Sulayem from 1986 to 1991.

BURNS

FOR

A LONG TIME HE CONFUSED SPEED WITH HASTE AND, WITHOUT MEANING TO, HE WAS APING AN IDOL WHO WENT BY THE NAME OF COLIN MCRAE. BUT YEAR IN, YEAR OUT, GOOD OR BAD, RICHARD WINS. HE HAS THE SPEED OF MCRAE AND THE DETERMINATION OF MAKINEN. THE NEW PRINCE OF WALES IS GROWING UP QUICKLY.

Rally driving is easy isn't it. It is just a matter of getting behind the wheel and taming those wild horses who want to drag you off the side of the mountain if you let them. It is easy, but it is also fun and the big joke in the service areas of England is that Richard Burns went to the same driving school as Colin McRae. Do you find that funny? It is all because the Englishman, like the Scotsman, had a tendency for throwing his car at the scenery in the days when the ink on his driving license was still wet. But joking aside, there is another important similarity between the two fast men of the forests: Richard and Colin are both part of that inner circle of British drivers who have won several world championship rallies. In fact they are the only two in this particular circle. Roger Clark also tasted the spoils of a world championship rally win, but just the once. So Richard Burns is a rare animal indeed and on top of that he is a really nice bloke. Physically, there is something of a cartoon character about him as though brought to life on film. He has a permanent cheeky smile on his face, as though his animator only had one expression in his pencil case. He is cool, kind, open and usually phlegmatic. He is tall and gangly, like a knitting needle, topped off with hair the colour of falling autumn leaves. More than anything, he looks very young; perhaps too young, as though he has skipped school to be with us. One day, while he was on a recce for the Safari, a Masai woman even looked surprised to see him behind the wheel. She thought he wasn't old enough to drive, but by then, he was already on his fourth Safari Rally.

But age is not the important issue. Richard Burns has fallen between two stones on this one. At times he adopted the role of a child prodigy, ahead of his time and at other moments he was a great white hope who looked like never delivering the goods, which is a strange duality to bear. As a lad, Richard was certainly not late and he was already rushing round the circuits before he was old enough to drive on the roads. "I started driving when I was eleven," he recalls. He was a member of the "under 17 club," an organisation run by the parents of children who had already shown some aptitude for driving. At least once a month, the happy kiddies would dash round circuits or airfields, just like grown-ups in grown-up cars. "I remember getting my hands on a Lotus Esprit," he says, the magic of that moment still etched on his face. At 13, he first tasted the heady pleasures of winning. Daddy had not spent his money in vain.

Other benefactors would help Richard the Lionheart on his way towards a brilliant career, including Pentii Airikkala for instance. The great driver lives not far from the Burns family home, as does Vatanen. Richard plucks up the courage and knocks on his door. Pentti would often take Richard along as a co-driver, on the school run to pick up his daughter and the school was quite some distance away. Another one to figure in those early days was David Williams, another good driver, who did great things in a Nissan 240RS and a Metro 6R4. David took a shine to the young lad. He started by giving him tyres and ended up buying him a Peugeot 205. He was on the road to success. Having been crowned British champion on more than once occasion, Burns deserved to be seen on a wider stage. That chance came courtesy of Subaru's David Richards in 1994, who ran a programme for him in the Asia-Pacific championship. However, rather than accelerate his career, it put the brakes on it. Richards did not keep Burns in 1995. He found a good drive with Mitsubishi, a team which did not have a big budget and was looking for young talent with promise. But Burns was in too much of a hurry. "I was too impatient to show what I could do and also too impatient to prove to Subaru that they had made a mistake." He did a very good impersonation of Demolition Man, the well known computer car crash game. It was not a success. He had a big crash in Thailand, he went off the road within the first few hundred metres in Indonesia and salvaged a second place in Malaysia..."I wanted to see just how badly Mitsubishi wanted me," he said with irony.

Mitsubishi is a team with a family environment and Andrew Cowan was convinced that the young son would calm down one day. You cannot learn about speed, but you can learn to use your intelligence. Then, finally, the light appeared at the end of the tunnel in New Zealand in 1996. Admittedly Makinen was out of the running, but nevertheless you had to be running second to pick up the win. New Zealand was not part of the world championship back then, but it was still a noteworthy drive and it was as though something finally clicked.

Then the following year, he finally set a fastest stage time on a world championship rally, in Argentina. The following year, bingo! He won in Kenya; his first success on a world championship rally.

"I stopped getting in a state over nothing," is his analysis of the situation. "My approach to the rallies was different. After all, I've got eyes, arms, a right foot and even a left one, so I have got all it takes to make a car go where I want it to go and not the other way round." All those bodyshop bills with Mitsubishi had finally been honoured and paid in full. As Andrew Cowan said: "he has the makings of a world champion." When he started competing in the world championship, Richard's ambition was to be the best of the second string drivers, but gradually he aimed higher in his ambitions. "I think in terms of pure speed, I am up there with the best. I just need more time. He built up a strong track record, winning the Safari and the RAC in 1998. For next season, the ambitious young man sets off again as the joint number one driver in the Subaru camp, alongside the big man himself, Juha Kankkunen. "I will be fighting for the title," he warns, at the end of a year which brought two wins and a phenomenal second place in Finland. "In testing, he works really methodically and this investment pays off during the rallies," explains David Richards. He is only twenty eight and almost his entire career stretches out before him. And he is already a championship runner up!

1992 RAC Rally
Winner of the Peugeot 205 GTI Cup in 1990 in his first full season of rallying, he took his first steps onto the world stage in his home event at the wheel of a Peugeot 309 GTI. (28th in 1990, 16th in 1991, DNF in 1992.)

1993 RAC Rally
At the age of 22, he became the youngest ever driver to win the British Championship, at the wheel of a Prodrive Subaru. He finished the RAC, held in very difficult snowy conditions in 7th place.

1994 Safari Rally
19th in the championship
Still with David Richards' team, he competed in the Asia-Pacific championship and in a few world championship events. For his first attempt at the Safari, he should have won Group N, but Subaru Japan chose to give the win to local star Patrick Njiru.

1995 RAC Rally
9th in the championship
While Colin McRae took the title for Britain, Richard completed the triumph for Subaru on the RAC Rally, getting his best finish on a world championship event (3rd.) His performance did not go unnoticed.

1996 Rally of Australia
9th in the championship
Having succumbed to the charms of the Mitsubishi team, Richard scored a convincing maiden win (New Zealand, "2-litre".) Despite a few too many crashes, Mitsubishi gave him time to learn his craft.

1997 New Zealand Rally
7th in the championship
For the first time in his career, he set a fastest stage time in Argentina before doing the same in New Zealand. For a while, Richards was also in the lead in Australia.

1998 Safari Rally
6th in the championship
Richard's first world championship rally win came on the difficult terrain of the Safari. But it was actually on the Monte Carlo, Swedish and Finnish rallies that the young Englishman made the biggest impression.

1998 RAC Rally
6th in the championship
He became the third British driver to win his national rally, following the footsteps of Clark and McRae. His win was somewhat overshadowed by the terrible misfortune which befell Carlos Sainz within metres of the finish.

1999 RAC Rally
2nd in the championship
To get away from Tommi Makinen, Richard returned to Prodrive where he had started off. He took three wins (Acropolis, Australia and Great Britain.) For 2000 he and his team are aiming for the title.

DOUBLE AND QUIT

It was a year of mixed fortunes for Citroen. On the one hand it scored two great wins with Philippe Bugalski in Catalunya and Corsica. However, it was not enough to get Citroen a ticket to ride in next year's world championship. It is a great shame that the Xsara WRC will never see a stage, but instead will languish in a museum.

This looked as though it would be the Xsara WRC's final corner. A 90 left on the way to the garage. A last lingering look back at a discrete little Parisian street, not far from the quai du Javel, before the left handed right angle, between a grocers and a small apartment block. There is a grey metal roller door which opens with all the speed of a safe. From there the car would plunge into the darkness, two floors down to an anonymous car park where a few rare Citroens are tucked away. It is a museum of sorts, except there are no visitors here, no commissionaires, but just a little bit of soul. There are even tears of moisture dripping from the roof, as if to add a note of nostalgia. It is a touch on the damp side and many of the cars are covered with a tarpaulin to keep the worst of it at bay.

The Xsara will be in good company, because there are some astonishing pieces in this forbidden underground city. The collection includes a cabriolet Landaulet B2, a four wheel drive 2CV which got to the top of the dunes at Pyla. Strange tracked desert vehicles in yellow, green and black, as well as Mistinguette's favourite car. On the sportier side, there are the DS that first tackled the African terrain and "Mille Pistes" Visas, the agile gazelles of the rocky tracks. A brutish BX 4TC dating from 1986, which was not a well conceived car. A rapid and triumphant rallye raid ZX, which did not leave much for its rivals in the desert.

It is sad to see these cars stopped in their tracks, especially before their time. "Sport is there to serve business, not the other way round," as Guy Frequelin is keen to point out. Competition boss "Freq" is certainly not anti-sport. On the contrary, he has tried everything. "Without getting into the business of internal rivalries," he assures us. For the company that is preventing him from running in the world championship is located in the same place at Velizy and goes by the name of Peugeot. It was a family quarrel, all musical chairs with only one chair for two. It was either Citroen or Peugeot. It was the result of internal politics. The PSA board could envisage no alternative, other than Peugeot and the WRC. But Frequelin, who soon learned it was as important to get round the board as it is to get round corners, found a small slice of the future for the Xsara. Close the grey door to the museum. The Xsara will be back there one day. For now, it will tackle the French championship.

Guy Frequelin, sitting in his Velizy office is only too happy to agree that "a sporting director is only there to apply the decisions taken from on high." Freq is a good soldier, who has learned to take orders, even if one gets the impression that under his gladiatorial exterior, which looks out of place in this day and age, he would like to speak his mind a bit more openly.

At first there were the rally raids. Not exactly an obvious choice, but a continuation: a bit like something you inherit and have to put up with, in order to keep the family name alive. Guy Frequelin, runner up in the 1981 world rally championship, had been recruited by Jean Todt to drive the Peugeots which would leave their yellow mark on the tracks that lead to Dakar. When Peugeot decided to leave it at that and head off to conquer the Le Mans 24 Hours, Citroen inherited the cars and, not wishing to make a fuss, fitted them out with a ZX body shell

CITROËN

While the Bulky Group B BX4TC never did anything special in the World Championship, the Xsara kit-car can be proud of its two wins in the hands of Philippe Bugalski.

and a lick of red paint and set off once again to win. That might be a slightly simplified version of events. But Citroen then came up against a Mitsubishi team which had just hit top form. Pierre Lartigue and the red army notched up 36 wins from 42 starts. Not bad. "We should still have been taking part in rally raids," sighs Frequelin. "But the decision by the Dakar organisers to ban prototypes pushed Citroen out after the 1997 event."

Guy Frequelin therefore returned to his office. He worked at it, studied the situation, came up with a suggestion, but maybe he let his dreams go too far, looking at a programme which required a minimum of around ten million pounds sterling. Because Citroen does not compete just to take part. "The competition is only justified when we win," says Frequelin.

In 1998, Citroen made do with the French championship with the two wheel drive Xsara kit car, winning the title, but only just, as it came up against Simon Jean- Joseph on full strength thanks to a 4x4 Subaru which was just the ticket as, more often than not, the weather was wet enough to give a duck rheumatism.

In 1999, Citroen had an easier time of it in the title chase. Patrick Magaud was even invited to stay at home, as the red team had matters so well in hand. It was left to Philippe Bugalski to get the job done. He certainly surprised the world championship competitors, when their paths converged in Catalunya and Corsica. The rest is history, but it was not enough to gain admittance to the full world championship in 2000. The WRC car, built in the utmost secrecy was therefore stillborn before it had even turned a wheel.

For Citroen's sporting director, it was time once again to don his suit and briefcase and to do a spot of lobbying, which is so much part of the sport. He did not convince FIA to leave the door open to the European championship. However, he did manage to persuade FFSA boss Jacques Regis and a new category was born - the FRC or French Rally Car. The FRC is just like the WRC except in name. On the programme is the entire French rally championship, except when it coincides with the European rally championship, which means the Antibes and Var rallies. On these events, the two wheel drive car will come out to play. It is not easy creating a future for yourself.

Bugalski: "It's a wonderful life"

It was the big surprise of the year. Philippe Bugalski took two wins, in Catalunya first and then in Corsica. It was a double achievement which had a whiff of revenge about it for a driver who has never really been given a fair crack at the world championship. Here we talk to a driver on top of his form.

Philippe, what was it like being back on a podium and looking down on Didier Auriol and Tommi Makinen, who have a few world titles between them?

"It was a big moment; the best in my career to date. On my left was Makinen and his three titles (He has added another one since then) and on my right, Auriol with one title. It was very pleasing. It is fabulous. On top of that, it was completely unexpected and it took some doing. It was a half surprise, but a surprise all the same. We thought we would be quite good. Then, on top of all that, we went and did it again two weeks later in Corsica. A lot of people thought that the stages in Catalunya were perfect for us because the weather was good and it was therefore dry and because the roads are quick and wide and they flow. However, in Corsica, where the roads are much narrower which suited us less well, we did it again."

The four wheel drive teams did not take long to have a few digs at you and to say that you were not playing by the rules; in particular that you had a big advantage in terms of your power to weight ratio.

"The rules are the rules. Fair or unfair, that's the way things are and it is the same for everyone. Citroen exploited it, did a very good job and would have been stupid not to. Today we have the best car on tarmac. Good for us and a shame for everyone else."

Your detractors also pointed out that it is too easy to concentrate on just three events, also suggesting that you were in breach of the recce rules.

"To start with, I have a clear conscience as far as the recces go. I know I did not cheat. On the other hand, even if I did go over the roads twice as much as the others, I would still be a long way back compared with those who are used to competing in the world championship. Let's see how McRae would get on if he came to try his hand in the French championship. It would be even easier for me. Our luck is that we are tackling the French championship on tarmac which is an advantage as a replacement to the extra testing we would do before the world championship events. We are perfectly at home on tarmac."

But would the two wheel drive Xsara have absolutely no chance on the loose?

"Under acceleration, when the power goes through four wheels instead of two, it changes everything. It's a question of the concept."

Are your two wins a sort of revenge for having missed your chances in the world championship?

"Of course I want to prove that I am very quick and that I deserve to be in the world championship. So yes, in some ways it is a form of revenge. But on the other hand, I am 36 years old, I am still at the wheel of a rally car and I am still enjoying myself. My one regret is that I am not going to be taking part in the world championship in a Citroen. I get on perfectly with the team and it has enormous potential."

Did your 1992 experience of the world championship with Lancia work against you in the long run?

"I signed with Lancia at the end of 1991. They were supposed to enter four cars, two with Martini and two with the Jolly Club. And then, all of sudden they decided to pull out two months later. So the programme was not at all as planned. I went from doing six or seven rallies to just three: the Monte Carlo where I finished fifth, Corsica where I was third and as a thank you, I was offered a run in Finland, which is just about the hardest of them all.

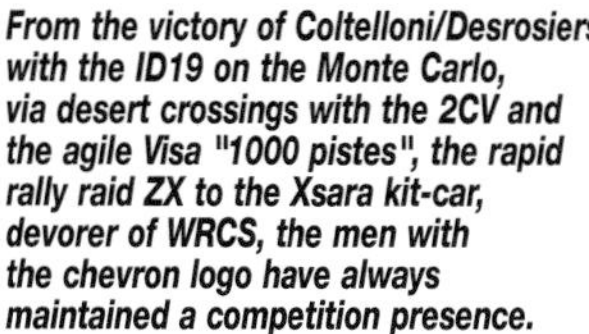

From the victory of Coltelloni/Desrosiers with the ID19 on the Monte Carlo, via desert crossings with the 2CV and the agile Visa "1000 pistes", the rapid rally raid ZX to the Xsara kit-car, devorer of WRCS, the men with the chevron logo have always maintained a competition presence.

"For months we had worked at Citroen's private tracks. They were great times. On top of that it was all secret. Then there was the launch on the day after Corsica..." Philippe Bugalski

Overall, I did not perform too well, but I had a few good stage times for someone who had no experience of the terrain. On top of that I was under orders not to break the car which had to go off somewhere or other for Kankkunen. I was told I would be well rewarded. Then, most of the time I was running on worn tyres. In short it was a poisoned gift. With hindsight, I know I should have pushed a lot harder. There would have been a nine in ten chance of going off, but it might have been better for my career."

But your two wins this season have apparently attracted some offers.

"Well, let's say I've been in touch with some teams. But I have not had a serious offer for the entire world championship. These teams just wanted to know what my plans were, nothing more. The problem with us Latin drivers is we are labelled as tarmac specialists and nothing more. Monte Carlo, Corsica, Spain, the San Remo; that's only four rallies. It doesn't take much for you to retire in the first one, crash in the second and you quickly find yourself in a difficult situation. So I would prefer a full programme. You only have to look at what happened to Simon Jean-Joseph at Ford. If you get it wrong, you are left to find a budget for a car that is less than the best. When you are 23 that is alright, but the older you get the harder it is. Anyway, I have always tried to be loyal. It is better than hopping around and risking hitting rock bottom."

How do you feel when you watch the rallies on television? Jealous, indifferent, sickened, depressed?

"Of course I want to be there. It is such a pleasure to drive a WRC. It is quite easy to drive and it reacts well. In comparison, a kit car is always on a knife edge and it lets go quickly and is not very forgiving. The cars look good and the stages are extraordinary. I know I could be there and I deserve to be. Overall, we are a handful of drivers who are all about equal. Nobody beats you by three seconds per kilometre. Some are there, not for the talent, but more by chance. I am comfortable with that."

Are you surprised that Gilles Panizzi found it difficult to get used to the loose in the world championship?

"Of course he is less comfortable on the loose. I had already noticed that in the French championship, as soon as the conditions get difficult, as soon as you had to improvise, Gilles found it harder than Francois Delecour and myself. It is not easy on gravel."

Where do you find the motivation to run in the French championship against opponents who are not as well equipped as you?

"To start with I want to win rallies and I do win a few. Of course, I am not flat out from start to finish because I have something of an edge. At the start I build up a lead and when it is a minute or two, then I just manage the event. But the advantage over circuit racing is that in a rally anything can happen at any corner: a stone, a puncture, a mud hole. There are all sorts of potential pitfalls. In circuit racing, if you have a one lap lead, it is easier to control the situation. In rallying you are on your own and it is harder to adapt to what the opposition is doing. Of course, in the French championship I cannot give my all to try and win, like I did in Corsica. But whatever the speed, there is still an enormous pleasure to be had at the wheel of a superb car in a fun environment with a wonderful noise from the engine. Then there is also the testing. At the end of the sessions, there is always a moment when I go flat out, to keep my hand in, where I find my reference points and seek out the limits of the car."

When Guy Frequelin told you that Citroen would not compete in the world championship, the roof of the Xsara must have collapsed on top of you.

"For months we had worked at Citroen's private tracks. They were great times. On top of that it was all secret. Then there was the launch on the day after Corsica, where the car ran and worked well without any problems. We were ready for it. Then Guy Frequelin called me into his office to give me the bad news. It all got a bit overwrought suddenly. So much work, such a big investment of time and motivation...."

What do you think of the different measure that have been taken by your management and by the governing bodies that have effectively consigned the Xsara WRC to the garage?

"As for the decision of the PSA group not to have Citroen up against Peugeot in the world championship, I think it was taken by people more intelligent than me. I cannot go against it. However, I am not so sure about the FIA's decisions. First you are allowed in the world championship, but the more the years go by the more you get squeezed and they force your hand and eventually, given the size of the budget needed to run, it forces out constructors who cannot do the whole series. We should be able to run when we like. Having one or two more cars on each rally would make it interesting. Then there is the question of us being ruled out of the European championship. It was an ideal way to give some value to the series, to get used to running on the loose and to be ready in case we could have gone in for the world series. Finally there is the matter of having to run the kit cars with an extra forty kilos in 2000. It's a lot. I think we upset things quite a bit with our wins. Politics ensued. We embarrassed people and they tried to destabilise us. If the weight is not enough then they will put a restrictor on us. They want to keep it for themselves. It is like a landowner who puts a fence around his nice land so that no one can bother him. Maybe our two wins did us more harm than good. But I'm alright. I have a nice life."

Maybe you will have more time to look after your horses.

"With the equestrian centre I bought in June, plus the horses I had behind my house, I now have fifty. I look after them. I get my boots on, I muck out the loose boxes and I put up fences. I act the peasant. I drive the tractor as well, but it could do with a bit of tuning. It gives me something else to think about. But I do not ride too much and I am careful. All dangerous sports are forbidden for me. Horse riding is not one of them, but I prefer to be careful."

Toyota's Ove Andersson had one horse called Auriol and another called Sainz. Do you indulge in anything similar?

"The last foal was born during the Catalunya rally, so what better name than Xsara.

Michelin

...The champions' choice

Michelin's longstanding commitment to world class rallying has been rewarded with victory in both the Drivers' and Manufacturers' championships for the second year running. The successes of Finland's Tommi Makinen and Toyota takes the French company's total score to twenty eight world crowns since the creation of the World Championship in 1973.

More often than not, success in any form of motor sport comes down to the combination of three different parameters- the driver, the car, both chassis and engine and the tyres. However, it is almost impossible to quantify the precise part played by each of these factors.

In the sphere of rallying, as in all the other disciplines in which it competes, Michelin is naturally quite proud to be a part of this triple alliance. Because, while the heat of battle often leads drivers to reach ever higher levels of performance and while the work of the manufacturers leads to an ever spiralling evolution of their cars' potential, it is impossible to disassociate these results from the important contribution made by Michelin and the constant development it applies to its products.

"In such a fiercely disputed championship, nobody can afford to just sit back on their laurels," adds Aime Chatard, the man in charge of the French firm's rallies programme. "In the course of 1999, we brought out a number of new products or significant evolutions of existing products in order to offer a complete and competitive range tailored for the broad range of conditions encountered in a World Championship season. Our determination to keep moving forward and the ongoing optimisation of our range will of course continue in 2000 when we will equip five WRC manufacturers: Ford, Hyundai, Mitsubishi, Peugeot and Skoda. Indeed, our preparations for next year began a long time ago!"

To win in rallying demands a long term commitment and faultless organisation to get to the end of a demanding calendar of events run on all sorts of terrain, which are never the same from one rally to the next. From the Monte Carlo rally in the middle of winter, although not exactly a snow rally, to the Rally of Great Britain, which ends the year and where one can expect variable conditions, the players on the championship stage move constantly from the cold to mild weather, from the Australian winter to the European summer. The roads also change, from tarmac to loose, which can either be smooth or car-breaking.

"To be competitive over a full season therefore demands a close association with a tyre manufacture capable of offering a full range of quality, adapted and technologically-advanced products," underlines four times world champion, Tommi Makinen. "Michelin, the inventor of the ATS system, meets all these criteria, not to mention the enormous effort it puts into the development of new solutions. I have been with Michelin for four years now and I know its products extremely well. The permanent presence of Dominique Bravy, the Michelin technician delegated to work with Mitsubishi, at both testing and on events is another key factor. When we are faced with a difficult choice to make, we discuss everything together. Sometimes he has the ideas, sometimes it's me. But the fact that we have now won four world championships together is a good pointer that our decisions have more often than not been the right ones and that our association works!

Indeed, while the fourteen rounds of the championship follow one another at a devilish pace, with four of the events concentrated in a seven week period from April to June, including the recces, there are also the long test sessions to be taken into account as well. These are aimed at trying out the latest developments in the tyres and checking how they suit the cars. Because, in order to perform well, they have to be perfectly adapted to the characteristics of the different cars which use them.

This is particularly critical on tarmac, where Michelin ruled the roost with three wins from three starts in 1999; in Catalunya, Corsica (wins for Philippe Bugalski and Citroen-Michelin) and San Remo (Makinen, Mitsubishi-Michelin.) Michelin also won every stage on these three events. This was partly due to the Michelin FP tyre - FP standing for "fort potentiel" or strong potential, which made its winning debut thanks

"I have been working with Michelin for four years now and I have a full understanding of their range. The constant presence of Dominique Bravy, the technician delegated to work with Mitsubishi in both testing and on the rallies is an important additional resource. When there is a difficult choice to be made, we always weigh up the pros and cons together. Sometimes I have the good ideas and sometimes it's him. But after four world championships, one can assume we have been right most of the time and that our relationship is efficient!"

Tommi Mäkinen

to Makinen in the 1998 Sanremo. It has left its mark as the tarmac tyre of the world championship.

Another Michelin product made its mark as the tyre of choice for the icy roads of the far north. For the second year running, competitors using the Michelin GE studded tyre monopolised the podium at the end of the Swedish Rally, where Makinen won. Once again, every single fastest stage time fell to the French firm!

On the loose, Michelin enjoyed the satisfaction of winning at least one event with each of its official partners in the 1999 World Rally Championship. They were Ford, thanks to Colin McRae on the Safari and in Portugal; Mitsubishi, with Makinen in New Zealand and Toyota with Didier Auriol's win in China. The latest version of the "dirt" tyres were joined during the season by a new product, the Michelin ZE, slightly narrower, with a more open tread pattern. It was very effective on harder surfaces.

Mud naturally played a part in deciding the outcome of some events, most notably in New Zealand and China. In both cases, judicious use of the Michelin WB allowed Tommi Makinen and Didier Auriol respectively to build their success at these crucial stages of the championship year.

But the full story of their adventures, as well as Toyota-Michelin's conquest of the constructor's title in the year they took their bow from the world rally stage, is well covered elsewhere in these pages.

Michelin and the 1999 World Rally Championship

The year in figures

28 The number of world titles (14 drivers, 14 manufacturers) won by Michelin since the creation of the World Championship in 1973 (Drivers' championship created in 1979).

9 The number of wins by Michelin's partners in 1999. On all types of terrain: ice/snow (Monte Carlo, Sweden), dry asphalt (Catalunya, Corsica, Sanremo), smooth gravel (Portugal, New Zealand), rough gravel (Safari) and mud (China).

6 The number of all-Michelin podiums in 1999. Including one 1-2-3-4-5-6 result (Corsica), two 1-2-3-4-5s (Safari, Sanremo), two 1-2-3-4s (Sweden, Catalunya) and one 1-2-3 (Portugal)!

29 The number of podium finishes obtained by Michelin's partners in 1999. From a possible total of 42 (14 rounds x 3).

PAI
FER
MITSUBISHI
Marlboro
MoviStar by maxon
PIRELLI
DARK DOG

EVERYONE HAD THEIR CHANCE, BUT SOME
MADE BETTER USE OF IT THAN OTHERS

Ford
Focus WRC

7. Colin McRae

IDENTITY CARD

- Nationality: *British*
- Date of birth: *5 August 1968*
- Place of birth: *Larnak (Scotland)*
- Resident: *Scotland, Monaco*
- Marital Status: *Married, 1 daughter*
- Hobbies: *Water-skiing, motocross*
- Co-driver: **Nicky Grist** *(British)*

CAREER

- First Rally: 1986
- Number of Rallies: 87
- Number of Victories: 18

1992 - 8th in championship
1993 - 5th in championship
1994 - 4th in championship
1995 - WORLD CHAMPION
1996 - 2th in championship
1997 - 2th in championship
1998 - 3th in championship
1999 - 6th in championship

It really looked as if Colin McRae was on his way back. Look how he started the season, with a new car that wasn't officially legal, but which certainly worried the competition. That form was confirmed two rallies later, on the rough roads of Kenya and again in Portugal. He showed considerable maturity, particularly on the Safari. It looked like he was going to be the man of the year, the only driver to challenge the one driver that he considers to be a rival: Makinen. And then nothing. The slightly egocentric aura with which he surrounds himself began to crumble. The Ford was promising, but it failed to live up to that promise. And McRae, the best paid rally driver ever, had only his bank balance to console him. Once again, he suffered the magnetic attraction of the demons at the side of the road. While the season up to Portugal was fantastic, thereafter it was equally disastrous. The points scores were one zero after another. Quick, give him a car that stays on the road.

8. Thomas Radstrom

IDENTITY CARD

- Nationality: *Swedish*
- Date of birth: *22 January 1966*
- Place of birth: *Vannas (Sweden)*
- Resident: *Umea (Sweden)*
- Marital Status: *Single*
- Co-driver: **Fred Gallagher** *(British)* Gunnar Barth *(Swedish)*

CAREER

- First Rally: 1989
- Number of Rallies: 27
- Number of Victories: 0

1996 - 15th in championship
1997 - 13th in championship
1998 - 19th in championship
1999 - 10th in championship

Remember the Acropolis rally, a few years ago, a fluorescent Toyota, well off the road? It's an image that has remained in people's minds. Thomas Radstrom was then making a name for himself in the World Championship. Time has passed, and the image might have faded. But the intrepid Radstrom still goes off, a lot. People forgive him because of his bespectacled studiousness and his chubby baby-face. And one must never forget that it isn't easy to drive a rally car quickly. But Thomas is paid to stay on the road. He has a very specific contract with Ford which means that he tackles only gravel events. But he hasn't really fulfilled expectations. He shined at home in Sweden, which is almost normal. He scored again on his return to Argentina. But then there was a succession of zero points scores. Australia was typical: he was in the points with no one pushing him, no one tantalisingly ahead. All he had to do was finish and he didn't. Sixth in Britain was a more suitable season-closer.

Ford
Focus WRC

8. Simon Jean-Joseph

IDENTITY CARD

- Nationality: *French*
- Date of birth: *9 June 1969*
- Place of birth: *Fort de France (Martinique)*
- Resident: *Fort de France (Martinique)*
- Marital Status: *Married, 3 childrens*
- Co-driver: **Fred Gallagher** *(British)*

CAREER

- First Rally: 1993
- Number of Rallies: 7
- Number of Victories: 0

1999 – No Classified

Just a word of warning: if Ford boss Malcolm Wilson wants to take a holiday in the sun, he would be well advised not to go to the French West Indies. People don't like to be made fun of there. And they don't feel that their favourite rallying son, Simon Jean-Joseph, was well treated by Ford. OK, we'll ignore the racist jokes from some of the more idiotic mechanics. It's some of the other things that have been surprising. Why employ a tarmac specialist to back up Colin McRae and then give him no chance, or almost no chance, to prove what he can do? Even worse, it has stalled a career which has scarcely begun. Simon was certainly naive enough to have faith in the marketing and financial pressures which had helped get him the drive. He thought he could prove himself in the events themselves, demonstrating the talent that he had shown in the French championship, and transposing that to the World events. But Malcolm Wilson thought otherwise. Jean-Joseph was scarcely given the opportunity to test. He did just three events, none of them with his regular co-driver. And that was it: bye-bye. What a waste!

8. Petter Solberg

IDENTITY CARD

- Nationality: *Norwegian*
- Date of birth: *18 November 1974*
- Place of birth: *Spydeberg (Norway)*
- Resident: *Norway*
- Marital Status: *Single*
- Co-driver: **Fred Gallagher** *(British)* Phil Mills *(British)*

CAREER

- First Rally: 1988
- Number of Rallies: 7
- Number of Victories: 0

1999 -18th in championship

Norway may not be thought of as being equal to its neighbour, the rallying capital of the world, Finland, but it has, at least, produced a new talent in Petter Solberg. His team leader, Malcolm Wilson, shows particular interest in Solberg and not just in the short term. He has a long term contract with Ford. For that reason, the driver himself is able quietly to obey team orders, certain of his future and under no pressure. But to be honest, Solberg hasn't produced much in the way of results so far. We will have to wait and see for him to fulfill his promise. As one of his rivals put it, "he's a hope for the future but one may have to wait a long time." Ford, however, is more positive. Malcolm Wilson even sang his praises after the Portuguese Rally where Solberg never really shone, happy to finish in eleventh place, 12 minutes behind the winner. "I simply wanted him to finish," said Wilson, "even in 20th place, as long as he finished." He will also have to show some pace one day.

Mitsubishi

Lancer Evolution VI

1. Tommi Mäkinen

IDENTITY CARD

- Nationality: *Finnish*
- Date of birth: *26 June 1964*
- Place of birth: *Puuppola (Finland)*
- Resident: *Puuppola, Monaco*
- Marital Status: *Married*
- Children: *1 son (Henry)*
- Hobbies: *golf, skiing, hiking*
- Co-driver: Risto Mannisenmaki *(Finnish)*

CAREER

- First Rally: 1987
- Number of Rallies: 83
- Number of Victories: 19

1990 - 20th in championship
1991 - 29th in championship
1993 - 10th in championship
1994 - 10th in championship
1995 - 5th in championship
1996 - **WORLD CHAMPION**
1997 - **WORLD CHAMPION**
1998 - **WORLD CHAMPION**
1999 - **WORLD CHAMPION**

Is Tommi Makinen simply the greatest rally driver ever? At the relatively tender age of 35, he has almost done everything one can with a steering wheel in one's hands, and one's feet on the pedals. His compatriot and friend, Juha Kankkunen, held the record for the great number of World Championship titles, four, but in winning his fourth, Tommi has gone one better because his have shown just how much he has dominated the sport by being consecutive. He had dreamt of winning the Monte Carlo rally, because without a win on that famous rally, his career couldn't really be complete. But he won that at the start of the year. So what does he dream of now? Retirement could beckon in a couple of year's time, but in the meantime, there is the feat of winning every rally in the championship at least once. Corsica, the Acropolis, New Zealand and Great Britain are among those that he hasn't yet won. It's quite a challenge, and it would be a great success for the man from Puuppola, a little village in the middle of Finland. Maybe that's why Tommi has remained the same since he first drove a car: simple, quiet, calm. He's just happier than ever!

8. Freddy Loix

IDENTITY CARD

- Nationality: *Belgian*
- Date of birth: *10 November 1970*
- Place of birth: *Tongres (Belgium)*
- Resident: *Millen (Belgium)*
- Marital Status: *Single*
- Hobbies: *Squash, mountain-bike*
- Co-driver: **Sven Smeets** *(Belgian)*

CAREER

- First Rally: 1993
- Number of Rallies: 36
- Number of Victories: 0

1996 - 8th in championship
1997 - 9th in championship
1998 - 8th in championship
1999 - 8th in championship

They call him Fast Freddy. He's the chosen son of a whole country, from Ypres to Brussels, which loves motor sport but which doesn't really have the background in the sport to promote that many drivers. The powerful Toyota team chose him to be their protege thanks to his speed and ability to adapt. He then found financial support from a cigarette company which invested a lot in his blossoming career. Freddy began his World Championship campaign in 1993, initially learning before intending to head for greater things. But six years and 30 or so top level rallies later and we're still waiting; Loix has yet to win. He's a nice, easy-going, amusing guy, so everyone wants him to win. But once again, there was a severe setback this year, his very nasty accident on the Safari. But then it's probably also a disadvantage competing in the same team but in the shadow of such a master as Makinen. They say that the Mitsubishi is totally set up for the Finn, particularly the differentials. And we know that Makinen left foot brakes, while Loix prefers to brake with his right foot. Furthermore, thanks to the Kenya accident, but perhaps also for financial reasons, Freddy missed a number of important tests. But these are excuses and they don't exact improve Freddy's record.

Mitsubishi
Carisma GT

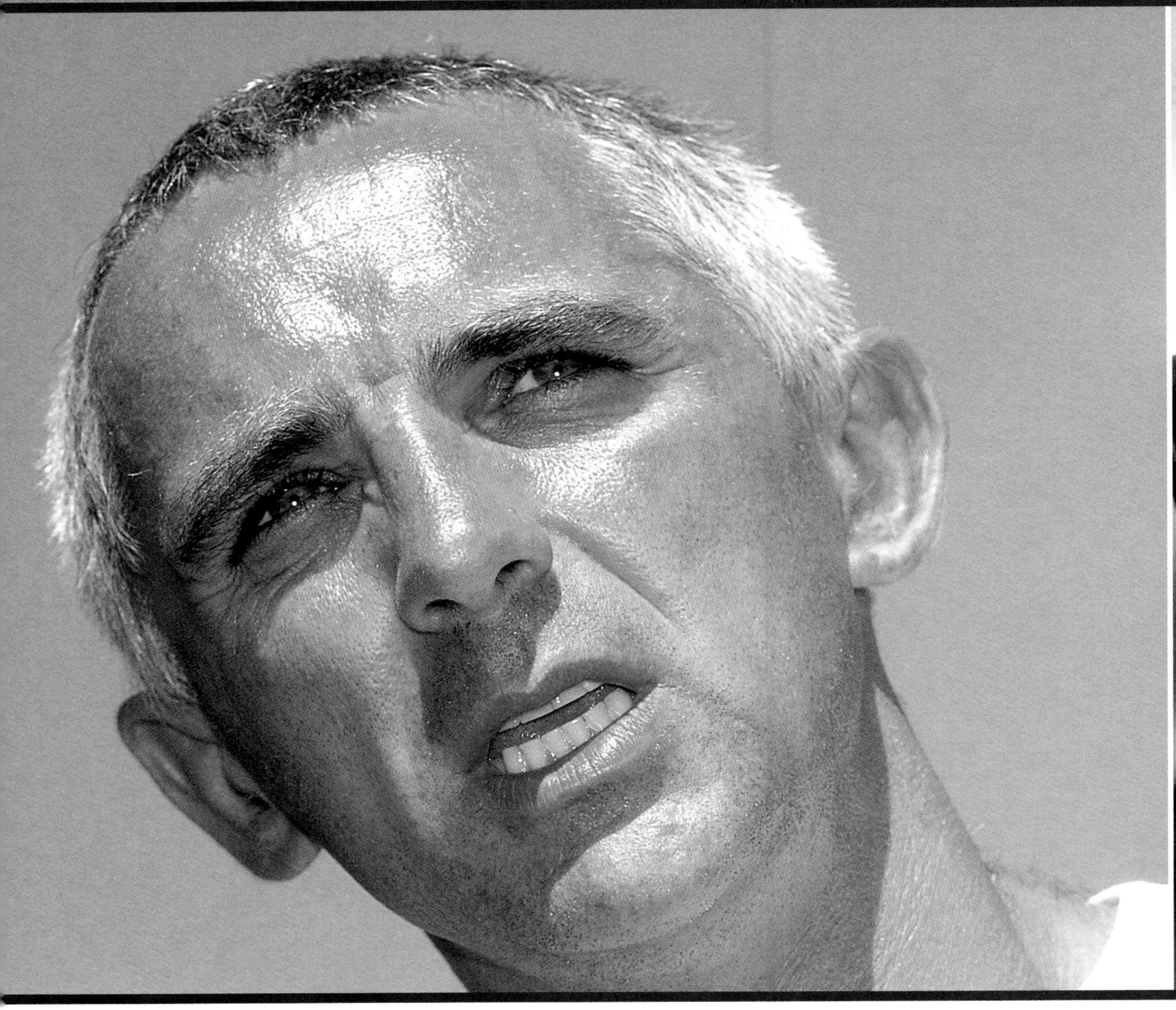

Peugeot

206 WRC

14. François Delecour

IDENTITY CARD

- Nationality: *French*
- Date of birth: *30 August 1962*
- Place of birth: *Cassel (France)*
- Resident: *Plan de la Tour (France)*
- Marital Status: *Single*
- Children: *2 (Anne-Lise, Gabriel)*
- Hobbies: *Jet-ski, mountain-bike*
- Co-driver: **Daniel Grataloup** *(French)*

CAREER

- First Rally: 1984
- Number of Rallies: 58
- Number of Victories: 4

1991 - 7th in championship
1992 - 6th in championship
1993 - 2nd in championship
1994 - 8th in championship
1995 - 4th in championship
1997 - 17th in championship
1998 - 10th in championship
1999 - 16th in championship

Perhaps Francois Delecour is condemned because he once made the wrong choice of car. Maybe it's because he went for the promising Ford Escort rather than signing a contract, going for a familiar, competitive car rather than a contract with Subaru. According to David Richards, who was offering the contract, "he would perhaps be World Champion," if he'd made the right choice. But he didn't, and there's no point dwelling on the fact. After all, perhaps that's what drives him on, the spirit of revenge. He's a rebel, a fighter who needs the spirit of adversity to spur him on. And he needs other things to perform at his best: he has to feel good, be wanted, liked. That's why he's only driven for two big teams: Ford and Peugeot. And he doesn't forgive those who have let him down. Add to that a certain propensity to tell the truth, all of it and one begins to realise why, in a world where diplomacy is important to one's career, Francois has been left on the sidelines from time to time. But Peugeot was on the look-out for someone, first of all for the French championship and then the World series and the two made an ideal pairing. When the road is unknown and wet, then Delecour is unbeatable. It was no mistake to hire him.

15. Marcus Gronholm

IDENTITY CARD

- Nationality: *Finnish*
- Date of birth: *5 February1968*
- Place of birth: *Espoo (Finland)*
- Resident: *Inkoo (Finland)*
- Marital Status: *Married*
- Children: *3 (Jessica, Johanna et Niclas)*
- Hobbies: -
- Co-driver: **Timo Rautiainen** *(Finnish)*

CAREER

- First Rally: 1989
- Number of Rallies: 29
- Number of Victories: 0

1996 -10th in championship
1997 -12nd in championship
1998 -16th in championship
1999 -15th in championship

There's a tempting comparison to be made that Marcus Gronholm is to the Peugeot 206 what Ari Vatanen was to the 205. That's not quite the full story. Vatanen might not have been well known in France, but he had already won the World Championship when he drove for Peugeot. Even so, Jean Todt was proud of his Finn. Similarly, Jean-Pierre Nicolas sings the praises of his Finn too. And he's not the only one. His teammates and competitors also speak highly of the great Marcus, not least because he has rapidly become part of the big family organisation that is the Peugeot team, into which he has easily integrated his lanky body. But also because he has proved, behind the steering wheel, to have an easy-going attitude that reveals talent. History relates that he scored the first points for the 206 over his native bumps, but he starred on the unfamiliar roads of the San Remo on a terrain he was discovering pretty much for the first time. He was the last left on the market, but Nicolas was more than happy to have signed him up. Well played.

Peugeot

206 WRC

15. Gilles Panizzi

IDENTITY CARD

- Nationality: *French*
- Date of birth: *19 September 1975*
- Place of birth: *Roquebrune Cap Martin (France)*
- Resident: *Monaco*
- Marital Status: *Married*
- Co-driver: **Hervé Panizzi** *(French)*

CAREER

- First Rally: 1990
- Number of Rallies: 16
- Number of Victories: 0

1997 - 9th in championship
1998 - 12th in championship
1999 – 10th in championship

He's like Zebedee, on his pogo stick: an uncatchable character who is everywhere at once. Fortunately the belts keep Gilles Panizzi firmly in his driving seat. He's a man in a hurry, ready to do anything he can to prove that he's an ace behind the wheel, as he swiftly ascends the heights of competition. He's afraid of no one, that's his strength. Doubts? What doubts? Jean-Pierre Nicolas won't easily forget the persistence of the unknown Panizzi, who had graduated through various Peugeot scholarship schemes and who endlessly telephoned to persuade the Peugeot boss to give him a works drive. This was when they were running two wheel drive 306s in the French championship. Panizzi rewarded him with two national titles. The next step was the World series. Gilles began by showing that he could easily adapt to four wheel drive, proving himself in a privateer Subaru on the Monte Carlo. He went on to confirm that performance on tarmac in Corsica and on the San Remo where he narrowly failed to win. Gravel remains a problem. His drive in Finland wasn't impressive but when one wants to succeed, one can and Gilles wants to very badly.

Seat

Cordoba WRC

9. Harri Rovanpera

IDENTITY CARD

- Nationality: *Finnish*
- Date of birth: *8 April 1966*
- Place of birth: *Jyvaskyla (Finland)*
- Resident: *Jyvaskyla (Finland)*
- Marital Status: *Married*
- Co-driver: **Risto Pietilainen** *(Finnish)*

CAREER

- First Rally: 1993
- Number of Rallies: 39
- Number of Victories: 0

1998 - 13th in championship
1999 - 9th in championship

Yet another Finnbut perhaps one who isn't on the right route. Harri Rovanpera was born in Jyvaskyla, home of the 1000 Lakes rally. It's where most of the promising Finns come from. And Harri seemed to be heading for stardom. He did really well in the two litre Seat in the two wheel drive championship, even if they were being beaten by the four wheel drive cars, and the Peugeot 306s and Citroen Xsaras when they appeared. But Harri was investing his future with a manufacturer who was making its marque in the championship and wanted to go to the top. Harri joined them but when it's all come down to it, Harri hasn't met Sally, or found success. There was a point in the Safari to begin with, two in Finland and in China and then lots of zeros. Apart from the points statistics, he had the disagreeable experience to be beaten by Liatti on gravel and nearly always beaten by Gardemeister. Furthermore, Seat criticised him for not developing the car. Harri nearly always seemed happy with his equipment, and spoke little. He vindicated himself somewhat at the end of the season, particularly on the Network Q, but by that stage it was too late.

10. Toni Gardemeister

IDENTITY CARD

- Nationality: *Finnish*
- Date of birth: *31 March 1975*
- Place of birth: *Kouvola (Finland)*
- Resident: *Finland*
- Marital Status: *Single*
- Co-driver: **Paavo Lukander** *(Finnish)*

CAREER

- First Rally: 1997
- Number of Rallies: 16
- Number of Victories: 0

1999 - 10th in championship

Seat
Cordoba WRC

He was hugely proud to be on the third step of the rostrum in New Zealand. It was a great picture. Above him were two of the old school, Tommi Makinen and Juha Kankkunen who were just as proud of the youngster. Of course, they had nationality in common. It's quite rare to have three drivers of the same nationality on the rostrum. But this was confirming an entire graduation system. Drivers in Finland try to get on together, not hinder one another's progress. It's very positive: I've profited from it, I'm going to help others profit from it. Running the system is former rally driver Mr Joukhi. He advises, helps, manages and positions, with the utmost modesty. Joukhi isn't alone, because there's an element of self-help in this graduation system from the drivers themselves, who contribute to the pyramid. Kankkunen and Makinen and have never been greedy, of course, but when you ask them about the system, they avoid answering. It's like helping a needy parent. But the results are there. Kankkunen is approaching retirement, Makinen is halfway through his career and Gardemeister is the latest graduate. One day he will be on the top step of the rostrum, with other young Finns beneath him.

10. Piero Liatti

IDENTITY CARD

- Nationality: *Italian*
- Date of birth: *7 May 1962*
- Place of birth: *Biella (Italia)*
- Resident: *Monaco, Biella(Italia)*
- Marital Status: *Married, 1 daughter (Lucrezia)*
- Hobbies: *skiing, motorbikes, mountain bike*
- Co-driver: **Carlo Cassina** *(Italian)*

CAREER

- First Rally: 1985
- Number of Rallies: 43
- Number of Victories: 1

1992 - 11th in championship
1993 - 26th in championship
1995 - 8th in championship
1996 - 5th in championship
1997 - 6th in championship
1998 - 7th in championship
1999 - 22nd in championship

Piero Liatti sometimes appears to be a bit of a day dreamer. There's always something which prevents life from being rosy. And when that happens, Piero clams up, forgets the few words of English he knows, smiles wistfully at questions and disappears inside his shell. That's the way his Subaru career ended, a drive engineered by Pirelli. And it's the same way that things ended with Seat. It all started so well. Piero smiled and looked happy. He got on well with his French engineer Benoit Bagur. But results weren't forthcoming. The Cordobas made progress, but not enough to challenge, say, the Subarus. Piero began to resent the fact. Communication ground to a halt. Bagur complained, Liatti replied, saying that he asked for modifications but they were refused. It was stalemate. While teammate Gardemeister did his best and scored the odd point here and there, Liatti looked miserable. The Italian seemed to have lost whatever it was that had made him so quick on the Monte Carlo, or the San Remo. Will he ever find it again?

Skoda

Octavia WRC

11. Armin Schwarz

IDENTITY CARD

- Nationality: *German*
- Date of birth: *16 July 1963*
- Place of birth: *Oberreichenbach (Germany)*
- Resident: *Monaco*
- Marital Status: *Single*
- Hobbies: *Sports and music*
- Co-driver: **Manfred Hiemer** *(German)*

CAREER

- First Rally: 1988
- Number of Rallies: 56
- Number of Victories: 1

1991 - 6th in championship
1994 - 7th in championship
1995 - Exclued (Toyota)
1997 - 8th in championship
1999 - No classified

Armin Schwarz is engaging person, constantly on the move. He goes off regularly, seemingly into the abyss of obscurity and then all of a sudden, yoohoo, there he is again. This time he re-emerged with Skoda, with whom he had found a drive. It's not exactly the best or even a well-funded team. In fact the cars probably lose a second per kilometer in comparison to the best, and that's not easy to make up. It certainly isn't like the good old days at Toyota where he enjoyed the odd competitive spell which allowed him to win the occasional rally. But Armin likes to drive although perhaps occasionally he tries to compensate for the lack of power by braking too late, with dire results. His comment, beside a wet road on the Sanremo, was perhaps the quote of the year: "my car is too wide for the road." And what he was suggesting happened; he went off, again. But let's point out that taking part in a partial programme doesn't strengthen either development or confidence. Skoda's three points in Greece and Great Britain were great reward for perseverance, but then it's always an uphill struggle for this brave team.

12. Emil Triner

IDENTITY CARD

- Nationality: *Czech*
- Date of birth: *15 March 1961*
- Place of birth: *Touzim (Czech Republic)*
- Resident: *Semcice (Czech Republic)*
- Marital Status: *Married*
- Children: *2*
- Hobbies: *Cycling, Motorsport*
- Co-driver: **Milos Hulka** *(Czech)*

CAREER

- First Rally: 1993
- Number of Rallies: 32
- Number of Victories: 0

1999 – No classified

He's known as Yul to his friends, because his surname rhymes with that of a famous American actor. But Yul, the driver, doesn't contribute a lot to the action. He doesn't speak English, rarely puts in a stunning performance and doesn't have a particularly exciting personality. But Emil - his real name - is Czeck, which is why he drives for Skoda. The brave, persevering team wanted a national driver. When they were battling over two litre honours, there were two of them, Emil Triner and Pavel Sibera. But they realised that to gain good results, they had to offer their drives to foreigners and first of all, Pavel Sibera found himself out of a drive. Triner, then, had to prove himself in the four wheel drive Octavia. It wasn't easy. Emil tried, but there were many obstacles to overcome: the lack of a rallying or even automobile culture in Checkoslovkia, the limited budget, the limited schedule, which didn't include ever event - they all worked against Emil. It's not certain whether he will keep his place in the team next year. The future of the former European two litre champion is in doubt.

Skoda
Octavia WRC

Subaru
Impreza WRC

5. Richard Burns

IDENTITY CARD

- Nationality: *British*
- Date of birth: *17 January 1971*
- Place of birth: *Reading (England)*
- Resident: *Reading (England)*
- Marital Status: *Single*
- Hobbies: *motorbikes, mountain-bike*
- Co-driver: **Robert Reid** *(British)*

CAREER

- First Rally: 1990
- Number of Rallies: 48
- Number of Victories: 5

1994 - 19th in championship
1995 - 9th in championship
1996 - 9th in championship
1997 - 7th in championship
1998 - 6th in championship
1999 - 2th in championship

He took a while to win in the World Championship. The first victory was the Safari in 1998 and that day, he remarked "they say that the first win is always the most difficult." To that, Phil Short of the Mitsubishi team added that "I think this is the first of quite a few." So how many more have followed, two years on? There was victory later that year in Britain and then the Acropolis, Australia and Britain again this year. To this record one should add Argentina, where teammate Kankkunen was scarcely fair. So there's no doubt that Richard Burns, Richard the Lionheart, really has arrived. "He has what it takes to be World Champion," said team boss Andrew Cowan. So now Richard is coming of age. He spent a long time learning without saying anything, but listening, observing and copying, while being perfectly polite and friendly. But then he began to take the initiative, daring to go for different settings on his car to Tommi Makinen. "Rallying teaches you humility," he admitted. He learned quickly and well. And now that Subaru is giving him more and more independence, he should blossom even more.

6. Juha Kankkunen

IDENTITY CARD

- Nationality: *Finnish*
- Date of birth: *2 April 1959*
- Place of birth: *Laukaa (Finland)*
- Resident: *Laukaa*
- Marital Status: *Married, 1 son (Tino)*
- Hobbies: *Golf*
- Co-driver: **Juha Repo** *(Finnish)*

CAREER

- First Rally: 1979
- Number of Rallies: 140
- Number of Victories: 23

1983 - 16th in championship
1984 - 24th in championship
1985 - 5th in championship
1986 - WORLD CHAMPION
1987 - WORLD CHAMPION
1989 - 3th in championship
1990 - 3th in championship
1991 - WORLD CHAMPION
1992 - 2th in championship
1993 - WORLD CHAMPION
1994 - 3th in championship
1995 - Exclued (Toyota)
1996 - 7th in championship
1997 - 4th in championship
1998 - 4th in championship
1999 - 4th in championship

Subaru
Impreza WRC

You can scarcely do better than Juha Kankkunen. Does he remember all his victories, all 20 or so of them? Having left Ford at the end of last season, and for no great reason, the great Juha bounced back magnificently by signing with Subaru for a few dollars more. Dave Richards, deprived of his number Colin McRae, was delighted that the Finn would be taking up the challenge. And Juha duly did exactly that, by winning in Argentina and then Finland. There was some doubt about the former victory, as he failed to understand team orders and allow teammate Richard Burns to win, or was he just remembering the similar incident in Indonesia with his then teammate Carlos Sainz a few years ago? He is still totally unflappable, still demanding, in vain, a cigar lighter to improve the creature comforts in his car. Life is comfortable. He enjoys his victories, plays golf when he wants and still precedes Sainz in the all-time winners league. So why should he go and do anything else?

11. Bruno Thiry

IDENTITY CARD

- Nationality: *Belgian*
- Date of birth: *8 October 1962*
- Place of birth: *Saint-Vith (Belgium)*
- Resident: *Les Awirs (Belgium)*
- Marital Status: *Married*
- Children: *2 sons (Adrien, Mathieu)*
- Hobbies: *Cycling, mountain bike*
- Co-driver: **Stéphane Prévot** *(Belgian)*

CAREER

- First Rally: 1989
- Number of Rallies: 53
- Number of Victories: 0

1992 - 16th in championship
1993 - 17th in championship
1994 - 5th in championship
1995 - 6th in championship
1996 - 6th in championship
1998 - 9th in championship
1999 - 10th in championship

What if Bruno Thiry had won the Tour de Corse a few years again, until he was robbed of victory? Would it have changed the career of the young Belgian? Because since then, he has been searching for that past. It's a shame, because as he nears 40 years of age, he's beginning to run out of time. He's too nice. Witness the way that he stood by and watched as Ford scuppered his plans so that Carlos Sainz could win. Now Thiry's future is in the balance. He didn't do much at Ford, nor at Subaru even though they appreciated his performances on tarmac. But his car seemed to attract the gremlins like a mobile lightning conductor. But team owners and sponsors don't appreciate bad luck. He won two points on the Monte Carlo, another in Portugal, but this was poor, particularly in comparison to his teammates. He paid dearly for these results by being sent on his way before the end of the season, but a lifebelt in the form of the Skoda and a fourth place in Britain may have given him another chance.

Toyota
Corolla WRC

3. Carlos Sainz

IDENTITY CARD

- Nationality: *Spanish*
- Date of birth: *12 April 1962*
- Place of birth: *Spain*
- Resident: *Madrid (Spain)*
- Marital Status: *Married*
- Children: *3 (Bianca, Carlos, Ana)*
- Hobbies: *Football, squash, tennis*
- Co-driver: **Luis Moya** *(Spanish)*

CAREER

- First Rally: 1987
- Number of Rallies: 123
- Number of Victories: 22

1988 - 11th in championship
1989 - 8th in championship
1990 - **WORLD CHAMPION**
1991 - 2th in championship
1992 - **WORLD CHAMPION**
1993 - 8th in championship
1994 - 2th in championship
1995 - 2th in championship
1996 - 3th in championship
1997 - 3th in championship
1998 - 2th in championship
1999 - 4th in championship

Statistics can be cruel. Carlos Sainz won four World Championship events in 1990, 1991 and 1992. He won two in 1995, 1997 and 1998, plus one or two here and there elsewhere. But whether they've been good years or bad years, Carlos has won. The only poor season before this one was 1993 - and this year was a lot like that one. So what had happened to the proud Spaniard who Francois Delecour nicknames 'His Excellency?' Is he a little demotivated, driving a Corolla when he remembers so well the dominant Celica? Have his reactions been dulled by age? He's not the type to explain. He remains demanding, fastidious, more than ever a master tactician. But Carlos Sainz has played only a supporting role this year, rarely disputing victory apart from with Makinen in Sweden. He could have retired when Toyota pulled out but he's decided to join Ford. So don't forget: Carlos may have not have been so quick this year, but he's still a knight of the sport, a giant. He was still battling with Kankkunen over who would win the most number of rallies this century. One poor season doesn't obliterate a dazzling career; he's still brilliant.

4. Didier Auriol

IDENTITY CARD

- Nationality: *French*
- Date of birth: *18 August 1958*
- Place of birth: *Montpellier (France)*
- Resident: *Millau (France)*
- Marital Status: *Married*
- Children: *2 (Robin, Diane)*
- Hobbies: *Golf, mountain bike*
- Co-driver: **Denis Giraudet** *(French)*

CAREER

- First Rally: 1984
- Number of Rallies: 108
- Number of Victories: 19

1988 - 6th in championship
1989 - 4th in championship
1990 - 2th in championship
1991 - 3th in championship
1992 - 3th in championship
1993 - 3th in championship
1994 - WORLD CHAMPION
1995 - Exclued (Toyota)
1996 - 25th in championship
1997 - 11th in championship
1998 - 5th in championship
1999 - 3th in championship

Didier Auriol might look like a man ready to retire, but then looks can deceive. He may be bald, on the wrong side of 40, with a nice country house in the South of France where he can watch the setting sun from the comfort of his balcony. But his career is very far from waning. And once again he proved it this year. He's become a self-styled spokesman for the drivers on safety and when the sporting balance is threatened. But as a competitor, as a former World Champion, he is still very much a force to be reckoned with when he's in tune with his car. He never gives up, always pushes. Take his win in China; "when he drives like that, he's unbeatable," said one resigned rival. He's regularly been ahead of his teammate Carlos Sainz, who tends to be regarded as the benchmark by the whole sport. And don't forget that Didier was Tommi Makinen's principal championship rival throughout the year, only demoted to third in the series in the very last event of the year.

Toyota
Corolla WRC

Scrutineering

	FORD FOCUS WRC	MITSUBISHI LANCER EV.VI	PEUGEOT 206 WRC
Technical Specification			
ENGINE			
TYPE	4 cylinders, 16 valves	4 cylinders, 16 valves, DOHC	4 cylinders in-line, 16 valves
BORE X STROKE	84,8 x 88 mm	85,0 x 88,0 mm	85,0 x 88,0 mm
CAPACITY	1988 cm3	1997 cm3	1997,5 cm3
TURBO	Garrett	Mitsubishi	Garrett - Allied Signal
MAX. POWER	300 bhp	300 bhp @ 6000 rpm	300 bhp
MAX. TORQUE	55 kg/m @ 4000 rpm	52 kg/m @ 3500 rpm	53,5 kg/m @ 3500 rpm
TRANSMISSION			
TYPE	Permanent 4-wheel drive	Permanent 4-wheel drive	Permanent 4-wheel drive
GEARBOX	6-speed sequential	6-speed sequential (INVECS)	6-speed sequential
SUSPENSION			
FRONT	Mc Pherson strut	Independent - Mc Pherson struts with helicoidal springs	Mc Pherson strut
REAR	Mc Pherson strut	Independent with pull rods and helicoidal springs	Mc Pherson strut
DAMPERS	Reiger	Ohlins	Peugeot
STEERING	Power-assisted rack and pinion	Power-assisted rack	Power-assisted rack
BRAKES	Ventilated discs, with 4 piston calipers (Front) - 4 pistons (Rear) with 8 piston calipers (Front) - 4 pistons (Rear)	Front - Ventilated discs with 6 piston calipers Rear - Ventilated discs with 4 piston calipers	Ventilated discs with 4 piston calipers
TYRES	Michelin	Michelin	Michelin
DIMENSIONS			
LENGTH	4152 mm	4350 mm	4005 mm
WIDTH	1770 mm	1770 mm	1770 mm
HEIGHT	1425 mm	-	1370 mm
WEIGHT	1230 kg	-	-
WHEELBASE	2635 mm	2510 mm	2468 mm
FRONT/REAR TRACK	1550 mm/1550 mm	1510 mm/1505 mm	1510 mm/1505 mm

POSITION
World championship for manufacturers
** 2 Litre*

FORD

1973 ...... 3th	1985 ...... 11th	1997 ...... 2th
1974 ...... 3th	1986 ...... 5th	1998 ...... 4th
1975 ...... 6th	1987 ...... 5th	1999 ...... 4th
1976 ...... 3th	1988 ...... 2th	
1977 ...... 2th	1989 ...... 13th	
1978 ...... 2th	1990 ...... 8th	
1979 ...... 1st	1991 ...... 4th	
1980 ...... 3th	1992 ...... 3th	
1981 ...... 3th	1993 ...... 2th	
1982 ...... 4th	1994 ...... 3th	
1983 ...... -	1995 ...... 3th	
1984 ...... 12th	1996 ...... 3th	

MITSUBISHI

1973 ...... 3th	198 ...... 14th	1996 ...... 2th
1973 ...... 16th	1985 ...... -	1997 ...... 3th
1974 ...... 11th	1986 ...... -	1998 ...... **1st**
1975 ...... 11th	1987 ...... -	1999 ...... 3th
1976 ...... 10th	1988 ...... 14th	
1977 ...... 10th	1989 ...... 4th	
1978 ...... 13th	1990 ...... 3th	
1979 ...... 13th	1991 ...... 3th	
1980 ...... 15th	1992 ...... 5th	
1981 ...... 14th	1993 ...... 5th	
1982 ...... 8th	1994 ...... -	
1983 ...... 16th	1995 ...... 2th	

PEUGEOT

1973 ...... 3th	1984 ...... 3th
1973 ...... 15th	1985 ...... **1st**
1974 ...... 13th	1986 ...... **1st**
1975 ...... 5th	1987 ...... -
1976 ...... 8th	1988 ...... 10th
1977 ...... 13th	1993* 3th
1978 ...... 8th	1994* 5th
1979 ...... 11th	1995* 1st
1980 ...... 8th	1996* 4th
1981 ...... 9th	1997* 3th
1982 ...... -	1998* 2th
1983 ...... 10th	1999 ...... 6th

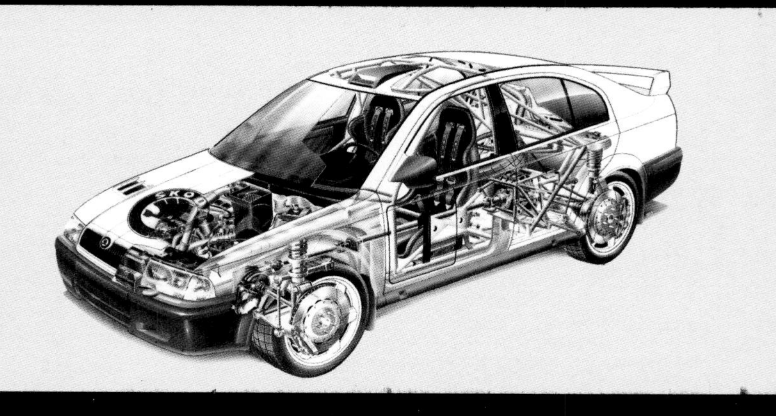

Technical Specification	**SEAT** CORDOBA WRC	**SKODA** OCTAVIA WRC	**SUBARU** IMPREZA WRC
ENGINE			
TYPE	4 cylinders, 16 valves	4 cylinders, 20 valves	Flat-4
BORE X STROKE	83 x 92,1	82,5 x 93,5 mm	92,0 x 75,0 mm
CAPACITY	1995 cm3	1999 cm3	1994 cm3
TURBO	Garett	Garrett	IHI
MAX. POWER	300 bhp @ 5300 rpm	296 bhp @ 6000 rpm	300 bhp @ 5500 rpm
MAX. TORQUE	48 kg/m	50,1 kg/m @ 3250 rpm	48 kg/m @ 4000 rpm
TRANSMISSION			
TYPE	Permanent 4-wheel drive	Permanent 4-wheel drive	Permanent 4-wheel drive
GEARBOX	6-speed sequential (INVECS)	6-speed sequential	Manual/semi automatic 6 speed (PRODRIVE)
SUSPENSION			
FRONT	Mc Pherson strut	Mc Pherson strut /Proflex	Mc Pherson strut
REAR	Mc Pherson strut	Mc Pherson strut /Proflex	Mc Pherson strut with longitudinal and transverse arms
DAMPERS	Ohlins	Proflex	Bilstein
STEERING	Power-assisted	Power-assisted rack	Power-assisted rack and pinion
BRAKES	Front - Ventilated discs, Asphalt Rear - Ventilated discs	Ventilated discs	Ventilated discs with 4 piston calipers Ventilated discs with 4 piston calipers
TYRES	Pirelli	Michelin	Pirelli
DIMENSIONS			
LENGTH	4150 mm	4511 mm	4340 mm
WIDTH	1770 mm	1770 mm	1770 mm
HEIGHT	1500	1429 mm	1390 mm
WEIGHT	1230	1240 Kg	1230 kg
WHEELBASE	2443 mm	2512 mm	2520 mm
FRONT/REAR TRACK	1520 mm/1520 mm	1580 mm/1576 mm	1590 mm/1590 mm

POSITION **World championship for manufacturers** ** 2 Litre*	SEAT	SKODA	SUBARU
	1977.......14th 1993*.....12th 1994*.....10th 1995*....4th 1996*....1st 1997*....1st 1998*....1st 1999 .....5th	1993*......2th 1994*......1st 1995*......3th 1996*......3th 1997*......2th 1999 ....7th	1983......7th 1984......9th 1985......12th 1986......8th 1987......10th 1988......9th 1989......12th 1990......4th 1991......6th 1992......4th 1993......3th 1994......2th 1995......**1st** 1996......**1st** 1997......**1st** 1998......3th 1999......2th

Scrutineering

Technical Specification	**TOYOTA** COROLLA WRC	**HYUNDAI** COUPE EV.2	**RENAULT** MEGANE MAXI
ENGINE			
TYPE	4 cylinders in line,16 valves DOHC	4 cylinders, 16 valves	4 cylinders, 16 valves
BORE X STROKE	85,44 x 86 mm	82 x 93,5 mm	84 x 90 mm
CAPACITY	1972,3 cm3	1998 cm3	1995 cm3
TURBO	Toyota, CT20	265 bhp	280 bhp
MAX. POWER	300 bhp @ 5700 rpm		25,8 kg/m @ 5900 rpm
MAX. TORQUE	51 kg/m @ 4000 rpm		
TRANSMISSION			
TYPE	Permanent 4-wheel drive		
GEARBOX	6-speed sequential	6-speed sequential	6-speed sequential
SUSPENSION			
FRONT	Mc Pherson strut	Mc Pherson strut /Proflex	Mc Pherson strut /Proflex
REAR	Mc Pherson strut	Mc Pherson strut	Mc Pherson strut
DAMPERS	Ohlins		
STEERING	Power-assisted		
BRAKES	Front - Ventilated discs Rear - Ventilated discs	Gravel - Ventilated discs with 4 piston calipers (Front) – Discs with 4 piston calipers (Rear) Asphalt - Ventilated discs with 6 piston calipers (Front) – Discs with 4 piston calipers (Rear)	Front - Ventilated discs with 12 piston calipers Rear - Ventilated discs with 2 piston calipers
TYRES	Michelin	Michelin	Michelin
DIMENSIONS			
LENGTH	4100 mm	4340 mm	3952 mm
WIDTH	1770 mm	1770 mm	1832 mm
HEIGHT	1365 mm	1313 mm	1313 mm
WEIGHT	1230 kg	995 kg	960 kg
WHEELBASE	2465 mm	2475 mm	2492 mm
FRONT/REAR TRACK	1564 mm/1556 mm	1465 mm/1450 mm	1606 mm/1608 mm

POSITION
World championship for manufacturers
** 2 Litre*

TOYOTA			HYUNDAI	RENAULT
1973 ......9th	1985 ......5th	1997 ......-	1996* 7th	1993* 6th
1974 ......4th	1986 ......6th	1998 ......2th	1997* 6th	1994* 3th
1975 ......7th	1987 ......7th	1999 ......**1st**	1998* 5th	1995* 2th
1976 ......6th	1988 ......5th		1999* 2th	1996* 2th
1977 ......5th	1989 ......2th			1997* 4th
1978 ......6th	1990 ......2th			1998* 4th
1979 ......5th	1991 ......2th			1999* 1st
1980 ......7th	1992 ......2th			
1981 ......8th	1993 ......**1st**			
1982 ......5th	1994 ......**1st**			
1983 ......6th	1995 ......-			
1984 ......4th	1996 ......-			

WORLD CHAMPIONSHIP RALLIES

1999

“A drunken night-time rodeo

ride...”

MONTE-CARLO

He was born in Finland, the land of forests and dirt tracks where champions are hewn from the trees, but for most of the year he now lives in Monaco, along wth so many other aces of the steering wheel who want to look after their money and reputation. So Makinen really did win his home event and a very important step so early in the season. But a neighbour called Gilles Panizzi gave him the odd headache, even taking the lead briefly. Sadly the two drivers were duelling with unequal equipment. A private entrant battling against a works car was never really going to pull off the miracle.

48.1

48.1
The Ford Focus WRC made a spectacular entrance in the hands of Colin McRae.

48.2
Still under the guidance of former driver Lasse Lampi, Tommi Makinen was on the right and icy road.

48.3
Harri Rovanpera took the Seat Cordoba WRC to its first ever stage win.

48.2

48.3

"If we are going to have to face up to them this season, then the sooner we kno

One has principles in the Principality. Forget to feed the meter and a little butterfly lands on your windscreen, which unfolds its wings to reveal an envelope. A polite note invites the culprit to place his forgotten five francs inside, which is not what one finds in neighbouring countries. The old-style ACM shares these customs and in its gentleman club lounges, its eminent members fight against FIA's modern ways of running a rally. They find the modern events banal and aseptic but, polite and law abiding they bow to the current format, at least on the surface. Because if you look at the first 48 kilometres of stages you will not find a single "Mickey Mouse" run designed for the benefit of the television cameras. The Monegasque organisers play by the book, but still sail pretty close to the wind. "It's a real Monte Carlo," analysed Panizzi. The old hands noticed that the Plan de Vitrolles-Faye which offered no respite, included a famous corner where Sainz and Aghini got it all wrong in 1993. As though out of respect for an era beloved of nostalgia freaks, two or three course openers, including Kankkunen's decided to visit the undergrowth at that point as the road was like a skating rink. It was by and large quite enough to warn the acrobats in the 1999 Monte. It was about to start all over again.

The image was straight out of 1993, with two openers stuck and damaged as though thrown down a ravine after a night of drunken rodeo riding. On top of that, we had the Toyotas of Sainz and Auriol. "When Denis said ice, I reacted too late," said the Frenchman. Others followed, although Sainz managed to keep going, with his bonnet grinning broadly and obscuring the driver's vision. Eight kilometres further on and the Toyota shot off the right side of the road, taking a telegraph pole with it. "To be honest, it's difficult to start a rally with such a long stage," cursed Sainz. "You have not got a rhythm going, you are not warmed up and you have not got your eye in yet. "A little bit luckier and less bothered was Auriol in the other Corolla, who enlisted the help of some strong armed men who ensured he did not spend the winter there. He even made it to the end of the stage, but with a 5 minute penalty. The final count was 14 retirements, including eleven crashes, notably Mitsubishi newboy Loix, who got it wrong on a bridge and holed the radiator. "I had to drop my wheels in the snow and the car got away from me," said the Belgian. Others avoided the ultimate penalty but left huge amounts of time up on the stage, such as McRae who was 3m20 down, as much for technical reasons as for weather related problems, Burns (4m 25.9) and Jean- Joseph (9m 23.5.) It wasn't quite Napoleon's retreat from Moscow as his cavalry officers only had one horsepower, but it looked like it. It was action-packed rallying, epic rallying, the rallying of legend. All the more so because, through no fault of the stage, by the end of the first kilometre, four top cars had their names really or as good as wiped from the time sheet. The night before, a road section accounted for two Skoda Octavia WCRs when the engine mapping failed; before the start ramp for Schwarz and hardly much further for Sibera, who went out at La Turbie. As for the two Ford Focus of McRae and Jean-Joseph they were ploughing along merrily, even if already excluded because of an illegal water pump. Should they have been allowed to start, knowing the inevitable penalty awaited them. "As far as I'm concerned," reckoned Makinen, "if we are going to go up against them this season then the sooner we know what they are like, the better." Quite so.

This meant there were plenty of egos as bruised as the bodywork after the opening stage. Almost alone in his serenity was Buster Makinen. His only contretemps came when a group of spectators got in his line of sight as he approached a service point and his Mitsu kissed a little wall, forcing his mechanics to change the bumper and front light cluster. The next morning came the real start and the Finn played the perfect balancing act. He decided to risk running without studs on a road which was hesitating between melting snow and thick soup. He judged it perfectly and Panizzi was a surprising second in his private Subaru Impreza, already 37.5s down. Panizzi had not finished yet and, constantly jiggling about with his springs but tightly strapped in, three stages later, he took the lead of a rally which Makinen already seemed to have in the bag. It was undoubtedly a worthy performance from the Frenchman, even if he was helped a bit by a warped brake disc slowing the Finn just when there was no service allowed between SS4 and SS5. Makinen did some DIY twiddling, dumping the disc and carried on as best he could. But he lost the lead. Panizzi was not spared either. He went a touch too far when ditch hooking but found some burly lads to put him back on course quickly enough to keep the lead by 5.9s; enough to dream anyway.

Panizzi is not the sort to have doubts and he was in confident mood..a little bit, but not that much. "I was there to learn and gain experience," he reminded his audience. Driving a WRC, choosing tyres, containing a multiple world champion and giving the factory cars a pasting as a privateer was too much. Gilles, who drives with his heart, threw in a few errors. It was too good to last. In SS6, the Subaru was still living the dream, keeping the Mitsubishi 50s down. It was a fire on ice display. Between Sisteron and Thoard, Makinen was on a piece of road he likes and goes well on when the mood takes him. Thanks to a good choice of tyre he closed the gap. Between Entrevaux and Saint-Pierre, Panizzi began to feel the pressure and spun, stalled and gave in. In the Turini, there was more of the same, when Panizzi was in trouble from snow thrown on the road by spectators who were hungry for incidents. "It didn't make the difference," admitted Panizzi with honesty. "He (Makinen) would have got me by at least thirty seconds." Back in Monaco, Panizzi lost touch with Makinen who was now 1m 45.6s ahead and he was beginning to catch worrying glimpses of Kankkunen in his mirrors. Further back, much further back, McRae, Delecour, Thiry and Auriol were tussling for the points scoring places.

The last day was actually just a morning, run over stages previously visited and there would be no heroics this time round. Panizzi was the unfortunate hero and if his talent had deserted him, so had his luck. His ice note crew missed a patch of black ice, hidden by a spectator's car and Panizzi paid for it with a couple of high speed rolls which led to retirement. It was unfair, but it meant Makinen could allow himself the odd spin with over two minutes in Kankkunen. The four times world champion took it easy and running along as though he was on a pleasant drive in his Subaru which seemed to fit him like a glove. "For an old man like me, it feels like a Rolls with its nice heater. Maybe it could do with a stereo system and a cigar lighter." Kankkunen has never won at Monaco, but he was nearly always in the points, as he was this time and very happy about it he was too. "This was one of the hardest Monte

hat they are worth the better." Tommi Makinen

Carlos I have known. Normally there are one or two stages which are hard to deal with because of changing conditions, the other being either dry or snow covered. But this time the conditions changed all the time. It wasn't easy."
Behind Makinen, who had what he described as "a dream start to the championship came a contented Kankkunen who did not have to worry too much about his pursuers. However, behind him it was a four-way shoot-out over the Turini. Delecour, McRae, Thiry and Auriol were crammed so tight together they looked like high flyers at a charity ball where everyone wants to be in the photo of do-gooders. There was a major bottleneck with just twelve seconds between them. Delecour was the least well equipped in a set up that reminded him of his early days: not enough tyres, not enough hands and not enough ice crews. He could therefore do nothing against McRae, then against his better off French rival Auriol. He thought he would have to give best to Thiry as well, but the Belgian had walked under too many ladders recently and a slow puncture in the final leg saw to his chances. However, the rally was not yet over, even if the cars were all in parc ferme. McRae and his illegal Focus would be disqualified, a decision confirmed on 1st February. This meant that Liatti, who had finished seventh, was promoted to sixth and a worthy point for Seat, who had made a good start to their first full season. Their joy was complete thanks to Rovanpera, who gave the marque its first ever stage fastest time. "We worked non-stop all winter for this," said Jaime Puig, the team's giant of a sporting director. "When the guys had too much work on, they never left it to the next day, but simply ordered pizza to keep them going." Then, rounding off this far from clear classification, Delecour and Thiry, who were not "nominated" by Ford and Subaru therefore were ineligible for constructors' points, although they could score on their own account. It was about as complicated as trying to get out of Monaco in the rush hour. By the time FIA simplifies it all, the cars will have six wheels.

FORD ON FORM ALREADY. It is always tempting to play with the times. What if we took away McRae's messed up times from the first two stages, just to see. 4m 16.4s compares with the 3m 16.8s which finally separated him from Makinen. It is clear that McRae could have won and indeed with four to his name, he won more stages than anyone else. But apart from brushing aside the problems of the first two stages, Ford would have had to brush aside the concerns of the FIA. Because the first diagnosis of its representative Jacques Berger would have to be confirmed by the Appeal Court of the FIA on 1st February. The accusation was that "a water pump which did not conform to the regulations had been relocated." Ford's extenuating circumstance was that "The Ford Motor Company Ltd. had no intention of doing anything illegal." For a moment it looked as though Ford had returned to the bad old days when it was often the laughing stock of the rally "paddock." But since Martin Whitaker had taken the reins of the American giant's competition operations, the laughing days had gone. The inefficient civil service of the Boreham department had been put to rest. Whitaker had copied the other teams by appointing an external preparation company, run by former Ford driver Malcolm Wilson. Ford had switched to commando tactics. At first, Wilson had hoped to stay put in his isolated little workshops near Carlisle, on the borders with Scotland. But a few words from old friend David Richards soon convinced him he had to move to motor sport's Silicone Valley to the north west of London. But it was not only the working practices and the place of work which changed.
Ford when for the best available driver and certainly paid through the nose for the privilege as McRae had pocketed an annual stipend of around three million pounds to stick in his sporran. As for the car, the venerable and outdated Escort made way for the fun and up-to-the-minute Focus. And from the good old glory days, Martini was back as a rally car sponsor with the level headed former mechanic Gunther Steiner as team manager All this meant Whitaker could afford to aim high. "We are entering a new era," he intoned. If proof was needed as to the new level of commitment, a miracle ensued which meant the new Focus was ready in time to line up on the start ramp for the Monte Carlo rally. The project only got the green light in December 1997. Just one year later, Malcolm Wilson had hung up his boss's suit and dug out some old racing overalls to test the little toy himself. It was clear, after just ten weeks of testing, that the Focus was damn quick and capable of getting to the very top step of the podium. McRae had not risked leaving Subaru for nothing: "it's more than we could have hoped for." It seemed that the huge Focus advertising campaign was about to get some serious validation.

DELECOUR GETS THE MAX FROM THE MIN. François Delecour has always been the sort to relish a challenge; to take on the big guns with a pea shooter; to go on a raid behind enemy lines. He like a situation where the man is more important than the machine, where the heart rules the wallet and a quick-fix overcomes strategic planning. In the past, he had regretted not making it to the start of his favourite rally, so Delecour was prepared to make all sorts of sacrifices to be there this time. While waiting for his 206 WRC to materialise, he took what he could find; in this case a Ford, prepared by First Willy Collignon and a small team of mechanics who bust a gut to get the job done. Gilles Panizzi, never one to let reality interrupt his dreams, even saw Delecour as a potential winner or almost. "François is Mr. Monte Carlo. It is always him against one or other, Delecour-Auriol or Delecour-Sainz or Delecour- McRae. He doesn't have factory levels of support, but he can be right up there. François certainly gave it his best shot: "it's a shame I lost so much time in the first one." Reality would kick in giving him more modest ambitions. His note maker, Pascal Enjolras in an ancient Sierra with 200,000 on the clock, broke down. The lack of info meant that he used all his old cunning to take a leap in the dark and borrow the Toyota choices. "No way could I count on the factory Fords to lend a hand." He was not surprised, but he was upset all the same. François is hungry to win, hungry for revenge on destiny, on himself and on the others. He wants to get back on track after two errors; one in a road traffic accident at a badly marked crossroads in the north of France and the other, when it came to choosing the team which should have given him the world title (Ford rather than Subaru.)
Delecour would not take a second Monte win to go with his 1994 victory. Although the man himself always reckons there was the one that got away under questionable circumstances, when the trophy went to Auriol, the team's main man at the time. He would however get to the finish as usual: eleven finishes from twelve starts. "Fourth isn't so bad," he said. "Anyway, it's something new, because I've never finished fourth." Delecour was back.

MONTE-CARLO

"A drunken night-time rodeo ride..."

50.1

Best of the best, Colin McRae was pleasantly surprised by the performance of the brand new Focus WRC..

50.2

Like many others, Didier Auriol lost any chance of victory right from the very start of the rally.

50.3 - 51.1

Tommi Makinen achieved his first target for the 1999 season, winning the Monte Carlo Rally.

50.4

The Ford Focus was thrown out of the final classification after it was deemed to have an illegal water pump.

50.1

50.2

50.3

50.4

51.1

51.2

51.2
Although outwardly similar, the Impreza WRC hid all sorts of interesting changes.

51.3
At the wheel of a private Subaru, Gilles Panizzi was the only one to challenge Makinen's domination.

51.4
It came as no surprise to find Makinen and Kankkunen, the two most experienced men in the field, occupying the first two places.

51.5
A slight knock and orders to keep it steady, prevented Simon Jean-Joseph from featuring in the top ten.

51.3

51.5

67TH MONTE-CARLO RALLY

TOP ENTRIES

1 Tommi Makinen - Risto Mannisenmaki
MITSUBISHI LANCER EV.6

2 Freddy Loix - Sven Smeets
MITSUBISHI CARISMA GT

3 Carlos Sainz - Luis Moya
TOYOTA COROLLA WRC

4 Didier Auriol - Denis Giraudet
TOYOTA COROLLA WRC

5 Richard Burns - Robert Reid
SUBARU IMPREZA WRC

6 Juha Kankkunen - Juha Repo
SUBARU IMPREZA WRC

7 Colin McRae - Nicky Grist
FORD FOCUS WRC

8 Armin Schwarz - Manfred Hiemer
SKODA OCTAVIA WRC

9 Harri Rovanpera - Risto Pietilainen
SEAT CORDOBA WRC

10 Piero Liatti - Carlo Cassina
SEAT CORDOBA WRC

11 Simon Jean-Joseph - Fred Gallagher
FORD FOCUS WRC

12 Pavel Sibera - Petr Gross
SKODA OCTAVIA WRC

16 Bruno Thiry - Stephane Prevot
SUBARU IMPREZA WRC

17 Gilles Panizzi - Herve Panizzi
SUBARU IMPREZA WRC

18 Gustavo Trelles - Martin Christie
MITSUBISHI LANCER EV.5

19 François Delecour - Dominique Savignoni
FORD ESCORT WRC

20 Isolde Holderied - Catherine François
TOYOTA COROLLA WRC

21 Henrik Lundgaard - Freddy Pedersen
TOYOTA COROLLA WRC

22 Andrea Dallavilla - Danilo Fappani
SUBARU IMPREZA WRC

23 Philippe Bugalski - Jean-Paul Chiaroni
CITROEN SAXO KIT CAR

24 Toni Gardemeister - Paavo Lukander
SEAT IBIZA KIT CAR

25 Jesus Puras - Marc Marti
CITROEN SAXO KIT CAR

26 Manfred Stohl - Peter Muller
MITSUBISHI LANCER EV.5

27 Marc Duez - Philippe Dupuy
MITSUBISHI CARISMA EV.5

28 Luis Climent - Alex Romani
MITSUBISHI CARISMA EV.5

62 Yves Loubet - Bruno Brissart
MITSUBISHI LANCER EV.5

87 Jurgen Barth - Claude Perramond
SUBARU VIVIO

1st leg of the 1999 world rally championships for constructors and drivers
1st leg of the constructors' "2 litre", production car drivers' and teams'world cups

Date: *17 - 20 January 1999*

Route: *1613,20 km divided into 4 legs, 14 stages all on tarmac (424,69 km)*

1st leg : Sunday 17th January, Monaco - Gap, 0 stage
2nd leg : Monday 18th January, Gap - Gap, 5 stages(161,16 km)
3rd leg : Tuesday 19th January, Gap - Monaco, 5 stages (154,49 km)
4th leg : Wednesday 20th January, Monaco - Monaco, 4 stages (109,04 km)

Starters/Finishers: *84/48*

An ephemeral performance from the new Skoda Octavia WRC. Schwarz never made it to the start ramp.

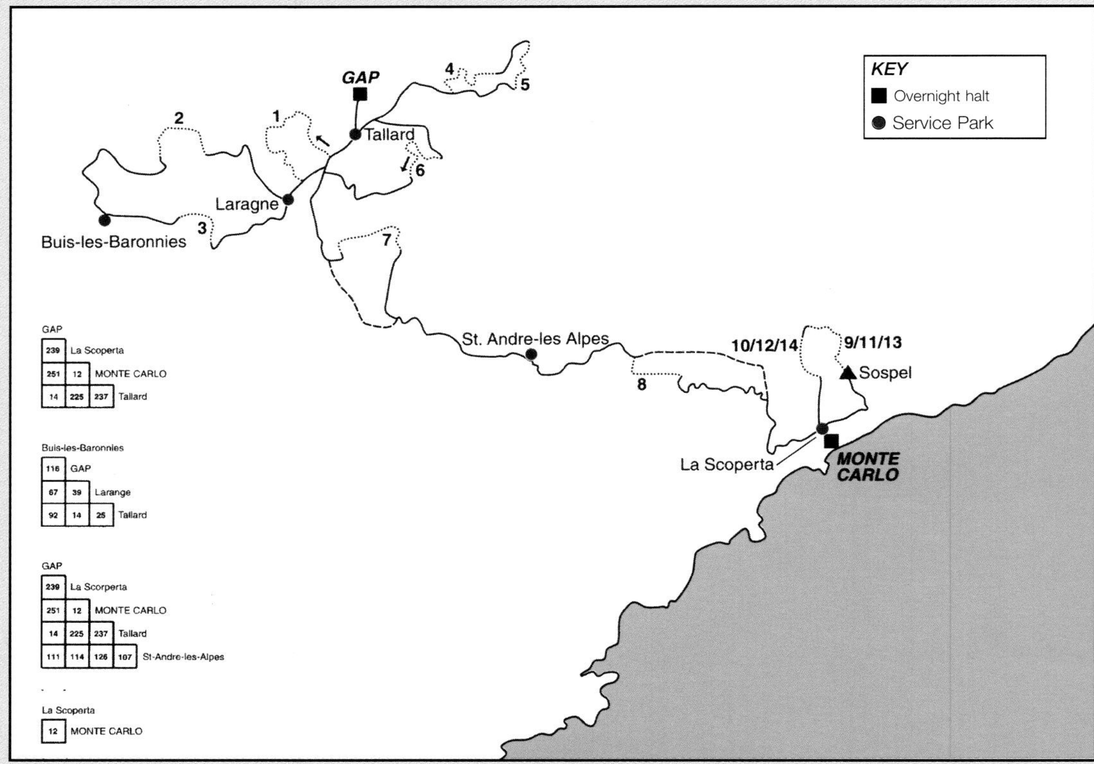

SPECIAL STAGE TIMES

SS.1 Plan de Vitrollss - Faye (48,28 km)
1. Makinen 34'36"4; 2. Panizzi 35'13"9; 3. Liatti 35'50"; 4. Kankkunen 35'54"4 ; 5. Thiry 36'01"8 ; Gr.N Loubet 37'18"9 ; F2 Gardemeister 37'14"

SS.2 L'Epine - Rosans (31,15 km)
1. Thiry 19'59"6 ; 2. Makinen 20'00"2 ; 3. Kankkunen 20'00"9 ; 4. Liatti 20'04"1 ; 5. Auriol 20'06"1 ; Gr.N Loubet 21'24"9 ; F2 Gardemeister 21'24"6

SS.3 Ruissas - Eygalayss (27,56 km)
1. Panizzi 18'50"3 ; 2. Rovanpera 19'07" ; 3. Auriol 19'21"2 ; 4. Makinen 19'23"7 ; 5. McRae 19'24"5 ; Gr.N Verini 20'01"5 ; F2 Maselli 19'48"3

SS.4 Prunièrss - Embrun (33,82 km)
1. McRae 20'50"3 ; 2. Auriol 21'17"7 ; 3. Delecour 21'18"1 ; 4. Jean-Joseph 21'19" ; 5. Kankkunen 21'26"2 ; Gr.N Duez 22'57"2 ; F2 Gardemeister 23'38"7

SS.5 Saint Clément - Saint Sauveur (20,35 km)
1.McRae 13'58" ; 2. Auriol 14'42"5 ; 3. Burns 14'47" ; 4. Makinen 14'54"8 ; 5. Delecour 14'59"5 ; Gr.N Duez 16'29"6 ; F2 Gardemeister 17'02"9

SS.6 Bayons (35,52 km)
1. Panizzi 24'13"1 ; 2. McRae 24'47"1 ; 3. Makinen 25'02"6 ; 4. Kankkunen 25'10"2 ; 5. Auriol 25'15"2 ; Gr.N Trellss 26'40"9 ; F2 Gardemeister 28'08"5

SS.7 Sisteron - Thoard (36,72 km)
1. Makinen 25'43"4 ; 2. Liatti 25'57"7 ; 3. Auriol 26'05"2 ; 4.Kankkunen 26'07"8 ; 5. Delecour 26'12"6 ; Gr.N Trellss 27'58" ; F2 Gardemeister 28'38"9

SS.8 Entrevaux - Saint Pierre (30,73 km)
1. Kankkunen 23'58"4 ; 2. Makinen 24'01"7 ; 3. Liatti 24'05"9 ; 4. McRae 24'16"1 ; 5. Burns 24'25"8 ; Gr.N Trellss 26'05"1 ; F2 Gardemeister 26'32"4

SS.9 Sospel - La Bollène 1 (33,65 km)
1. Makinen 27'20"1 ; 2. Kankkunen 27'27"6 ; 3. Auriol 27'36"1 ; 4. Thiry 27'41"3 ; 5. Delecour 27'47"2 ; GR.N Trellss 30'02"3 ; F2 Gardemeister 30'50"6

SS.10 Lantosque - Lucéram 1 (20,87 km)
1. McRae 15'22"7 ; 2. Auriol 15'24"9 ; 3. Delecour 15'36"5 ; 4. Makinen 15'36"9 ; 5. Panizzi 15'48"2 ; Gr.N Trellss 17'12" ; F2 Maselli 17'29"2

SS.11 Sospel - La Bollène 2 (33,65 km)
1. Auriol 28'06"2 ; 2 Thiry 28'16" ; 3. Kankkunen 28'25"4 ; 4. Liatti 28'36"3 ; 5. Delecour 28'38"5 ; Gr.N Duez 29'58"7 ; F2 Maselli 31'50"9

SS.12 Lantosque - Lucéram 2 (20,87 km)
1. McRae 15'43"2 ; 2. Burns 15'63"2 ; 3. Makinen 16'07" ; 4. Kankkunen 16'07"5 ; 5. Lundgaard 16'14"2 ; Gr.N Duez 18'10"1 ; F2 Maselli 17'13"2

SS.13 Sospel - La Bollène 3 (33,65 km)
1.Rovanpera 26'53"4 ; 2. Auriol 26'53"8 ; 3. Liatti 26'55"4 ; 4. Delecour 26'59"8 ; 5. Thiry 27'01"4 ; Gr.N Spiliotis 28'45"6 ; F2 Maselli 29'00"3

SS.14 Lantosque - Lucéram 3 (20,87 km)
1. Auriol 15'19" ; 2. Delecour 15'25"8 ; 3. Thiry 15'29"9 ; 4. McRae 15'31"3 ; 5. Burns 15'43" ; GR.N Arnaud 17'07"8 ; F2 Maselli 16'35"2

RESULTS AND RETIREMENTS

	Driver/Co-Driver	Car	Gr	Total Time
1	**Tommi Makinen - Risto Mannisenmaki**	**Mitsubishi Lancer Ev.6**	**A**	**5h16m50,6s**
2	Juha Kankkunen - Juha Repo	Subaru Impreza WRC	A	5h18m35,3s
3	Didier Auriol - Denis Giraudet	Toyota Corolla WRC	A	5h20m43,4s
4	François Delecour - Dominique Savignoni	Ford Escort WRC	A	5h20m51,8s
5	Bruno Thiry - Stephane Prevot	Subaru Impreza WRC	A	5h20m53,1s
6	Piero Liatti - Carlo Cassina	Seat Cordoba WRC	A	5h23m48,7s
7	Harri Rovanpera - Risto Pietilainen	Seat Cordoba WRC	A	5h23m52,9s
8	Richard Burns - Robert Reid	Subaru Impreza WRC	A	5h26m15,2s
9	Henrik Lundgaard - Freddy Pedersen	Toyota Corolla WRC	A	5h30m56,8s
10	**Marc Duez - Philippe Dupuy**	**Mitsubishi Carisma Ev.5**	**N**	**5h43m31,2s**
14	**Toni Gardemeister - Paavo Lukander**	**Seat Ibiza Kit Car**	**A**	**5h53m50,3s**
Start	Armin Schwarz - Manfred Hiemer	Skoda Octavia WRC	A	Electronics
Start	Pavel Sibera - Petr Gross	Skoda Octavia WRC	A	Electronics
SS.1	Carlos Sainz - Luis Moya	Toyota Corolla WRC	A	Accident
SS.1	Freddy Loix - Sven Smeets	Mitsubishi Carisma GT	A	Accident
SS.1	Jesus Puras - Marc Marti	Citroen Saxo Kit Car	A	Engine
SS.1	Luis Climent - Alex Romani	Mitsubishi Carisma Ev.5	A	Accident
SS.1	Manfred Stohl - Peter Muller	Mitsubishi Lancer Ev.5	A	Accident
SS.5	Philippe Bugalski - Jean-Paul Chiaroni	Citroen Saxo Kit Car	A	Transmission
SS.5	Andrea Dallavilla - Danilo Fappani	Subaru Impreza WRC	A	Accident
SS.11	Gilles Panizzi - Herve Panizzi	Subaru Impreza WRC	A	Accident
SS.11	Yves Loubet - Bruno Brissart	Mitsubishi Lancer Ev.5	N	Engine

GOSSIP

• GROUP ANYWAY

No reason why these boys should get away trouble-free. The Group N competitors had their fair share of problems right from the start: out went Stohl and Climent, while Trelles lost a lot of time. Duez escaped the eye of the storm and only had to hold it all together to get back to his Monaco home in the lead.

• WOMEN

Isolde Holderied and Catherine François were 15th, but they did not win the Coupe des Dames, as it does not exist any longer.

• SERIES

Mitsubishi racks them up. Fifth consecutive win, but Lancia's record is still out of reach with 12 wins in a row.

• JUST THE TICKET

Makinen and Panizzi were naughty boys on a road section and had to negotiate with the law. Panizzi was a bit too chatty and his lengthy conversation meant he had to "pay" a 20s penalty for late arrival at the service point.

• F1

They might leave close by, but well done all the same to Hakkinen and Coulthard who got up bright and early to watch some of the Monte Carlo rally.

• CITRON PRESSE

It was a short trip, if not as short as the Skodas' for the little Saxo Kit cars. Puras went off on SS1 and Bugalski's diff let go on SS5.

EVENT LEADERS

SS.1 - SS.3	Makinen
SS.4 - SS.7	Panizzi
SS.8 - SS.14	Makinen

BEST PERFORMANCES

	1	2	3	4	5	6
McRae	4	1	-	2	1	1
Makinen	3	2	2	3	-	1
Auriol	2	4	3	-	2	1
Panizzi	2	1	6	6	1	3
Kankkunen	1	1	2	4	1	1
Thiry	1	1	1	1	2	-
Rovanpera	1	1	-	-	-	1
Liatti	-	1	3	2	-	1
Delecour	-	1	2	1	1	4
Burns	-	1	1	-	2	1
Jean-Joseph	-	-	-	1	-	1
Lundgaard	-	-	-	-	1	2

CHAMPIONSHIP CLASSIFICATIONS

Drivers	
1. Tommi Makinen	10
2. Juha Kankkunen	6
3. Didier Auriol	4
4. François Delecour	3
5. Bruno Thiry	2
6. Piero Liatti	1
Constructors	
1. Mitsubishi	10
2. Subaru	7
3. Seat	5
4. Toyota	4
Group N	
1. Marc Duez	13
2. Gustavo Trelles	8
3. Christophe Spiliotis	5
Two Litres	
1. Renault	10
Team's Cup	
no finishers	

PREVIOUS WINNERS

1973	Andruet - "Biche" Alpine Renault A 110
1975	Munari - Mannucci Lancia Stratos
1976	Munari - Maiga Lancia Stratos
1977	Munari - Maiga Lancia Stratos
1978	Nicolas - Laverne Porsche 911 SC
1979	Darniche - Mahe Lancia Stratos
1980	Rohrl - Geistdorfer Fiat 131 Abarth
1981	Ragnotti - Andrie Renault 5 Turbo
1982	Rohrl - Geistdorfer Opel Ascona 400
1983	Rohrl - Geistdorfer Lancia rally 037
1984	Rohrl - Geistdorfer Audi Quattro
1985	Vatanen - Harryman Peugeot 205 T16
1986	Toivonen - Cresto Lancia Delta S4
1987	Biasion - Siviero Lancia Delta HF 4WD
1988	Saby - Fauchille Lancia Delta HF 4WD
1989	Biasion - Siviero Lancia Delta Integrale
1990	Auriol - Occelli Lancia Delta Integrale
1991	Sainz - Moya Toyota Celica GT-Four
1992	Auriol - Occelli Lancia Delta HF Integrale
1993	Auriol - Occelli Toyota Celica Turbo 4WD
1994	Delecour - Grataloup Ford Escort RS Cosworth
1995	Sainz - Moya Subaru Impreza 555
1996	Bernardini - Andrie Ford Escort Cosworth
1997	Liatti - Pons Subaru Impreza WRC
1998	Sainz - Moya Toyota Corolla WRC

“Like a bullfight without a kill..

,

SWEDISH

We expected Tommi Makinen, we got Tommi Makinen of course. The Finn was comfortably in his element on snow and was too strong, much too strong even for Carlos Sainz, who was extremely motivated by the thought of being the first Latin to dominate on snow in Sweden. The Spaniard was still chasing the holy grail of at least one win on each of the rallies making up the world championship. Sweden would not be added to the list this time, even though he richly deserved to win. Maybe next year, unless the insatiable Tommi Makinen, the nordic Speedy Gonzales does it once again.

56.1

56.1 - 2

As expected, Tommi Makinen was untouchable.

56.3

Kenneth Eriksson retired on the last stage, when he had the 2 litre class in his pocket.

"Tommi is unbeatable. I just regret not pushing harder in Jutbo, because maybe I could have worried him."

Carlos Sainz

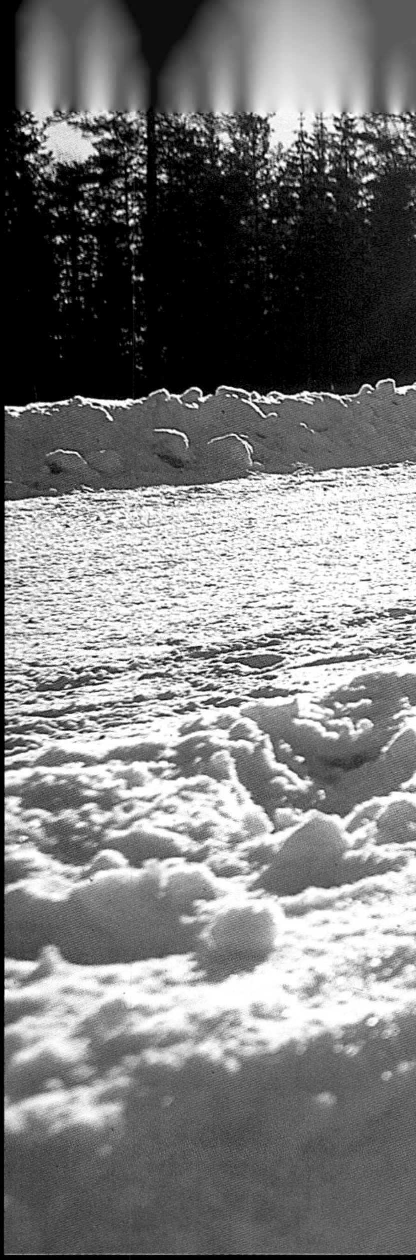

56.3

THE SCENERY LOOKS LIKE a stage prop with pine trees and bushes crumbling under the weight of a white winter. And the road goes on forever in one long flat line. With his right hand on the wheel, the chase car driver risks fiddling with the radio in the vain hope of finding an English voice. There aren't any. All he can hear is the monotonous refrain on Swedish radio stations tuned into the rally: "Tommi Makinen leder totalt." Leder totalt, the number one, the overall leader. In Swedish or Swahili or whatever language you care to name, it would have been the same story. It was Eriksson's turn to wear the winner's crown. It was a case of one turn for me and one for you with Tommi Makinen since 1995. But with Eriksson languishing behind the wheel of a Hyundai and the Swedish Rally being the private hunting ground of the Scandinavians, it could only be Makinen and it was. "It was much harder than last year," he would pretend once it was all over. "It was a close fight and it required maximum concentration all the time with no let-up."

Tommi was not entirely wrong. After all, a proud Iberian tried to be the first Latin driver to succeed and he believed he could do it. Carlos Sainz even led the field as they come out of SS1 and then again after SS7. "The domination of the nordic drivers is not unbeatable," he claimed before the start. "Someone has to beat them and it will be me."

Sainz, the intelligent matador almost delivered on his promise. For a whole day, he seemed to be toying with Makinen. But who was the beast due to die and who was the one holding the cape? Four fastest times for Carlos, three for Tommi and one for Radstrom. Ever professional, Sainz even chose to lose a few tenths so as not to reach Karlstad in the lead and have to clear the road the next day. It had been a bullfight without a kill. The first bandilleros had gone in, but not too deep, just to test the beast and to get a point of reference. Further back, Radstrom was already 21.7s adrift. "He's the favourite," predicted Auriol. "He's at home. He knows the route perfectly and that is so important here." Five months a year, the Swede drives on roads where you cannot see the tarmac. However, the studious looking Radstrom with his specs is still a tenderfoot with only eighteen world championship starts to his name and he is still learning about his Ford. On top of that, the new and potent Focus is still experiencing growing pains. The result is a somewhat chaotic event with a prang in SS3 necessitating changes to much of the engine sub-frame and the engine was a bit wheezy. Could it be a problem with the water pump -see the Monte-? "I don't think so," says Malcolm Wilson. "From what we can see and from the telemetry the new, revised water pump doesn't seem to have any effect on the power output." Radstrom should not hide behind his miserable expression because there are reasons to be cheerful as, on the first night, he is within striking distance of Makinen and Sainz. And if he listens carefully, he can hear the experienced co-driver Fred Gallagher heap praise on him which should make him blush to the same colour as his ears, turned red in the cold. "Thomas is very talented. That's obvious. He reminds me of Bjorn Waldegard and I hope he will be as successful as Bjorn."

But for this year at any rate, Radstrom was powerless against Makinen and Sainz. He was not the only one to throw in the towel quite early on. Auriol soon got the message. The Frenchman was 32.2s down, which was not that bad on paper, but he had made a bad start. He was struggling a bit, perhaps because of a new balance on the front differential. "I am not driving the way I would like. I am always thinking about the car, because I don't like it. But it is me and my driving I should be concentrating on." McRae is in much worse shape. He hasn't tipped it over, but he has managed to break the windscreen on a post and smash the left rear wheel. The only good point: the water pump which was the centre of attention in Monte Carlo is now legal and working fine. The Subarus are way off the pace, with a poor tyre choice impeding forward motion. "It's a disaster," said Kankkunen. "After ten kilometres it's as though the tyres are punctured," added Thiry. The Seats of Gronholm and Rovanpera had fuel feed problems and were also out of the running. But who was going to stop Makinen anyway from reigning over the event? Only a nasty troll with four toes and nothing else and as the trolls only come out at night, there was not much chance of that happening.

The Finn only had one real opponent and that was the road itself. The paradox on these roads that the driver has to guess more than see, is that although grip is at a minimum, speeds are at a maximum. The Swedish rally runs at one of the highest average speeds on the calendar. There are no drops and there are hardly any tight corners. The walls of snow act like safety barriers. There is no Mediterranean on the right or pampas on the left. "It's quick," is McRae's brief summary, "but you can get away with some mistakes and you can use the banks to get straightened up. The important thing is to adapt your style to the snow and ice and to constantly plan ahead and to do everything quicker than on tarmac or on the loose." It is almost like a bobsleigh event. In fact, Auriol tried his hand at that over the winter, tucked in behind Bruno Mingeon, the French world champion. It was all made to measure for Tommi. So he had to lead on the road on the second day. So what? He still won five stages out of six. It was just the ticket to establish his supremacy and turn his opponents ambitions into vain illusions. Sainz' little calculation to ensure he didn't have to act the snow plough did not really

pay off. Tommi also made the most of his very favourite stage, the 47.650 km long Jutbo. "Maybe I should have got a bit closer to worry him," mused Sainz. "It's hard for someone who dreams of winning every rally at least once before retirement." But he did not manage it and Sainz finished second, just as he did in 1996, 97 and 98! On the third and final day, Makinen was supreme and even lifted off a bit in the final two stages to make sure of being crowned King of Sweden for the third time and taking his seventeenth world championship win. On top of that, he also extended his lead in the championship. Not a bad weekend's work all in all!

Behind the duelling leaders, another race was in progress. McRae went out in SS9, let down by his engine, although he remained confident for the future: "we should win one by the middle of the season." So with the Subarus in deep and disastrous bother, it was left to Radstrom and Auriol to keep an eye on third place. In fact the top two battling pairs shared the top four places on the 19 stages, with the exception of a fourth spot for Hagstrom.

Auriol was never really in the same league as Makinen, but as the kilometres flew by, so the confidence grew and he actually stole two stages, SS17 and SS19. "Il could not have gone any quicker," he said after 17. "I have rarely been off the road so often," he added after 19. A perfectionist to his fingernails, he had even asked his note makers, his brother Gerard and Thierry Barjou, to indicate the corners where he could save the odd fraction by cutting the corner. It was not enough and he would be less than three seconds off Radstrom, at the wheel of a fat but efficient Focus, which weighed in at 70 kilos more than Makinen's Mitsu. Didier looked a bit grumpy and was thirsty, not just for the local acquavit but also for a result. "That's unfinished business. A little podium would have been just the ticket." Still, there was always next year.

IS MAKINEN TOO MUCH? It could be a road safety campaign: do not fall asleep at the wheel! That was pretty much what Carlos Sainz was saying. The man from Madrid was bored and worried that the championship might be getting boring. "Tommi is too dominant. It's very annoying." He was not the only one to complain. Colin McRae added his own two cents worth. "Tommi will win the title more easily than ever before and that's no use to anyone." Are we dreaming here? Why not arrange and fix the results like they do in Eastern European soccer games. Maybe the sport needs a Bernie Ecclestone sitting in a nice warm motorhome, fiddling with the bells and whistles, controlling the power of the engines, or throwing ice in secret traps surrounded by garden gnomes to cause accident and incident and run the whole thing like a computer game. Hang on a minute. Whoa there! If Tommi and Mitsubishi have won five rallies out of six maybe it's the others who are at fault. Mitsubishi is certainly not the best funded team. Makinen certainly does not care: "It's not my fault. I cannot do anything about it." After all, it was much worse in the Lancia days and that era did more for the image of rallying than any other. Go on Carlos, get to work.

PIRELLI DEFLATED. Tyreology.... a strange science. If the car demolishes the opposition and wins, then that is normal and the tyres have simply done their job. However, if the car is all over the shop and comes in last then that's the fault of the tyres. This rule is even more cruel in Sweden, where grip is ever more important than anywhere else. Michelli, who kit out Mitsubishi, Toyota and Ford have won, while Pirelli, on the Subarus and Seats have lost. And the famous glamour girl calendar reserved for the great and the good will not be enough to console David Richards, the demanding Prodrive boss who runs the Subarus. But is Pirelli solely to blame?

Let us look at the facts. It does seem that Makinen and Sainz are able to perfectly control their slides, like ice skaters on a rink, while Kankkunen, who is no slouch, is driving as though he has had one Vodka too many or is simply out for a bit of fun, bouncing off the snow banks and the ditches with a rear end which seems desperate to overtake the front of the car. The result is that, as we all know, the crowd pleasing style is not the quickest and Kankkunen, Burns and Thiry's stage times are disastrous; at least one second off Makinen's pace. It would be a very strange coincidence if they had all had a bad day at the office at the same time. For their part, the off-song trio were happy to lay the blame.

It would seem that while the studs stayed in the Pirellis better than in others, the rubber compound was a touch too soft allowing the tyre to flex too much. It was a case of soft chewing when the ideal would have been some nougat! "In testing it had worked well," lamented David Richards.

The fact is that producing studded tyres to suit the snow and ice found in Sweden is not an easy task which is why some of the tyres ended up in ribbons. All sorts of parameters have to be considered: the rubber of course, the temperature, the tread pattern, the size of the rubber blocks and their position, the length, shape and material used for the studs. It is a major headache for the boffins and all that for pretty much just one rally. It seemed that Pirelli had hobbled Subaru, whereas it had been the opposite the previous year. Wait for next year.

SWEDISH

"Like a bullfight without a kill..."

58.1 - 59.1

More aggressive than ever, Didier Auriol took all the risks, but ended up 2.5 second behind Radstrom.

58.2

Thomas Radstrom gave Ford the podium he had been unable to claim on the Monte.

58.3

The Swedish Rally went off the rails for Subaru, with the most of the blame being laid at Pirelli's door.

59.2

Despite taking some imaginative lines, Petter Solberg managed to get his car to the finish.

59.3

With eleven cars in the top eleven places in the production car category, Mitsubishi appeared to have things covered.

59.4

Kankkunen and Burns were locked in battle with the young Englishman finally getting the better of his older team-mate.

58.1

58.2

58.3

59.1

59.2

59.3

59.4

48TH RALLY SWEDISH

TOP ENTRIES

1 Tommi Makinen - Risto Mannisenmaki
MITSUBISHI LANCER EV.6

2 Freddy Loix - Sven Smeets
MITSUBISHI CARISMA GT

3 Carlos Sainz - Luis Moya
TOYOTA COROLLA WRC

4 Didier Auriol - Denis Giraudet
TOYOTA COROLLA WRC

5 Richard Burns - Robert Reid
SUBARU IMPREZA WRC

6 Juha Kankkunen - Juha Repo
SUBARU IMPREZA WRC

7 Colin McRae - Nicky Grist
FORD FOCUS WRC

8 Thomas Radstrom - Fred Gallagher
FORD FOCUS WRC

9 Harri Rovanpera - Risto Pietilainen
SEAT CORDOBA WRC

10 Marcus Gronholm -Timo Rautiainen
SEAT CORDOBA WRC

11 Bruno Thiry - Stephane Prevot
SUBARU IMPREZA WRC

12 Pasi Hagstrom - Tero Gardemeister
TOYOTA COROLLA WRC

14 Petter Solberg - Philip Mills
FORD ESCORT WRC

15 Sebastian Lindholm – Asto Aho
FORD ESCORT WRC

17 Krzysztof Holowczyc - Jean-Marc Fortin
SUBARU IMPREZA WRC

19 Jouko Puhakka - Jakke Honkanen
MITSUBISHI LANCER EV.4

20 Stig-Olov Walfridsson - Jan Svanstrom
MITSUBISHI LANCER EV.4

22 Gustavo Trelles - Martin Christie
MITSUBISHI LANCER EV.5

23 Manfred Stohl - Peter Muller
MITSUBISHI LANCER EV.5

25 Luis Climent - Alex Romani
MITSUBISHI LANCER EV.3

27 Kenneth Eriksson - Staffan Parmander
HYUNDAI COUPE EV.2

29 Per Svan - Johan Olsson
OPEL ASTRA KIT CAR

30 Alister McRae - David Senior
HYUNDAI COUPE EV.2

33 Toni Gardemeister - Paavo Lukander
SEAT IBIZA KIT CAR

34 Stig Blomqvist - Benny Melander
FORD PUMA VK.2

36 Markko Martin - Toomas Kitsing
FORD ESCORT WRC

49 Hamed Al Wahaibi - Tony Sircombe
MITSUBISHI CARISMA GT

65 Abdullah Bakhashab – Michael Park
TOYOTA CELICA GT-FOUR

2nd leg of the 1999 world rally championships for constructors and drivers
2nd leg of the constructors' «2 litre», production car drivers' and teams'world cups

Date: *12 - 24 February 1999*

Route: *1478,40 km divided into 3 legs, 19 stages on snow covered loose surface roads (384,30 km)*
1st leg : Friday 12th February, Karlstad – Torsby – Karlstad, 8 stages (142,65 km)
2nd leg : Saturday 13th February, Karlstad – Borlange, 6 stages (142,85 km)
3rd leg : Sunday 14th February, Borlange – Hagfors – Karlstad, 5 stages (98,80 km)

Starters/Finishers: *102/64*

Poland's Holowczyc was the first winner of the 99 teams cup at the wheel of a new Impreza WRC.

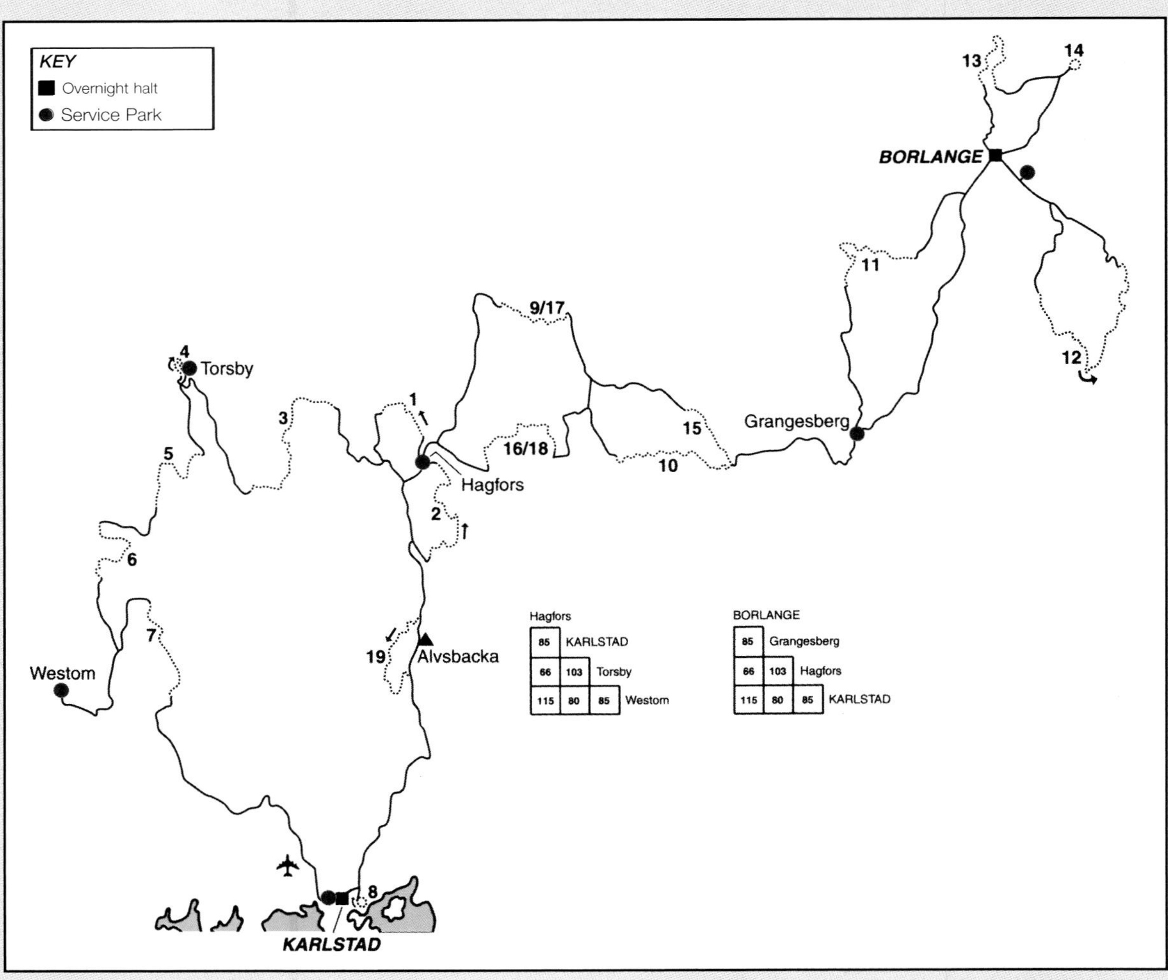

SPECIAL STAGE TIMES

SS.1 Malta (11,88 km)
1. Sainz 5'56"8; 2. Radstrom 5'58"7; 3. Makinen 5'58"8; 4. Auriol 6'03"; 5. McRae 6'06"2; Gr.N Puhakka 6'21"9 ; F2 Eriksson 6'27"

SS.2 Sunnemo (30,87 km)
1. Makinen 15'17"; 2. Sainz 15'19"5; 3. Auriol 15'25"2; 4. Radstrom 15'27"6; 5. McRae 15'30"9; Gr.N Puhakka 16'20"7 ; F2 Eriksson 16'37"9

SS.3 Hamra (30,69 km)
1. Makinen 16'30"9; 2. Radstrom 16'34"9; 3. Sainz 16'36"4; 4. McRae 16'41"1; 5. Auriol 16'43"; Gr.N Walfridsson 17'46"4 ; F2 McRae 18'05"1

SS.4 Torsby (2,79 km)
1. Sainz 2'13"; 2. Makinen 2'13"9; 3. Auriol 2'14"4; 4. Radstrom 2'16"5; 5. McRae 2'17"3; Gr.N Walfridsson 2'23"7 ; F2 Eriksson 2'27"

SS.5 Bjalverud (21,58 km)
1. Radstrom 11'07"8; 2. Sainz 11'08"9; 3. Auriol 11'11"6; 4. Makinen 11'11"9; 5. McRae 11'24"; Gr.N Pykalisto 11'56"8 ; F2 Eriksson 12'10"2

SS.6 Mangen (22,09 km)
1. Sainz 12'30"8; 2. Makinen 12'33"1; 3. Auriol 12'34"3; 4. Radstrom 12'34"5 ; 5. Burns 12'56" ; Gr.N Walfridsson 13'23"8 ; F2 Eriksson 13'23"8

SS.7 Langjohanstorp (19,44 km)
1. Sainz 10'00"7 ; 2. Makinen 10'01"9 ; 3. McRae 10'04"3 ; 4. Radstrom 10'07"1 ; 5. Auriol 10'09"3 ; Gr.N Walfridsson 10'44"8 ; F2 Svan 10'48"8

SS.8 Kalvholmen (2,10 km)
1. Makinen 1'48"2 ; 2. McRae 1'49"8 ; 3. Auriol 1'50"1 ; 4. Radstrom et Hagstrom 1'50"3 ; Gr.N Walfridsson 1'55"1 ; F2 McRae 1'56"8

SS.9 Sagen 1 514,76 km)
1. Makinen 8'01"9 ; 2. Sainz 8'02"8 ; 3. Auriol 8'03"6 ; 4. Radstrom 8'03"9 ; 5. Rovanpera 8'12"3 ; Gr.N Walfridsson 8'34"2 ; F2 Svan 8'41"9

SS.10 Fredriksberg (27,83 km)
1. Makinen 16'15"6 ; 2. Radstrom 16'17"8 ; 3. Auriol 16'23"8 ; 4. Sainz 16'25" ; 5. Hagstrom 16'42" ; Gr.N Walfridsson 17'25"4 ; F2 Eriksson 17'27"5

SS.11 Nyhammar (27,83 km)
1. Makinen 14'49"7 ; 2. Radstrom 14'53"9 ; 3. Sainz 14'56"1 ; 4. Auriol 14'58" ; 5. Kankkunen 15'17"9 ; Gr.N Passonen 15'56" ; F2 Eriksson 16'10"9

SS.12 Jutho (47,65 km)
1. Makinen 27'36"7 ; 2. Auriol 27'43"9 ; 3. Sainz 27'48"8 ; 4. Radstrom 27'55"3 ; 5. Burns 28'24" ; Gr.N Puhakka 29'44"9 ; F2 Svan 30'13"6

SS.13 Skog (22,82 km)
1. Sainz 12'57"7 ; 2. Makinen et Radstrom 12'58"3 ; 4. Auriol 12'59"7 ; 5. Burns 13'12" ; Gr.N Puhakka 7'16"9 ; F2 Joki 14'16"1

SS.14 Lugnet (2 km)
1. Makinen 1'58"2 ; 2. Radstrom 1'58"8 ; 3. Auriol 1'59"5 ; 4. Sainz 1'59"6 ; 5. Kankkunen 2'02"1 ; Gr.N Puhakka 2'08" ; F2 Eriksson 2'14"4

SS.15 Stromsdal (13,93 km)
1. Makinen 6'51"8 ; 2. Radstrom 6'53"8 ; 3. Sainz et Auriol 6'54"1 ; 5. Kankkunen 6'59" ; Gr.N Puhakka 7'16"9 ; F2 Svan 7'23"4

SS.16 Rammen 1 (23,81 km)
1. Sainz 12'24"6 ; 2. Auriol 12'26"5 ; 3. Makinen 12'29"5 ; 4. Radstrom 12'30"2 ; 5. Hagstrom 12'41"4 ; Gr.N Walfridsson 13'16"9 ; F2 Svan 13'23"8

SS.17 Sagen 2 (14,76 km)
1. Auriol 7'59"1 ; 2. Makinen 8'02"3 ; 3. Sainz 8'02"9 ; 4. Radstrom 8'03" ; 5. Hagstrom 8'11"2; Gr.N Walfridsson 8'37" ; F2 Svan 8'34"4

SS.18 Rammen 2 (23,81 km)
1. Sainz 12'22"7 ; 2. Auriol 12'23"1 ; 3. Radstrom 12'25"5 ; 4. Makinen 12'27" ; 5. Hagstrom 12'38"5 ; Gr.N Puhakka 13'12"5 ; F2 Svan 13'26"9

SS.19 Mangstorp (22,49 km)
1. Auriol 11'53"7 ; 2. Radstrom 11'55"5 ; 3. Sainz 12'02" ; 4. Makinen 12'08"4 ; 5. Kankkunen 12'14"7 ; Gr.N Puhakka 12'53"1 ; F2 Gardemeister 13'10"7

RESULTS AND RETIREMENTS

	Driver/Co-Driver	Car	Gr	Total Time
1	**Tommi Makinen - Risto Mannisenmaki**	**Mitsubishi Lancer Ev.6**	**A**	**3h29m15,6s**
2	Carlos Sainz - Luis Moya	Toyota Corolla WRC	A	3h29m33,7s
3	Thomas Radstrom – Fred Gallagher	Ford Focus WRC	A	3h29m53,4s
4	Didier Auriol – Denis Giraudet	Toyota Corolla WRC	A	3h29m55,9s
5	Richard Burns – Robert Reid	Subaru Impreza WRC	A	3h35m04,9s
6	Juha Kankkunen – Juha Repo	Subaru Impreza WRC	A	3h35m10s
7	Pasi Hagstrom – Tero Gardemeister	Toyota Corolla WRC	A	3h37m39,6s
8	Markko Martin – Toomas Kitsing	Ford Escort WRC	A	3h38m57,6s
9	Freddy Loix - Sven Smeets	Mitsubishi Carisma GT	A	3h39m21,8s
10	Bruno Thiry – Stephane Prevot	Subaru Impreza WRC	A	3h39m48,9s
13	**Jouko Puhakka – Jakke Honkanen**	**Mitsubishi Lancer Ev.4**	**N**	**3h44m48,5s**
15	**Krzysztof Holowczyc – Jean-Marc Fortin**	**Subaru Impreza WRC**	**A**	**3h45m03,7s**
21	**Per Svan – Johan Olsson**	**Opel Astra Kit Car**	**A**	**3h50m10,8s**
SS.2	Marcus Gronholm – Timo Rautiainen	Seat Cordoba WRC	A	Engine
SS.3	Sebastian Lindholm – Asto Aho	Ford Escort WRC	A	Accident
SS.3	Stig Blomqvist – Benny Melander	Ford Puma VK.2	A	Accident
SS.6	Abdullah Bakhashab – Michael Park	Toyota Celica GT-Four	A	Suspension
SS.9	Colin McRae – Nicky Grist	Ford Focus WRC	A	Engine
SS.12	Alister McRae – David Senior	Hyundai Coupe Ev.2	A	Engine
SS.19	Kenneth Eriksson – Staffan Parmander	Hyundai Coupe Ev.2	A	Engine

GOSSIP

• ERIKSSON ROBBED
Kenneth Eriksson thought he had the two litre class in the bag when he was robbed after his car did a "Sainz at the RAC" on him. His Hyundai's engine died on him on the very last stage. Victory was handed to Per Svan and his Opel Astra kit-car, just as in 1993, 94 and 95.

• IN-HOUSE
The Nordic Mitsubishi drivers fought it out between them in Group N and the winner was Stig-Olof Walfridson in a Carisma shod with Russian tyres!

• GIRAUDET SPEAKS
Denis Giraudet is evidently something of a philosopher- codriver. Auriol's man had this to say on the subject in Rallyes Magazine: "The power of the voice fascinates me. It can have the purity of Gerard Philippe or the seduction of Sacha Guitry or the diabolical eloquence of Philippe Henriot. Among my fellow co-drivers there are some who have that perfect voice which brings together surgical precision and the sensitivity of an orchestra conductor."

• REPORT
There were no extra points allocated for the final stage, 3, 2, 1, as envisaged by FIA. This involved the use of a television and the organisers were not given sufficient notice to set one up.

• KANKKUNEN EQUALS ALEN
129th world championship rally for Juha Kankkunen, therefore joins the great, but never champion driver, Markku Alen.

• THE HONESTY OF LOIX
A comment from the not very quick Freddy Loix, who was learning about Swedish roads for the first time: "My Mitsubishi is too powerful for me."

• THIRY THE GUINEA-PIG
Bruno Thiry was experimenting with an electro-hydraulically controlled semi-automatic gearbox. It was so complicated, the Belgian almost missed the start of the first stage. He got going after eighteen seconds, with just two to spare according to the regulations.

EVENT LEADERS

SS.1	Sainz
SS.2 – SS.6	Makinen
SS.7	Sainz
SS.8 – SS.19	Makinen

BEST PERFORMANCES

	1	2	3	4	5	6
Makinen	9	5	2	3	-	-
Sainz	7	3	6	2	-	-
Auriol	2	3	9	3	2	-
Radstrom	1	8	1	9	-	-
McRae	-	1	1	1	4	-
Burns	-	-	-	-	5	7
Hagstrom	-	-	-	-	5	1
Kankkunen	-	-	-	-	-	4
Lindholm	-	-	-	-	-	2
Rovanpera	-	-	-	-	-	1
Loix	-	-	-	-	-	1
Martin	-	-	-	-	-	1
Solberg	-	-	-	-	-	1

CHAMPIONSHIP CLASSIFICATIONS

Drivers	
1. Tommi Makinen	20
2. Juha Kankkunen	7
2. Didier Auriol	7
4. Carlos Sainz	6
5. Thomas Radstrom	4
Constructors	
1. Mitsubishi	20
2. Toyota	13
3. Subaru	10
4. Seat	5
5. Ford	4
Group N	
1. Marc Duez	13
1. Jouko Puhakka	13
3. Gustavo Trelles	9
Two Litres	
1. Renault	19
2. Volkswagen	16
Team's Cup	
1. Turning Point Rally Team Krzysztof Holowczyc	10

PREVIOUS WINNERS

1973	Blomqvist - Hertz SAAB 96 V 4
1975	Waldegaard - Thorszelius LANCIA STRATOS
1976	Eklund - Cederberg SAAB 96 V 4
1977	Blomqvist - Sylvan SAAB 99 EMS
1978	Waldegaard - Thorszelius FORD ESCORT RS
1979	Blomqvist - Cederberg SAAB 99 TURBO
1980	Kullang - Berglund OPEL ASCONA 400
1981	Mikkola - Hertz AUDI QUATTRO
1982	Blomqvist - Cederberg AUDI QUATTRO
1983	Mikkola - Hertz AUDI QUATTRO
1984	Blomqvist - Cederberg AUDI QUATTRO
1985	Vatanen - Harryman PEUGEOT 205 T16
1986	Kankkunen - Piironen PEUGEOT 205 T16
1987	Salonen - Harjanne MAZDA 323 TURBO
1988	Alen - Kivimaki LANCIA DELTA HF 4WD
1989	Carlsson - Carlsson MAZDA 323 4WD
1991	Eriksson - Parmander MITSUBISHII GALANT VR-4
1992	Jonsson - Backman TOYOTA CELICA GT-FOUR
1993	Jonsson - Backman TOYOTA CELICA TURBO 4WD
1994	Radstrom - Backman TOYOTA CELICA TURBO 4WD
1995	Eriksson - Parmander MITSUBISHI LANCER EV.2
1996	Makinen - Harjanne MITSUBISHI LANCER EV.3
1997	Eriksson - Parmander SUBARU IMPREZA WRC
1998	Makinen - Mannisenmaki MITSUBISHI LANCER EV.4

"An elephant had wiped its

feet..."

SAFARI

Colin McRae had predicted a win for the new Focus around the middle of the season. He was wrong as victory arrived earlier and on the toughest event of all. The Safari is the best proving ground in the world for a rally car which is unlikely to have to answer such difficult questions anywhere else. It is a car breaker par excellence; a rally where mechanics, even the bald ones, end up pulling their hair out. A win third time out was a major achievement, all the more so as Colin McRae won it as much with his head as with his right foot. It seemed that in the land of the big game hunter, he had learned to repress

his killer instinct. Well done to him and well done to the car. His trophy room would have looked even nicer and victory would have been even sweeter if Tommi Makinen had not been kicked out for receiving outside assistance, which robbed the event of some of its spectacle..

64.1

"The Safari is all about consistency. You have to be controlled." Colin McRae

"HAKUNA MATATA" yawned the Lion King, which translates from the Swahili as "no problem. Let's take you through the Safari in a cartoon strip on three pages; one per leg.

First page
1st picture. Black faces with woolly hats down to their ears are huddled around a red car and red "Mitsubishi" with Makinen written on the rear window. A double puncture. What language are they talking? Finnish or Swahili? Machetes appear and cut off the rubber, no doubt to make into sandals. But this looks like outside assistance, prohibited in the regulations. "I cannot stop them," whines Tommi. But it would have taken him longer without this extra manpower. Makinen would gain a few seconds but would lose everything and was disqualified after the finish. A camera had caught the incident and after a while, Toyota threw in a protest. "Our drivers are told to stop outside the inhabited areas," explained Donaldson, the Toyota team manager, "precisely so that the locals don't come out and help when it's not wanted."
2nd picture. A car flattened as though an elephant had wiped its feet on it. It is a red Mitsubishi. Loix's Number Two. He is speaking, so he is alright. He tells of a jump at 170 km/h over a forgotten bump and the fact he was flat rather than on the brakes. He also explains that at times, Flemish can be a confusing language. His co-driver, Sven Smeets mentioned a "hek," but "hek" means a barrier. Freddy got confused, jumped and got a fright. A helicopter gets bigger as it gets nearer to take Loix to hospital, where nothing was found. That did not stop Belgian radio from talking about two broken bones; one in the neck and one in the back. Apparently, Loix was fine immediately after the crash. But when he went to undo his belts, still hanging upside down, he fell onto the roof of his car, punishing his neck and back enough to miss his favourite rally in Portugal.
3rd picture. A blue car, a Subaru is stationery. Hardly a rare sight at the side of the road in Kenya. But the car is covered in stickers and has racing numbers on its sides. Kankkunen, for it is he, is smoking a cigarillo, making sure he does not set fire to surrounding savannah. "It's a shame, because the car was capable of winning with the perfect ride height for Kenya and a perfect centre of gravity." But here he was on foot with an engine that expired without warning. Just has happened earlier to Thiry and maybe Burns soon? For the moment the Brit was flying in the lead, by thirty seconds from Sainz and McRae.

Second page
4th picture. The troops do not look happy. The boys in blue had already lost two cars and they cannot count on the last one. Burns was not paying too much attention to his engine. "If it happens it happens," he said philosophically, commenting on the misfortunes which had befallen his team mates. In the end, it was his suspension which let him down. At first Burns thought he had a puncture, but it was more serious. He fiddled around for a while as best he could, trying to take the weight off the rear suspension. After an hour of sweating away at it he got back behind the wheel. But all this African style service achieved little. The car drove off only to stop again, this time for good. The suspension had let go and the men in blue could pack their bags. Their trip was over.
5th picture. To say the Spaniard was sweating would have been an understatement. Carlos Sainz was tomato red with the exertion. He was suffocating with sweat pouring off him. At his age, every effort is a little bit harder to deal with and as victory starts to slip from his grasp there is nothing to be cool about. Sainz was in the lead though. But a puncture, then another and a third, finally buried his hopes in the scrub. As Thiry said before the start: "In Sweden it was the war of the studs, here it will be the war of the punctures." Sainz's ambitions had gone flat and here he was third, behind McRae and Auriol. Caramba! He could console himself with the fact that on the last three occasions he had not even made it to the finish. Once it had been in a Ford, a venerable Ford.

Third page
6th picture. They thought they had seen him driving with one arm out the window. They were wrong. Colin McRae was making sure of his win, but making sure in the Safari is like counting on a single thin rope when climbing Mount Kenya. Colin is just being careful. "The Safari is all about consistency," he explained. "You have to be controlled. He never tried to match the pace of Burns or Sainz, running at 140 km/h average speed. For once, Colin used his head and hung back, maybe down to the calming influence of Nicky Grist. Steering clear of trouble, the Scotsman did not set a single fastest time, but he hardly encountered a single stone, or animal or difficulty. He slightly damaged the suspension on the first day, but "luckily the car is built like a tank," and he had a few inevitable punctures. It is not a lot when you are crossing darkest Africa. So there he was, comfortably in the lead with a fifteen minute lead, driving to victory. It was almost like being back in the colonial days and the time of English hegemony. For the past three years, the Brits had made the Safari their own: McRae 1997 and now 1999 and Burns 1998. At the finish line, the Union Jack was flying once again above the crowd.

64.2

Picture 7. On the television screens, the film of Makinen's impromptu service crew is shown over and over again. Tommi cannot bear to look and stares at the ground: 2853 kilometres and all for nought; for a second place that was taken away from him in an air-conditioned room with cool drinks to slake deep thirsts. Everyone behind him thus moved up a place on the finish order. Toyota had been beaten on what had been very much their event, with Auriol, Sainz and Duncan all in a bunch behind McRae.
Picture 8. It was Elaine Wilson, always at Malcolm's side through the good and the bad days, the thick and the thin, who said it in between the champagne and the slaps on the back, in between the bubbles of happiness and the tears of irrepressible joy: "if I could put this feeling in a bottle and have a whiff of it every morning." It's good to win. "This is even better than the first time," said McRae. "Winning with such a new car! I was confident but not that much." Ford had come to Kenya with learning in mind, but preliminary tests saw them raise their sights. It was not in vain. "My most dangerous rival in the championship will be Colin," summarised Makinen. "I have been for a while," replied McRae, "but being it and having a car to prove it with is even better." Portugal could not come soon enough.

65.1

64.1 - 65.1-2

Right from the first section, Tommi Makinen picked up two punctures and had to stop to change wheels. The locals came out uninvited to help. The incident was captured on film, Toyota protested and the Makinen was disqualified.

64.2

Petter Solberg, Malcolm Wilson's newest recruit was having his first run on the last remaining legendary rally on the championship.

65.3

Before the start, the clever money was on victory for Makinen or Burns, as both men were past winners here.

65.2

FROM THE SNOW TO THE SUN for Solberg. There he was almost north of the polar circle, getting ready for a local rally with a thread-bare private budget. Here he came to the other side of the equator to take part in the toughest rally in the world, driving for the Ford factory.

65.3

In an instant, Petter Solberg's life turned round. The Norwegian owed it all to a fall down some stairs. Those stairs were in the luxurious surroundings of a Nairobi hotel and they caught out Thomas Radstrom not long before the start of the event. The sad and painful news was revealed by an X-ray in the Nairobi hospital. His left leg was broken.

Even though he was the first to drive the Focus, Malcolm Wilson could not contemplate driving himself. The boss starting thinking and ringing round. Ari Vatanen was one possibility, but in the end he settled on Solberg. It was Christmas for Petter, who had been a diligent student in Sweden, where he handed back his Ford in eleventh place. "Petter drove with great maturity there," justified Wilson. "He was able to contain his pace to get to the finish. He has all the makings of a great driver."

Solberg, who comes from a country where rallies are run under very strict rules, unlike neighbouring Finland and Sweden, naturally jumped with both feet into the first plane to Nairobi.

"I feel very sorry for Thomas, but it is such a great opportunity for me. It is both stressful and exciting. To take part in a rally like this, after having driven in just three world championship events is a big deal. I have to do a good job and make the most of this opportunity."

Solberg was given one vital piece of advice, to get to the end of the 2,650 kilometre route. He took things steadily, making it difficult to judge his performance. He was no doubt champing at the bit, but he settled for obeying orders, running tenth for much of the time, eventually bringing home the points that go with fifth place. He was never higher than fifth in the timed sections, where he was forty five minutes down. His frustration must have taken some of the sparkle off his pleasure. Solberg deserves another shot and Malcolm Wilson has promised him just that. "He has a five year deal with us," affirmed Wilson. He also knows he has time to learn and that he is under no obligation to deliver results in the short term. He is learning a lot and that is fine."

face at a speed which have blown every radar trap in Nairobi.

FACE TO FACE. Mitsubishi and Subaru said nothing about it, but the jungle drums did the talking for them: Tommi Makinen had a nasty encounter on the recce with Robbie Head. It is not that the two drivers hate one another, in fact they hardly know one another. They were both in their favourite cars, with Head being a test driver for Subaru and they should never have come face to face a speed which have blown every radar trap in Nairobi.

From what can be ascertained, Makinen arrived in a hurry at the start of a section, which Subaru was using as testing base. And of course, Tommi was going in the opposite direction to Robbie. At first the Finn agreed to wait. Then he decided to risk it, promising to be careful and asking the Subaru mechanics to warn the other driver on the radio. But the radio message never got through and maybe Tommi was not concentrating hard enough. The two cars met coming round a corner. Most of the damage was of a mechanical nature, although Head had a few minor cuts. Pride was badly dented however, but not as badly dented as the wallets once FIA got hold of the story. FIA didn't like it, not one little bit. Makinen was stuck with a ten thousand dollar fine and Subaru had to cough up twice as much. It would seem that some were judged more guilty than others.

AFRICAN SAGA. It is a symbol of a past that has gone forever. While the Safari still hangs on (but for how long?) Africa's other famous event the Ivory Coast Bandama rally is dying. Once, an integral part of the world championship, it was a model of a demanding event, it was a showcase for heros, it was an inevitable African saga. The rally is no longer on the world championship calendar. It is hardly on any calendar at all and with just twenty cars entered for its 2500 kilometres, it was on a major diet. The quality was certainly not there. Ambrosino and Servant were barrelling along in little 106s, on loan from Peugeot Sport who were using them to test the odd component for the 206. It was enough to dominate the ramshackle collection of old four wheel drive cars which made up the rest of the field. Rallying has gone out of fashion in the Ivory Coast. Ambro and the others spend their time jet skiing on the high seas or in the lagoons or messing around with karts. The cars stay locked in the garages because "there is no money left," according to one of Ambrosino's friends. Africa certainly has more important matters to deal with, but despite this there is an African championship. The three times champion is a native of Zimbabwe, Satwant Singh who splits his time between a Hyundai Elantra and a Subaru Impreza. There are eight rounds planned for 1999, but some would never get off the ground. The first round was the Tara rally in Namibia, organised by Surinder Thatthi, who in the grand tradition of these things is not only in charge of the rally, but also co-driver to the reigning champion and president of the confederation of African motor sport. He is keeping a close watch on what is going on in Durban and the official South African Rally. That will be an event which conforms to the same rules as the other events on the world championship. The writing is on the wall and the Safari Rally should be quaking in its boots. Its only hope is that ecological pressure in Europe allows for more rallies in faraway places.

In the meantime, African motor sport continues with its own idiosyncracies. Jonathan Toroitich, son of Kenyan president, Arap Moi is also reckoned to be making a return to competition. The gentleman-farmer who had been the national champion back in 1997, had hung up his helmet. But then, his co-driver Ibraham Choge was killed last year on a cut throat road not far from Kapsabet. So, Jonathan, even if he is not a real star at the wheel, wants to give it another shot. That way he can pay homage to his friend who his now flying far higher and faster than he would be even if he drove over Mount Kilimanjaro. As long as there are characters like that....

SAFARI

"An elephant had wiped its feet..."

66.1
Harri Rovanpera was hit by all manner of problems and had hoped for better than sixth place.

66.2
Ian Duncan ensured good grouping for the Toyotas in Colin McRae's wheel tracks.

66.3
Broken suspension forced Richard Burns to retire just when he had taken the lead.

66.4
In the fast sections to the south of Nairobi, Freddy Loix had a very big crash.

66.1

66.2

66.3

67.1

67.1
Once again this year, Didier Auriol got very close to rolling in the special stage layed out in the suburbs of Nairobi.

67.2
Starting like a bullet from a gun, Al-Wahaibi made sure of the Group N category.

67.3
Kankkunen and Sainz would have very different events: retirement for the former and a podium finish for the latter.

67.4
Thomas Radstrom was unavailable, but Petter Solberg was a perfect replacement.

7.2

67.4

3

47TH SAFARI RALLY

3rd leg of the 1999 world rally championships for constructors and drivers
3rd leg of the constructors' «2 litre», production car drivers' and teams'world cups

Date: *25 - 28 February 1999*

Route: *2650,24 km divided into 3 legs, 13 sections run on loose surface roads (1009,91 km)*
1st leg : Thursday 25th and Friday 26th February, Nairobi – Plains Park – Nairobi, 5 sections (349,85 km)
2nd leg : Saturday 27th February, Nairobi – Equator Park – Nairobi, 4 sections (382,77 km)
3rd leg : Sunday 28th February, Nairobi – Plains Park – Nairobi, 4 sections (277,29 km)

Starters/Finishers: *45/24*

TOP ENTRIES

1 Tommi Makinen - Risto Mannisenmaki
MITSUBISHI LANCER EV.6

2 Freddy Loix - Sven Smeets
MITSUBISHI CARISMA GT

3 Carlos Sainz - Luis Moya
TOYOTA COROLLA WRC

4 Didier Auriol - Denis Giraudet
TOYOTA COROLLA WRC

5 Richard Burns - Robert Reid
SUBARU IMPREZA WRC

6 Juha Kankkunen - Juha Repo
SUBARU IMPREZA WRC

7 Colin McRae - Nicky Grist
FORD FOCUS WRC

8 Petter Solberg - Fred Gallagher
FORD FOCUS WRC

9 Harri Rovanpera - Risto Pietilainen
SEAT CORDOBA WRC

10 Piero Liatti – Carlo Cassina
SEAT CORDOBA WRC

11 Bruno Thiry - Stephane Prevot
SUBARU IMPREZA WRC

12 Ian Duncan – Dave Williamson
TOYOTA COROLLA WRC

14 Hamed Al Wahaibi - Tony Sircombe
MITSUBISHI CARISMA GT

15 Luis Climent - Alex Romani
MITSUBISHI LANCER EV.3

16 Frederic Dor – Kevin Gormley
SUBARU IMPREZA WRC

17 Manfred Stohl – Kay Gerlach
MITSUBISHI LANCER EV.5

18 Jonathan Toroitich – Mahesh Saleh
TOYOTA CELICA Turbo 4WD

20 Hideaki Miyoshi – Eido Osawa
SUBARU IMPREZA

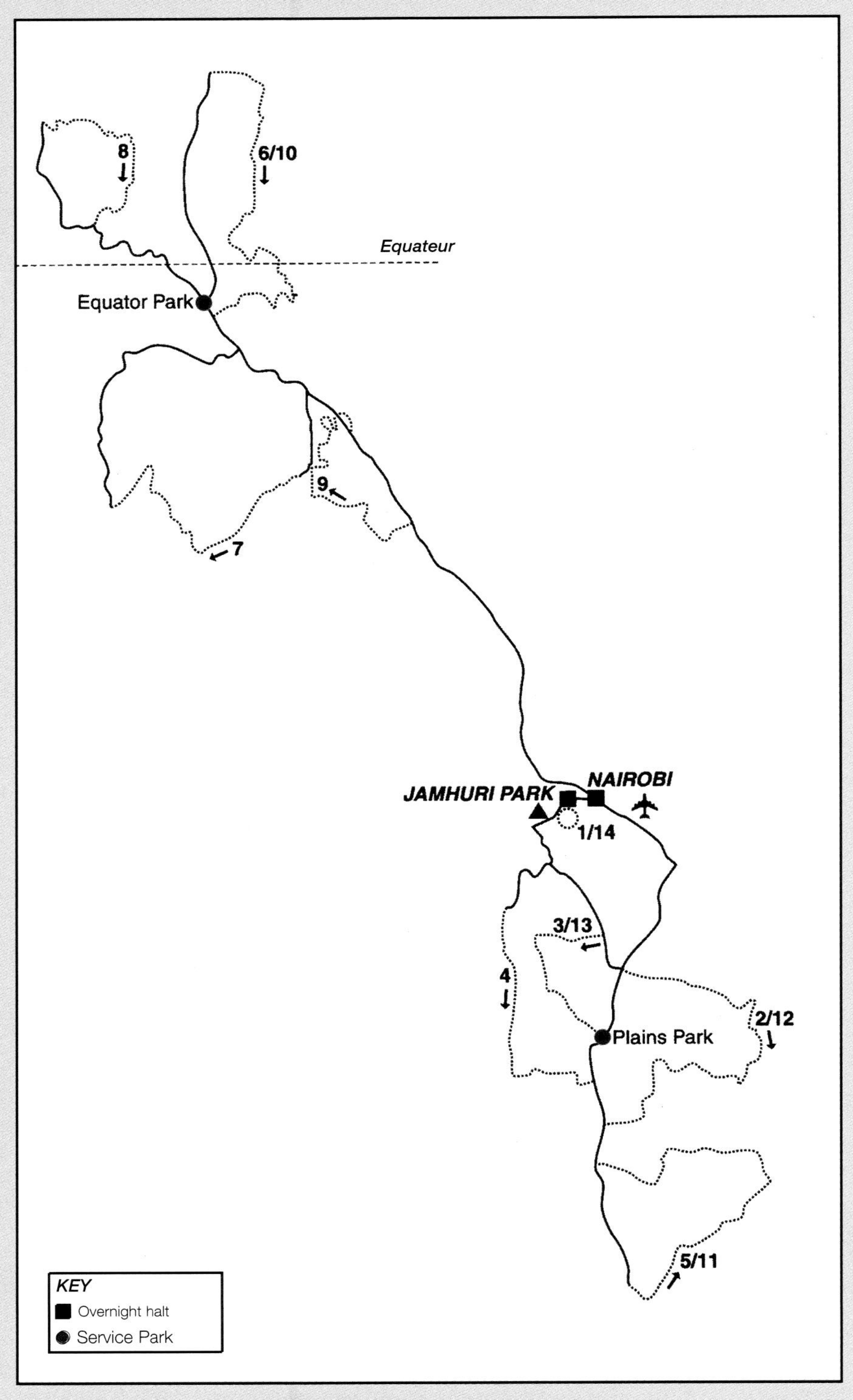

Having driven a steady rally, Frederic Dor just missed out on a points finish.

SPECIAL STAGE TIMES

CS.1 Super Spéciale 1 (2,42 km)
1. Kankkunen 1'53"4 ; 2. Burns 1'54"4 ; 3. Sainz 1'54"5 ; 4. McRae 1'55"2 ; 5. Liatti 1'55"4 ; Gr.N Al Wahaibi 2'01"1

CS.2 Isinya 1 (112,40 km)
1. Burns 48'25"7 ; 2. Sainz 48'26"1; 3. Auriol 49'19"3 ; 4. Kankkunen 49'36"5 ; 5. McRae 50'44"5 ; Gr.N Al Wahaibi 56'02"3

CS.3 Olooloitikosh 1 (49,06 km)
1. Sainz 22'38"7 ; 2. Burns 23'22"6 ; 3. McRae 23'23"5 ; 4. Makinen 23'26"7 ; 5. Rovanpera 24'57"5 ; Gr.N Al Wahaibi 27'03"9

CS.4 Hunter Lookout (72,56 km)
1. Burns 36'11" ; 2. Sainz 36'27"7 ; 3. McRae 36'53"7 ; 4. Duncan 37'13'7 ; 5. Makinen 37'28"5 ; Gr.N Al Wahaibi 42'41"8

CS.5 Lenkili 1 (113,41 km)
1. Makinen 59'57"3 ; 2. McRae 1h00'01"9 ; 3. Burns 1h00'12"5 ; 4. Auriol 1h00'17"8 ; 5. Sainz 1h01'05"9 ; Gr.N Al Wahaibi 1h09'37"3

CS.6 Elmenteita (89,13 km)
1. Burns 42'56"2 ; 2. Makinen 43'13"1 ; 3. McRae 43'10"9 ; 4. Auriol 43'25"4 ; 5. Liatti 44'21"7 ; Gr.N Al Wahaibi 51'47"2

CS.7 Nyaru (87,59 km)
1. Sainz 56'26" ; 2. Auriol 56'53" ; 3. McRae 57'18"4 ; 4. Rovanpera 57'21"8 ; 5. Duncan 57'28" ; Gr.N Al Wahaibi 1h03'08"

CS.8 Morendat (81,40 km)
1. Makinen 41'03" ; 2. McRae 41'43"6 ; 3. Auriol 43'27"4 ; 4. Duncan 44'17'1 ; 5. Rovanpera 44'38"8 ; Gr.N Climent 50'56"2

CS.9 Marigat (124,65 km)
1. Sainz 1h01'03"9 ; 2. Makinen 1h03'48"4 ; 3. Liatti 1h04'15"9 ; 4. McRae 1h04'19"3 ; 5. Duncan 1h04'52"9 ; Gr.N Al Wahaibi 1h11'59"9

CS.10 Lenkili 2 (113,41 km)
1. Auriol 1h00'22" ; 2. Makinen 1h00'22"7 ; 3. Sainz 1h00'51"3 ; 4. Duncan 1h01'42" ; 5. Liatti 1h02'42" ; Gr.N Climent 1h08'20"

CS.11 Isinya 2 (112,40 km)
1. Duncan 50'22" ; 2. Makinen 50'35"9 ; 3. Auriol 50'36"9 ; 4. Rovanpera 51'10"8 ; 5. Sainz 51'11"2 ; Gr.N Al Wahaibi 53'02"

CS.12 Olooloitikosh 2 (49,06 km)
1. Makinen 22'59" ; 2. Sainz 23'25"4 ; 3. Auriol 24'29" ; 4. McRae 24'58" ; 5. Duncan 25'15"; Gr.N Al Wahaibi 28'14"

CS.13 Super Spéciale 2 (2,42 km)
1. Makinen et Sainz 1'56"9 ; 3. Rovanpera et Dor 1'58"2 ; 5. Duncan 1'59" ; Gr.N Al Wahaibi 2'03"6

RESULTS AND RETIREMENTS

	Driver/Co-Driver	Car	Gr	Total Time
1	**Colin McRae – Nicky Grist**	**Ford Focus WRC**	**A**	**8h41m39,1s**
2	Didier Auriol – Denis Giraudet	Toyota Corolla WRC	A	8h56m05,3s
3	Carlos Sainz – Luis Moya	Toyota Corolla WRC	A	8h59m46,3s
4	Ian Duncan – Dave Williamson	Toyota Corolla WRC	A	9h05m35,7s
5	Petter Solberg – Fred Gallagher	Ford Focus WRC	A	9h26m28,2s
6	Harri Rovanpera – Risto Pietilainen	Seat Cordoba WRC	A	9h40m08,4s
7	**Frederic Dor – Kevin Gormley**	**Subaru Impreza WRC**	**A**	**9h41m38,2s**
8	**Hamed Al Wahaibi – Tony Sircombe**	**Mitsubishi Carisma GT**	**N**	**10h05m09s**
9	Luis Climent – Alex Romani	Mitsubishi Lancer Ev.3	N	10h08m24,2s
10	Hideaki Miyoshi – Eido Osawa	Subaru Impreza	N	10h42m00,8s
18	**Phineas Kimathi – Abdul Sidi**	**Hyundai Coupe**	**A**	**13h26m16,2s**
SC.2	Bruno Thiry – Stephane Prevot	Subaru Impreza WRC	A	Electronics
SC.3	Juha Kankkunen – Juha Repo	Subaru Impreza WRC	A	Electronics
SC.3	Freddy Loix – Sven Smeets	Mitsubushi Carisma GT	A	Accident
SC.7	Richard Burns – Robert Reid	Subaru Impreza WRC	A	Suspension
SC.11	Piero Liatti – Carlo Cassina	Seat Cordoba WRC	A	Engine
Finish	Tommi Makinen – Risto Mannisenmaki	Mitsubishi Lancer Ev.6	A	Excluded

GOSSIP

• AL WAHAIBI'S PREMIERE
"I knew nothing about rallying, but I wanted to try some motor sport, so as there are no circuits at home.." But of course. It is easy to find a career in the Sultanate of Oman. And it produced, at the fifteenth rally, a win in Group N. Well done to Hamed Wahaibi and his Mitsu Evo V, who dealt with the experienced Spaniard Luis Climent and his Evo III.

• BETWEEN FRIENDS
No official entries in the two litre class. It was a battle between four local Hyundais and victory went to the only one to make it to the finish, that of Kimathi, in a modest 21st place overall.

• WALDEGAARD WAS THERE
The indefatigable Bjorn Waldegaard did the Safari as a note car. In the past he used to win it.

• THUMBS UP
Colin McRae did the rally with a bandage on a broken thumb.

• LOST HELICOPTER
It is quite common for the helicopters to find it difficult to keep up with the cars, if the wind is in the opposite direction. But the pilot of the chopper due to precede Makinen and warn him of any danger, got lost for a while. This meant Makinen had to do the first leg without his guardian angel flying overhead.

EVENT LEADERS

SC.1	Kankkunen
SC.2	Burns
SC.3 - SC.4	Sainz
SC.5 - SC.6	Burns
SC.7 - SC.13	McRae

BEST PERFORMANCES

	1	2	3	4	5	6
Makinen	4	4	-	1	1	-
Sainz	3	4	2	-	2	-
Burns	3	2	1	-	-	-
Auriol	2	1	4	2	-	1
Duncan	1	-	-	3	4	2
Kankkunen	1	-	-	1	-	-
McRae	-	2	4	3	1	2
Rovanpera	-	-	1	2	2	2
Liatti	-	-	1	-	3	2
Dor	-	-	1	-	1	2
Solberg	-	-	-	-	-	3

CHAMPIONSHIP CLASSIFICATIONS

Drivers
1. Tommi Makinen ... 20
2. Didier Auriol ... 13
3. Colin McRae ... 10
3. Carlos Sainz ... 10

Constructors
1. Toyota ... 23
2. Mitsubishi ... 20
3. Ford ... 17
4. Subaru ... 10
5. Seat ... 7

Group N
1. Marc Duez ... 13
1. Jouko Puhakka ... 13
1. Hamed Al Wahaibi ... 13

Two Litres
1. Renault ... 19
2. Volkswagen ... 16
3. Hyundai ... 10

Team's Cup
1. Turning Point Rally Team ... 10
Krzysztof Holowczyc
1. F.Dor Rally Team ... 10
Frederic Dor
3. Valencia Terra Mar Team ... 6
Luis Climent

PREVIOUS WINNERS

1973	Mehta - Drews Datsun 240 Z
1974	Singh - Doig Mitsubishi Colt Lancer
1975	Andersson - Hertz Peugeot 504
1976	Singh - Doig Mitsubishi Colt Lancer
1977	Waldegaard - Thorszelius Ford Escort RS
1978	Nicolas - Lefebvre Peugeot 504 v6 Coupé
1979	Metha - Doughty Datsun 160 J
1980	Metha - Doughty Datsun 160 J
1981	Metha - Doughty Datsun Violet GT
1982	Metha - Doughty Datsun Violet GT
1983	Vatanen - Harryman Opel Ascona 400
1984	Waldegaard - Thorzelius Toyota Celica Turbo
1985	Kankkunen - Gallagher Toyota Celica Turbo
1986	Waldegaard - Gallagher Toyota Celica Turbo
1987	Mikkola - Hertz Audi 200 Quattro
1988	Biasion - Siviero Lancia Delta Intégrale
1989	Biasion - Siviero Lancia Delta Integrale
1990	Waldegaard - Gallagher Toyota Celica GT-Four
1991	Kankkunen - Piironen Lancia Delta Integrale
1992	Sainz - Moya Toyota Celica Turbo 4WD
1993	Kankkunen - Piironen Toyota Celica Turbo 4WD
1994	Duncan - Williamson Toyota Celica Turbo 4WD
1995	Fujimoto - Hertz Toyota Celica Turbo 4WD
1996	Makinen - Harjanne Mitsubishi Lancer EV.3
1997	McRae - Grist Subaru Impreza WRC
1998	Burns - Reid Mitsubishi Carisma GT

“From the river of forgetfulness

ame the revelation...”

PORTUGAL

Just as in 1998, Colin McRae came out on top at the end of the Portuguese Rally and just as in 98, he built up a big lead by the end of the first day to make life easier for himself, but unlike 98, he was in a Ford Focus WRC. The car's win in only its fourth appearance was much more convincing than its previous victory in Kenya, because the Portuguese stages were a fairer representation of typical world championship conditions. The Toyota drivers, plus Burns and especially Gronholm, who was making a

big impact with Mitsubishi, tried in vain to stop the rot. Thanks to a fifth place finish, Makinen just managed to hang onto his championship lead.

72.1

WITH ITS ROWS of little granite built houses, Ponte de Lima is a pretty little village, overlooking the blue of the river Lima which flows under a rickety bridge. From the river of forgetfulness (its original name) came the revelation in the middle of the first leg. That was when the Ford Focus WRC showed its true potential. We knew it was quick, but not how quick. "Objectively, I am a bit surprised." Sprawling on a plastic chair, his face towards the sun, Colin McRae was working on his tan. There were no outward signs of delight on his calm features as he unwound. There was no sense of triumph. At Ponte de Lima, when the rally was just four stages old, the Scotsman had been quickest on all of them Given the distance covered up to that point, it was easy to draw a conclusion: he was running half a second quicker than Burns and Auriol who were second and third respectively.

Leaving the quaint fortified village with the sun bouncing off its rococo churches, McRae continued to confirm the sure-footedness and speed of the Focus, which was leaving the opposition struggling in its wake. Auriol could only shrug his shoulders, amusement mixed with impotence. Gronholm preferred to put it down to the driver rather than the car, while Burns blamed the total package.

But these three drivers never gave up the fight. Finally finding the Subaru to his liking, Richard Burns in second place set two quickest times and refused to be intimidated. In the Toyota camp, the Corolla's handling had been improved after problems in the morning with some fine tuning. Gronholm was plain magnificent at the wheel of the Mitsubishi he was learning about on the move. While they were charging, Makinen seemed to be down in the dumps, dragging along a sadness totally in keeping with this country's traditional Fado songs, thanks to erratic behaviour from the front diff. But the necessary repairs could only be carried out at the final service point, which had the longest time allowance.

The second leg of the Portuguese Rally was a complete contrast to the calm and untroubled atmosphere that reigned over the bucolic run to the south of Porto. Even though the last two stages were cancelled because of problems caused by too many spectators, it was a day of struggle and strife. The sweaty faces of the gladiators revealed the true picture. Auriol's tanned head was constantly dripping with sweat. Makinen's breathing was short and painful, while Gronholm's wide eyed stare showed the fear. The risk was plain to see thanks to the damaged bodywork on Thiry's Subaru. It was all spelt out in the order as they chased McRae. Sainz and Auriol were giving it their all, followed by Burns and then there was Makinen, finally happy with his Mitsubishi again, but settling for a points finish. McRae managed to stay ahead of this talented bunch, even though he was also first car on the road, generally reckoned to be a major disadvantage in Portugal. He was handing out quite a lesson, leading Sainz by 33s and Auriol by 35s at the end of the second leg.

The final leg did not change much. McRae had it all under control, while his opponents tried to shine, with Makinen mounting an assault on fourth place. Despite three fastest times from four stages, the Finn could not shift Burns. The two points which came his way from fifth place were enough to keep in the lead in the championship. Also on a charge was Auriol, desperate to try and take second place off Sainz in the final stage. His ardour almost ended in a roll, with the Toyota tipping onto two wheels as Auriol regained control, with the help of a rock, to take a magnificent fastest time. It was not enough and he had to settle for third place on the podium.

A PROMISING FOCUS. Surprising but illegal on the Monte; triumphant, but under unusual circumstances in Kenya, the Ford Focus was quite simply stunning in the fourth round of the championship, taking a very convincing and most unexpected win, on classic rally roads. There was no exaggeration from Ford drivers and management when they said that, "none of us thought we could be so competitive." It was a very complete package, with six fastest times, a big lead, high speed and reliability all on the agenda. "And the car is just in its early stages," explained the team boss Malcolm Wilson. "In the weeks and months to come, it will make even more progress. I can tell you there is plenty of room for improvement!" Looking at his baby after the event, Gunther Steiner, the Focus' Italian technical coordinator, criticised by some observers for having no engineering qualification, had a huge grin from ear to ear. "Our next job is to put the car on a diet," he explained, turning serious all of a sudden. Because that was the main problem with this brand new car as could be seen quite clearly, when the car

72.1

Harri Rovanpera won the high-jump prize on the "Fafe bump."

73.1

While his brother was the overall winner, Alister McRae won the 2 litre class for Hyundai.

73.2

Various problems compromised Bruno Thiry's rally and the Belgian had to settle for sixth place.

73.3

Marcus Gronholm was standing in for Freddy Loix, still recovering from his Safari shunt.

73.1

73.2

"And the Ford is still in its infancy in terms of development."

Malcom Wilson

73.3

was weighed during the rally: Sainz's Corolla, 1237 kilos, which is seven over the minimum limit, against 1313 for McRae's Focus, or a whopping 83 kilos over the limit! The other area rip for development is the engine. "We can increase both power and driveability," continued Steiner. "Because, so far, we have concentrated on reliability rather than outright performance. We are working on this, small steps at a time."

Triumphant in this demanding if conventional rally, the win was a useful pointer for the rest of the season, proving that the long Focus was more than up to the challenge. In Portugal, Mitsubishi made a very rare technical error; Subaru struggled with an old car and inconsistent tyres; the Toyota drivers found it difficult to set up their Corollas and Ford pounced on all those weaknesses. But the American company had set itself a very high target given that the WRC car had only turned a wheel for the first time back on 21st October of the previous year. Just what they had achieved was summed up at the last service area, normally the site of all manner of tinkering. "Nothing to do," was McRae's impressive order when he pulled in.

DREAM, BRAVE SCOT! Gronholm, the luxury stand-in. It is considered bad form for the misfortunes of some to make the happiness of others, but after Loix's African accident, Gronholm got lucky. Shortly before the rally, Andrew Cowan did indeed ring Jean-Pierre Nicolas, his opposite number at Peugeot, to ask if he could borrow the Finn to fill the seat. Mitsubishi was evidently not worried about offering a drive in what is reckoned to be the top cockpit in the world championship to a driver from a team which will soon be a major challenger. No doubt, after the Portuguese rally, Gronholm underwent a longer debrief with his Peugeot employers than with his temporary bosses at Mitsubishi. Putting aside the remarks about industrial espionage, the driver was delighted to have been called up for this event where, in 1998, he had actually led for a brief while at the wheel of his privately entered Toyota Corolla WRC. "Mitsubishi has given me a fantastic opportunity and I thank Jean-Pierre Nicolas for letting me take it up." It was the same sort of opportunity used to such good effect by Panizzi and Delecour, those two solo flying artists putting on a good show on the Monte, earlier in the year. Just like them, Gronholm was note perfect. Right from the opening stages and only two days after first trying the Carisma GT during the shakedown, he was fighting it out in the lead group, finishing the opening leg in fifth place. Makinen could do no better than ninth because of diff problems. Sadly for big Marcus, the brakes gave up the ghost before a fatal transmission problem forced him to retire on the second day. The Mitsubishi is reckoned to be an easy car to drive, although built around the needs of Makinen, it can be hard for others to get the most out of it - just ask Burns and Loix, so Gronholm's performance had impressed everyone. Maybe Peugeot had already found its future world champion.

TAKE HEART MR. MCRAE. This Portuguese rally finished up as a family affair with Colin McRae taking overall honours, while little brother Alister flew home with the cup for the two litre class in his luggage. But above all, this win had given Colin renewed hope in the fight for the championship. Crowned once before in 1995, he has never stopped chasing after a second title. So far in vain. But it now seemed the winning Focus might be the car to help him reach his target. "The car ran faultlessly," he said at the finish. "The fact it is so quick on the loose, means it is should be the same on tarmac. All the same, it's incredible that our Focus has been so successful so soon in its career, when there is still so much development to come." With two wins in a row and no doubt more to come, McRae was now in Makinen's wake in the championship. The world champion, with wins in Monte Carlo and then Sweden was still leading, but only by two little points from the Ford driver. It looked as though a fascinating duel was in prospect between Makinen and McRae, rated by many as the two best drivers in the world. We would see. The Scotsman was definitely on a high and on the green hills of Lusitania, there was much talk of a test in a Formula 1 car. He had not been ridiculous back in 1996 at the wheel of a Jordan and so Ford was quite keen to try him in the cockpit of the Stewart. "If I am competitive, then I will have to consider what direction my career should go in. If I can do it, then there is no reason why I could not end up in Formula 1." Dream on brave Scot. The test was scheduled for the day after the British Grand Prix, but in the end it did not take place. So now Colin you are condemned to rallying where you please the fans and cause commentators to despair. Mind you, it would be good to see a wild man having a crack at the over- civilised world of Formula 1. Apparently the test will now take place in 2000.

74.1

Richard Burns was brilliant in fending off Tommi Makinen.

74.2

Although his car was fitted with a new evolution engine, Didier Auriol reckoned he could not tell the difference.

74.3

Piero Liatti bit the dust before retiring.

74.1

74.2

74.3

PORTUGAL

"From the river of forgetfulness came the revelation..."

75.1-6

Colin McRae, Pernilla Walfridsson and Carlos Sainz tackled the Baltar spectator stage without problems, but Abdullah Bakashab was a touch over optimistic, hitting the scenery. With no help from the spectators caged behind bars, retirement followed.

75.1

75.2

75.3

75.4

75.5

75.6

32ND PORTUGUESE RALLY

TOP ENTRIES

1 Tommi Makinen - Risto Mannisenmaki
MITSUBISHI LANCER EV.6

2 Marcus Gronholm - Timo Rautiainen
MITSUBISHI CARISMA GT

3 Carlos Sainz - Luis Moya
TOYOTA COROLLA WRC

4 Didier Auriol - Denis Giraudet
TOYOTA COROLLA WRC

5 Richard Burns - Robert Reid
SUBARU IMPREZA WRC

6 Juha Kankkunen - Juha Repo
SUBARU IMPREZA WRC

7 Colin McRae - Nicky Grist
FORD FOCUS WRC

8 Petter Solberg - Phil Mills
FORD FOCUS WRC

9 Harri Rovanpera - Risto Pietilainen
SEAT CORDOBA WRC

10 Piero Liatti - Carlo Cassina
SEAT CORDOBA WRC

11 Armin Schwarz - Manfred Hiemer
SKODA OCTAVIA WRC

12 Emil Triner - Milos Hulka
SKODA OCTAVIA WRC

14 Bruno Thiry - Stephane Prevot
SUBARU IMPREZA WRC

15 Rui Madeira - Nuno Da Silva
SUBARU IMPREZA

16 Krzysztof Holowczyc - Jean-Marc Fortin
SUBARU IMPREZA WRC

17 Markko Martin - Toomas Kitsing
FORD ESCORT WRC

18 Pasi Hagstrom - Tero Gardemeister
TOYOTA COROLLA WRC

19 Pedro Chaves - Sergio Paiva
TOYOTA COROLLA WRC

21 Frederic Dor - Didier Breton
SUBARU IMPREZA WRC

23 Luis Climent - Alex Romani
SUBARU IMPREZA

24 Abdullah Bakashab - Michael Park
TOYOTA COROLLA WRC

25 Volkan Isik - Erkan Bodur
TOYOTA COROLLA WRC

27 Matthias Kahle - Dieter Schneppenheim
TOYOTA COROLLA WRC

28 Adruzilo Lopes - Luis Lisboa
PEUGEOT 306 MAXI

29 Kenneth Eriksson - Staffan Parmander
HYUNDAI COUPE EV.2

30 Jose Macedo - Miguel Borges
RENAULT MEGANE MAXI

31 Alister McRae - David Senior
HYUNDAI COUPE EV.2

32 Martin Rowe - Derek Ringer
RENAULT MEGANE MAXI

34 Toni Gardemeister - Paavo Lukander
SEAT IBIZA KIT CAR

35 Tapio Laukkanen - Kaj Lindströn
RENAULT MEGANE MAXI

36 Gustavo Trelles - Martin Christie
MITSUBISHI LANCER EV.5

37 Manfred Stohl - Peter Muller
MITSUBISHI LANCER EV.5

40 Hamed Al Wahaibi - Tony Sircombe
MITSUBUSHI LANCER EV.5

43 Pernilla Walfridsson - Ulrika Mattsson
MITSUBISHI LANCER EV.4

4th leg of the 1999 world rally championships for constructors and drivers
4th leg of the constructors' "2 litre", production car drivers' and teams'world cups

Date: *21 - 24 March 1999*

Route: *1809,01 km divided into 3 legs, 23 stages on loose surface roads (399,51 km)*
1st leg : Sunday 21st et Monday 22nd March, Porto – Carbeceiras de Basto – Porto, 9 stages (162,58 km)
2nd leg : Tuesday 23rd March, Porto – Arganil – Porto, 10 stages (180,28 km)
3rd leg : Wednesday 24th March, Porto – Felgueiras – Porto, 4 stages (59,85 km)

Starters/Finishers: *117/56*

Thanks to numerous accidents befalling his rivals, Volkan Isik took the Team's cup.

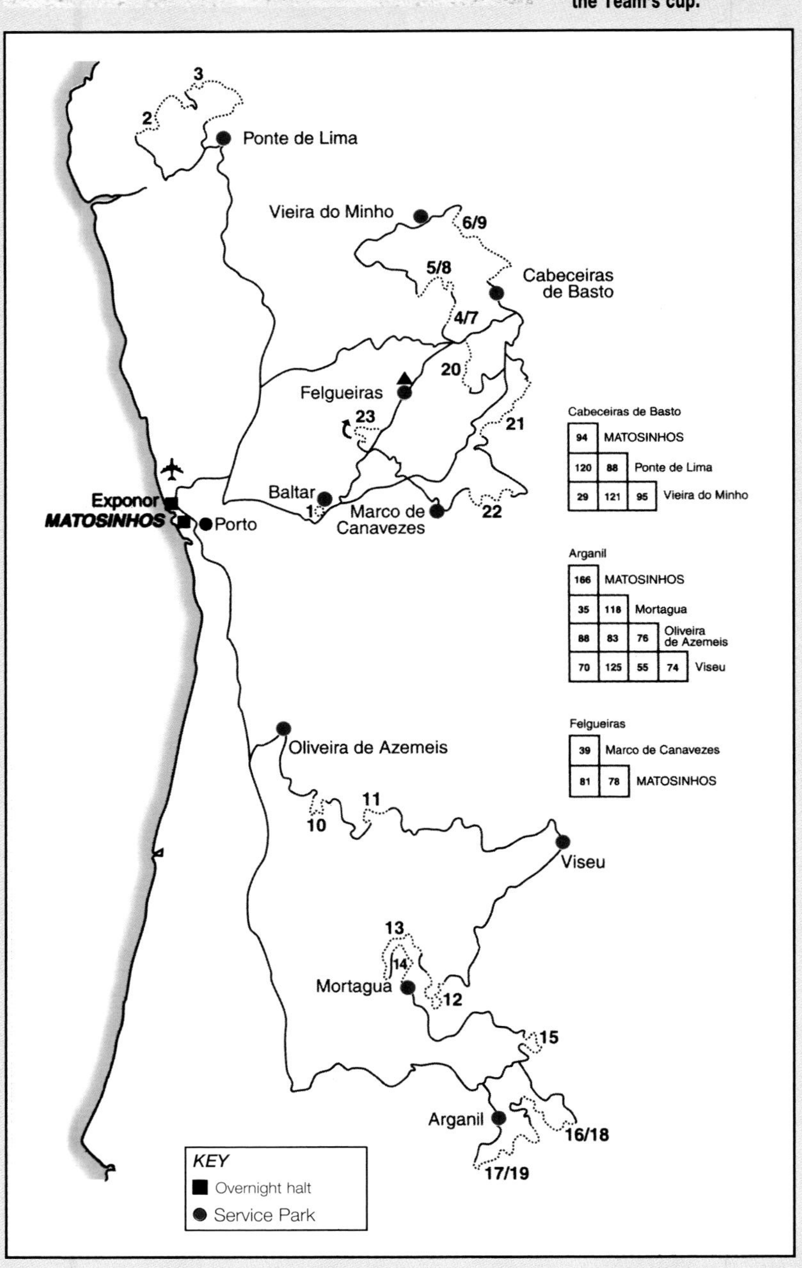

SPECIAL STAGE TIMES

SS.1 Baltar (3,2 km)
1. McRae 3'12''3 ; 2. Gonhölm 3'12''7 ; 3. Sainz 3'13''2 ; 4. Auriol 3'14''3 ; 5. Makinen 3'14''4 ; Gr.N Stohl 3'25''6 ; F2 Lopss 3'27''9

SS.2 Ponte de Lima Sste (23,64 km)
1. McRae 15'38''2 ; 2. Burns 15'51'' ; 3. Gronholm 15'56''5 ; 4. Sainz 15'58''8 ; 5. Kankkunen 16'01''6; Gr.N Stohl 16'56''3 ; F2 Laukkanen 16'53''4

SS.3 Ponte de Lima Osste (25,84 km)
1. McRae 18'39''2 ; 2. Auriol 18'52''4 ; 3. Sainz 18'58''2 ; 4. Gronholm et Burns 18'59''8 ; Gr.N Campos 20'02''3 ; F2 Eriksson 20'17''2

SS.4 Lameirinha 1 (15,2 km)
1. Sainz 10'06''5 ; 2. Gronholm 10'10''3 ; 3. McRae 10'11''3 ; 4. Auriol 10'12''8 ; 5. Burns 10'13'' ; Gr.N Galli 10'41''7 ; F2 Lopss 10'36''3

SS.5 Luilhas 1 (10,55 km)
1. McRae et Burns 7'51''7 ; 3. Sainz 7'52''6 ; 4. Auriol 7'53''6 ; 5. Gronholm 7'54''5 ; Gr.N Galli 8'10''6 ; F2 Macedo 8'09''9

SS.6 Cabreira 1 (27,6 km)
1. McRae 18'11''1 ; 2. Sainz 18'15''6 ; 3. Burns 18'18''3 ; 4. Auriol 18'23''1 ; 5. Liatti 18'24''6 ; Gr.N Puhakka 19'20''7 ; F2 McRae 19'23''3

SS.7 Lameirinha 2 (15,2 km)
1. Auriol 10'03''5 ; 2. Burns 10'04''2 ; 3. McRae 10'05'' ; 4. Sainz 10'06'' ; 5. Gronholm 10'07'' ; Gr.N Campos 10'37''5 ; F2 Lopss 10'37''7

SS.8 Luilhas 2 (10,55 km)
1. Burns 7'45''9 ; 2. Auriol 7'46''7 ; 3. Sainz 7'48''8 ; 4. Gronholm 7'48''9 ; 5. Thiry 7'51''2 ; Gr.N Campos 8'12''2 ; F2 Lopss 8'09''4

SS.9 Cabreira 2 (27,6 km)
1. McRae 18'03''9 ; 2. Makinen 18'09''9 ; 3. Auriol 18'10''9 ; 4. Burns 18'13''5 ; 5. Kankkunen 18'14''8 ; Gr.N Campos 19'13''6 ; F2 McRae 19'08''7

SS.10 Sever do Vouga (14,83 km)
1. Auriol 11'15''5 ; 2. Makinen 11'16''1 ; 3. McRae 11'18''6 ; 4. Gronholm 11'19''9 ; 5. Rovanpera 11'22''9 ; Gr.N Campos 11'49''1 ; F2 Lopss 11'55''1

SS.11 Oliveira de Fradss (11,26 km)
1. Burns 7'43''4 ; 2. Makinen 7'43'5 ; 3. Gronholm 7'43''9 ; 4. Auriol 7'44'' ; 5. Sainz 7'44''8 ; Gr.N Puhakka 8'05''6 ; F2 Lopss 8'12''3

SS.12 Aguieira (23,33 km)
1. Auriol et Puhakka 16'53''1 ; 3. Makinen 16'53''7; 4. McRae 16'57''2 ; 5. Sainz 16'58''5 ; F2 McRae 18'01''

SS.13 Mortazel (18,81 km)
1. Sainz 12'29''1 ; 2. Makinen 12'29''1 ; 3. Burns 12'29''8 ; 4. McRae 12'31'' ; 5. Rovanpera 12'33''4; Gr.N Puhakka 13'20''2 ; F2 Lopss 13'09''7

SS.14 Mortagua (17,24 km)
1. Sainz 11'41''7 ; 2. Makinen 11'42''1 ; 3. Auriol 11'43''2 ; 4. Burns 11'47''4 ; 5. McRae 11'48'' ; Gr.N Trellss 12'34''2 ; F2 Lopss 12'21''8

SS.15 Tabua (13,49 km)
1. Makinen 8'23'' ; 2. Auriol 8'27''4 ; 3. Gronholm 8'27''5 ; 4. Sainz 8'27''9 ; 5. Burns 8'29'' ; Gr.N Campos 8'58''5 ; F2 Lopss 8'49''3

SS.16 Coja 1 (20,96 km)
1. Sainz 13'03''8 ; 2. Auriol 13'04''8 ; 3. Makinen 13'04''9 ; 4. McRae 13'08'' ; 5. Burns 13'08''8 ; Gr.N Campos 14'12''1 ; F2 Lopss 13'53''9

SS.17 Salgueiro - Gois 1 (19,7 km)
1. Burns 11'30''6 ; 2. Sainz 11'31''2 ; 3. Makinen 11'32''6 ; 4. McRae 11'33'5 ; 5. Auriol 11'35'' ; Gr.N Campos 12'44''3 ; F2 Lopss 12'28''6

SS.18 Coja 2 et SS. 19 Salgueiro - Gois 2
Annuléss (public trop nombreux)

SS.20 Celorico de Basto (11,84 km)
1. Makinen 7'31''9 ; 2. Sainz 7'32''8 ; 3. Auriol 7'33''3 ; 4. McRae 7'36''3 ; 5. Burns 7'38''1 ; Gr.N Campos 8'01'' ; F2 Lopss 8'02''1

SS.21 Fridao (14,2 km)
1. Makinen 10'12'' ; 2. McRae 10'16''6 ; 3. Sainz 10'16''9 ; 4. Auriol 10'19''9 ; 5. Burns 10'20''2, Gr.N Campos 11'03''2 ; F2 Eriksson 11'03''1

SS.22 Aboboreira (17,96 km)
1. Makinen 12'13''2 ; 2. Auriol 12'14''1 ; 3. Sainz 12'14''2 ; 4. Burns 12'17''4 ; 5. McRae 12'23''5 ; Gr.N Campos 13'12''7 ; F2 McRae 13'06''4

SS.23 Lousada – Barrosas (15,85 km)
1. Auriol 11'53''4 ; 2. Sainz 11'54''5 ; 3. Makinen 11'57''9 ; 4. Burns 12'01''1 ; 5. McRae 12'02''7 ; Gr.N Campos 13'02'' ; F2 Eriksson et McRae 13'00''

RESULTS AND RETIREMENTS

	Driver/Co-Driver	Car	Gr	Total Time
1	**Colin McRae – Nicky Grist**	**Ford Focus WRC**	**A**	**4h05m41,7s**
2	Carlos Sainz – Luis Moya	Toyota Corolla WRC	A	4h05m54s
3	Didier Auriol – Denis Giraudet	Toyota Corolla WRC	A	4h05m58,2s
4	Richard Burns – Robert Reid	Subaru Impreza WRC	A	4h06m37,1s
5	Tommi Makinen – Risto Mannisenmaki	Mitsubishi Lancer Ev.6	A	4h06m46,1s
6	Bruno Thiry – Stephane Prevot	Subaru Impreza WRC	A	4h13m11,4s
7	**Volkan Isik – Erkan Bodur**	**Toyota Corolla WRC**	**A**	**4h15m07,5s**
8	Matthias Kahle – Dieter Schneppenheim	Toyota Corolla WRC	A	4h15m15,9s
9	Rui Madeira – Nuno da Silva	Subaru Impreza	A	4h15m51,5s
10	Luis Climent – Alex Romani	Subaru Impreza	A	4h17m10,3s
12	**Miguel Campos – Miguel Ramalho**	**Mitsubishi Carisma GT**	**N**	**4h22m11s**
13	**Alister McRae – David Senior**	**Hyundai Coupe Ev.2**	**A**	**4h22m49,7s**
SS.3	Krzysztof Holowczyc – Jean-Marc Fortin	Subaru Impreza WRC	A	Accident
SS.6	Pasi Hagstrom – Tero Gardemeister	Toyota Corolla WRC	A	Accident
SS.8	Emil Triner – Milos Hulka	Skoda Octavia WRC	A	Clutch
SS.10	Armin Schwarz – Manfred Hiemer	Skoda Octavia WRC	A	Clutch
SS.11	Piero Liatti – Carlo Cassina	Seat Cordoba WRC	A	Accident
SS.12	Markko Martin – Toomas Kitsing	Ford Escort WRC	A	Gearbox
SS.16	Pedro Chaves – Sergio Paiva	Toyota Corolla WRC	A	Engine
SS.16	Juha Kankkunen – Juha Repo	Subaru Impreza WRC	A	Engine
SS.16	Marcus Gronholm – Timo Rautiainen	Mitsubishi Carisma GT	A	Transmission
SS.16	Harri Rovanpera – Risto Pietilainen	Seat Cordoba WRC	A	Accident

GOSSIP

• KANKKUNEN STRUGGLES

It was a rally to forget for Juha Kankkunen. Never happy with the handling of his Subaru Impreza WRC, the four times world champion was never in the race. He was beaten by his engine and chose to pack it in after fifteen stages. Sad, when his last win dated back to this event all of five years ago.

• HARD, VERY HARD FOR SKODA

In the final stage of the first leg, both Skoda Octavia's retired at the same time with broken gearboxes. Their return to competition, having been absent since the Monte, was difficult with many clutch and engine management problems. However, a few of Schwartz's times showed that the big Czechs had some potential.

• THE MCRAES ON ALL FRONTS

The McRae family did the grand slam with Colin's little brother Alister winning the two litre class at the wheel of his Hyundai from his team-mate Kenneth Eriksson. This meant that the Korean constructor had taken its first world championship win and was first equal in the Two Litre World Cup with Renault. The Hyundaï's had it easy after the very talented Adruzilo Lopes retired his Peugeot at the start of the second leg.

• SOLBERG CONTINUES BUT DOES NOT SHINE

Once again Radstrom is replaced at the wheel of the second works Focus by the young Norwegian Petter Solberg. He found it hard to get as much out of the car as his team-leader McRae and only once featured in the top six on a stage. He finished eleventh, 11m 32.5s down but it was enough to give Ford an extra point in the championship to add to the ten from its win. Apparently, Malcolm Wilson reckons Solberg has a great future.

• SUBARU SPIES ON MICHELIN

Before the Portuguese rally, the Subaru team carried out no less than two tarmac tests with the Impreza, using customer Michelins, bought on the quiet because of their Pirelli contract in order to compare them with the Italian rubber. Every time, the stopwatch produced the same result: an improvement of 0.8s per kilometre. In Portugal, Subaru found it hard to disguise its anger towards its tyre supplier. It was an ugly sight.

MICHELIN

EVENT LEADERS

SS.1 – SS.23	McRae

BEST PERFORMANCES

	1	2	3	4	5	6
McRae	6	1	4	4	3	-
Makinen	4	6	3	-	1	
Auriol	4	5	3	6	1	1
Sainz	4	4	6	4	1	2
Burns	4	2	2	4	7	-
Gronholm	-	2	3	3	2	3
Kankkunen	-	-	-	-	2	4
Rovanpera	-	-	-	-	2	4
Thiry	-	-	-	-	1	2
Liatti	-	-	-	-	1	-
Isik	-	-	-	-	-	3
Madeira	-	-	-	-	-	1
Solberg	-	-	-	-	-	1
Kahle	-	-	-	-	-	1

CHAMPIONSHIP CLASSIFICATIONS

Drivers

1. Tommi Makinen	22
2. Colin McRae	20
3. Didier Auriol	17
4. Carlos Sainz	16
5. Juha Kankkunen	7

Constructors

1. Toyota	33
2. Ford	28
3. Mitsubishi	22
4. Subaru	13
5. Seat	7

Group N

1. Gustavo Trelles	17
2. Marc Duez	13
2. Jouko Puhakka	13
2. Hamed Al Wahaibi	13
2. Miguel Campos	13

Two Litres

1. Hyundai	26
1. Renault	26
3. Volkswagen	16

Team's Cup

1. F.Dor Rally Team Frederic Dor	14
2. Valencia Terra Mar Team Luis Climent	10
2. Toyota Mobil Team Turkey Volkan Isik	10
2. Turning Point Rally Team Krzysztof Holowczyc	10

PREVIOUS WINNERS

1973	Therier - Jaubert Alpine Renault A 110
1974	Pinto - Bernacchini Fiat 124 Abarth
1975	Alen - Kivimäki Fiat 124 Abarth
1976	Munari - Maiga Lancia Stratos
1977	Alen - Kivimäki Fiat 131 Abarth
1978	Alen - Kivimäki Fiat 131 Abarth
1979	Mikkola - Hertz Ford Escort RS
1980	Rohrl - Geistdorfer Fiat 131 Abarth
1981	Alen - Kivimaki Fiat 131 Abarth
1982	Mouton - Pons Audi Quattro
1983	Mikkola - Hertz Audi Quattro
1984	Mikkola - Hertz Audi Quattro
1985	Salonen - Harjanne Peugeot 205 T16
1986	Moutinho - Fortes Renault 5 Turbo
1987	Alen - Kivimaki Lancia Delta HF 4WD
1988	Biasion - Cassina Lancia Delta Integrale
1989	Biasion - Siviero Lancia Delta Integrale
1990	Biasion - Siviero Lancia Delta Integrale
1991	Sainz - Moya Toyota Celica GT-Four
1992	Kankkunen - Piironen Lancia HF Integrale
1993	Delecour - Grataloup Ford Escort RS Cosworth
1994	Kankkunen - Grist Toyota Celica Turbo 4WD
1995	Sainz - Moya Subaru Impreza
1996	Madeira - Da Silva Toyota Celica GT-Four
1997	Makinen - Harjanne Mitsubishi Lancer Ev.4
1998	McRae - Grist Subaru Impreza WRC

“This radiant cat with golder

wings..."

CATALUNYA

The domination of the two Citroen Xsaras was complete, during an event which saw Puras lead at first, before Bugalski took over after the Spaniard went out with mechanical problems. After several attempts, a Kit-Car finally triumphed in a World Championship event, much to the shame of the leading players in the series. Remarkably, this meant that while Didier Auriol had to settle for the six points which went with his second place, his team Toyota

picked up the ten points. Strange rules which finally worked in favour of the double chevron team. It had not won at this level since 1971 and finally, its most loyal driver won his first world championship rally.

THE CHEVRONS WERE TOO STRONG! Jesus Puras is a strange cove. His profile is reminiscent of a mynah bird and his smile makes you think of Buster Keaton. And here he comes, at the entrance to the Girona service area with a huge and happy grin on his face, as well as a look of slight embarrassment at it all. He blushes a bit before passing comment: "Yes of course, I am more surprised than anyone. Honestly, I never expected to do so well. I am in the lead. Great!" Puras is modest about his achievement. Others would be definitely more expansive. The first leg of the Catalunya Rally had been marked by the total domination of the Xsara Kit-Car and he was the quickest of their drivers, everywhere. From the delicate Sierra of the Gavarres, where springtime encourages nature to put on an astonishing display of greenery, then in the foothills of the Pyrenees; more austere and with traces of lingering snow on its highest peaks, the two little red rockets, his and Bugalski's, were hardly ever troubled on their way to first and second on this first leg. Their day had been a long inexorable march to the front, hardly troubled but for a few little benign glitches: a harmless spin for Bugalski, excessively worn tyres for Puras, who had to watch his braking towards the end of the run, but nothing serious.

The stars of the series would have wished more troubles on them, as they were totally subdued. No doubt, some of them must have burst out laughing at the start of the second leg. As they tried to leave Lloret del Mar, the town which was hosting the rally, the lead Citroen resolutely refused to fire up and get on with the job, despite all the pushing from its crew. It was in vain and the beast refused to roar into life. "The battery was perfect, the starter turned the engine over," explained Citroen's technical director Jean-Claude Vaucard. "But it just refused to start." That was it - retirement was the only result. But as one Xsara fell by the wayside, another took up the baton with Bugalski going into the lead. Auriol was the only one who could keep up. Sometimes, figures speak louder than words.

Gratalops-Escaladei, 45 kilometres of narrow, fast road - 29m 08.9s for Bugalski with Auriol next at 2.8s with Burns third over 20 seconds down. To stay with the Xsara, the Toyota driver was having to take some big risks. "There a left in 6thwhere we came that close to the grass," he said, indicating a tiny gap between two fingers. Two more centimetres and we would have been in the trees. We were going so quickly, it wouldn't have been one roll, it would have been fifteen. Ow, ow, ow! As for the others, they were nowhere and Makinen, Burns and Rovanpera all added to their woes with one minute penalties for jumped starts.

Despite a great display on the third leg from Tommi Makinen, Bugalski's win was never in doubt. Back up there in fighting mood, once he had sorted his Mitsubishi to his liking, the world champion was putting everyone else in the shade. "Tommi isn't driving, he's flying," said an admiring Sainz. Having tried all he knew to stop the rot, the Spaniard was out after his Corolla died on the road section after the final stage. Bugalski did get to the finish as a winner for the first time in his long career.

BUGALSKI, FIRST. Back in Lloret de Mar as the winner after a three day epic fight, Philippe Bugalski had just written his own little chapter in the history of world motorsport. And not just for one reason.

The simplest: never since 1971, had a driver taken a Citroen to a win in a classic rally. It happened in Morocco in prehistoric times almost. The World Championship did not even exist back then and the winners were Deschaseaux and Plassard in their amazing SM Coupe, which looked like a camel in the desert.

The most insolent: never before had one of these peppy two wheel drive machines, called Kit-Cars, managed to trounce the WRC 4x4 cars in a world championship event. It was not for want of trying, especially in the case of Peugeot and its 306 Maxi.

Finally, the most personal: Philippe Bugalski had never won a world championship rally. Yes, he did win in Corsica in 1996, but back then the event was not part of the championship.

So, when he finally took the Xsara to the top rung of the podium, his smile was that of a radiant cat with golden wings as large as the shoulders of a piano mover and "little Bug" could afford to smile. The shouts and cheers were loud enough to drown out even the sea. The French Champion looked proud up there, with Makinen on his left and Auriol on his right, with four world championship titles between them. "That feels good," he said with a grin. It was a perfect introduction to the winner's enclosure, after a drive built on tenacity, determination and skill. The facts speak for themselves: nineteen stages and nine fastest times for the Citroen drivers, five for Bug and four for the unfortunate Puras. No other driver was ever in the lead. Citroen had been dominant, beating the entire world championship field. As for the driver, this result made up for the disappointment for his all too brief time and badly prepared time with Lancia in 1992. This time he did it and Bug can finally add that all important, "world championship rally winner" to his cv, at the age of 35 and after 17 years of competition.

FRUSTRATION FOR MONSIEUR AURIOL. Auriol was second behind Bugalski, but his team was telling anyone who would listen that Toyota had won. Because there was a slight sense of unease in the presence of the victorious Citroen. At the finish, the little bald guy was keen to

"There's a left in 6th'. Two more centimetres and we were in the trees. We were going so quickly, it wouldn't have been one roll, it would have been fifteen."

Didier Auriol

80.2

80.3

80.1

explain his own misgivings. "I've got nothing against Citroen or Bugalski, but I have got something against FIA. Citroen has a Kit-Car which is not eligible for world championship constructors' points, which are reserved for the WRC, but Bugalski gets all his drivers' points. The French driver was beginning to feel like the turkey at the feast. His team had picked up ten points, but he only had six to Bug's ten, even though the Citroen driver is not even taking part in the championship. The main problem with this system is that Auriol is in the fight for the title at the end of the season and misses out for the sake of those missing four points, Auriol will definitely regret the two tier points system. Nevertheless, as the only driver to hang on to the Citroen's tail pipes, his performance did not go unnoticed. The Italian magazine Rombo, with its extensive rally coverage publishes its own scoring system at the end of every rally. Their main writer, Guido Rancati has a pen which he can wield like a scalpel and is a maker and breaker of reputations. The drivers rarely complain about his scoring system and they all read his reviews religiously. When it came to this event he wrote, "above and beyond" next to Auriol's name and the accompanying paragraph began with the word, "Inspired." By comparison, although he was the winner, Philippe Bugalski was scored as a 9.5 out of 10, which was more than honorable, it was exceptional.

It was not a crazy verdict. When you consider that, on dry tarmac, the Corolla WRC is no match for the Xsara Kit-Car, Auriol's performance was nothing short of magnificent. For three whole days, he was the only one to worry the Citroens. Makinen and McRae were brilliant at times, and the Frenchman's team-mate Sainz was also thereabouts, but only Auriol was consistently quick. He also had a very clear picture of what to expect. He had predicted that the Bug-Xsara machine would be the big favourite. Inspired but also divine.

THE AL-WAHAIBI REVELATION. In the rally that marked the startling Citroen win, there was another victory almost as impressive if much less noticeable, but it still surprised the little world of the world championship. A pocket sized driver, all smiles, not only took a totally unexpected victory in Group N, but also took the lead in this championship for production cars. Hamed Al-Wahaibi, a native of Muscat in the Sultanate of Oman certainly upset the very conservative establishment in this category. On the Catalan roads, one had expected victory to go to a specialist Spaniard or once again, the tireless Gustavo Trelles, rather than this strange driver from a country whose motor sport habits are a mystery. Son of a very good Oman family, working mainly in the real estate business, "Hamed Said Al-Wahaibi" to be precise, he came late to motor sport and started out on two wheels. Sent to California to finish his studies, he began by racing bikes on really tough circuits like Laguna Seca. Given a lecture by his family, who objected to him spending the money which should have gone on his studies, not to mention the risk to his life on these dangerous contraptions, the young man was ordered home in disgrace. But a love for all things mechanical, which began when he whizzed around the family farm on a tractor, would not desert him. A comeback was always on the cards and he went to study the subject properly at the Jim Russell racing school at Donington Circuit in England. He was quicker than all the other students on his course and then decided to switch to rallying. The roads in the Middle East hardly see any traffic. He tackled the regional championship, rife with cheating and an unequal field made up of mega rich drivers with no real interest in the sport and true amateurs who felt out of their depth. He made a lot of enemies denouncing the parlous state of the sport, upsetting the front runners by beating them to the Group N crown. By then he was bored, but his blind ambition and unshakeable faith and his skill at the wheel opened the doors to the world championship. In 1998, he tried his hand at Group N on five world championship events and proved he was not out of his depth. For 1999, he put together his own organisation, paid for more by family money rather than by the cigarette company whose logo adorned his bonnet. He employed the technical talents of Ralliart Germany who provided him with an excellent Lancer Evo. 5 which he drove with verve. Missing out on the Monte, he had a difficult start in Sweden where he finished eighth before pulling off a great win on the Safari, an event where admittedly, luck can play more a significant part. But best of all, this Catalan success on tarmac, something of an unknown quantity to him, proved that Trelles finally had an opponent worthy of the name. "He thinks I feel threatened," laughed the Uruguayan driver, "but in fact, I'm playing with him." But Al-Wahaibi was already dreaming of the title. And why not? He has the talent. It would be a first as no Arab driver has ever been crowned world champion in a motor sport category. It will happen one day and it will have started with this very nice young lad.

80.1

Because of crowd control problems, Makinen was the only one to tackle the first stage.

81.1

Philippe Bugalski's performance was not well received by all the big boys in the world championship.

81.2

After a surprising performance in Monte Carlo, the Seats appeared to have run out of steam.

82.1
Constant problems in the final three stages saw Carlos Sainz drop out of the points.

82.2
As in Portugal, Tommi Makinen went absolutely flat out on the final leg, to ensure third place on the podium.

82.3
Simon Jean-Joseph was hindered by a whole host of mechanical problems.

82.4
Oriol Gomez and his Megane put Renault back in the lead in the 2 litre class.

83.1
Didier Auriol felt cheated at not picking up the winner's ten points, while Toyota got them for the constructors' championship.

83.2
Freddy Loix made a successful comeback but the Belgian moved over for his team mate towards the end of the rally.

82.1

82.2

82.3

82.4

CATALUNYA

"This radiant cat with golden wings..."

83.3

Despite a mediocre start to the season, David Richards was optimistic about the future events.

83.4

Harri Rovanpera was handicapped by his tyre choice, while learning more about tarmac.

83.5

At the end of the first leg, Armin Schwarz and his surprising Skoda was ahead of the two factory Subarus.

83.3

3.1

83.4

83.2

83.5

35TH SPANISH RALLY

TOP ENTRIES

1 Tommi Makinen – Risto Mannisenmaki
MITSUBISHI LANCER EV.6

2 Freddy Loix – Sven Smeets
MITSUBISHI CARISMA GT

3 Carlos Sainz – Luis Moya
TOYOTA COROLLA WRC

4 Didier Auriol – Denis Giraudet
TOYOTA COROLLA WRC

5 Richard Burns – Robert Reid
SUBARU IMPREZA WRC

6 Bruno Thiry – Stephane Prevot
SUBARU IMPREZA WRC

7 Colin McRae – Nicky Grist
FORD FOCUS WRC

8 Simon Jean-Joseph – Fred Gallagher
FORD FOCUS WRC

9 Harri Rovanpera – Risto Pietilainen
SEAT CORDOBA WRC

10 Piero Liatti – Carlo Cassina
SEAT CORDOBA WRC

11 Armin Schwarz – Manfred Hiemer
SKODA OCTAVIA WRC

12 Pavel Sibera – Petr Gross
SKODA OCTAVIA WRC

14 Juha Kankkunen – Juha Repo
SUBARU IMPREZA WRC

15 Henrik Lundgaard – Freddy Pedersen
TOYOTA COROLLA WRC

16 Philippe Bugalski – Jean-Paul Chiaroni
CITROEN XSARA KIT CAR

17 Jesus Puras – Marc Marti
CITROEN XSARA KIT CAR

18 Adruzilo Lopes – Luis Lisboa
PEUGEOT 306 MAXI

19 Oriol Gomez – Oriol Julia
RENAULT MAXI MEGANE

21 Kenneth Eriksson – Staffan Parmander
HYUNDAI COUPE EV.2

23 Alister McRae – David Senior
HYUNDAI COUPE EV.2

25 Luis Climent – Alex Romani
SUBARU IMPREZA

26 Volkan Isik – Erkan Bodur
TOYOTA COROLLA WRC

27 Isolde Holderied – Catherine François
TOYOTA COROLLA WRC

28 Abdullah Bakashab – Michael Park
TOYOTA COROLLA WRC

30 Gustavo Trelles – Martin Christie
MITSUBISHI LANCER EV.5

31 Manfred Stohl – Kay Gerlach
MITSUBISHI LANCER EV.5

34 Hamed Al Wahaibi – Tony Sircombe
MITSUBUSHI LANCER EV.5

36 Pernilla Walfridsson – Ulrika Mattsson
MITSUBISHI LANCER EV.5

5th leg of the 1999 world rally championships for constructors and drivers
5th leg of the constructors' «2 litre», production car drivers' and teams'world cups

Date: *19 - 21 April 1999*

Route: *1713,31 km divided into 3 legs, 19 stages on tarmac roads (396,01 km)*
1st leg : Monday 19th April, Lloret de Mar – Manlleu – Lloret de Mar, 8 stages (135,30 km)
2nd leg : Tuesday 20th April, Lloret de Mar – Mora La Nova – Lloret de Mar, 6 stages (169,43 km)
3rd leg : Wednesday 21st April, Lloret de Mar – Manlleu – Lloret de Mar, 5 stages (91,28 km)

Starters/Finishers: *104/56*

Didier Auriol was the only driver to have scored point on every round in the early part of the season.

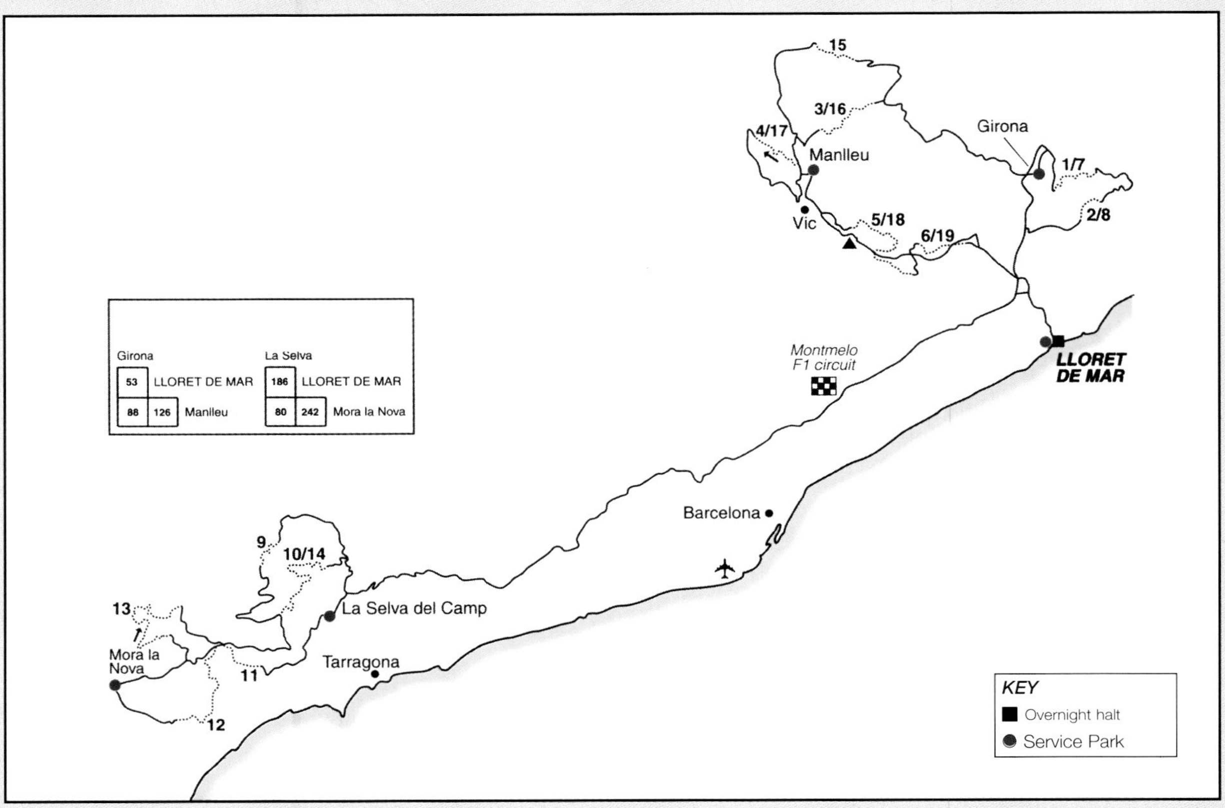

SPECIAL STAGE TIMES

SS.2 Santa Pellaia 1 (11,66 km)
1. Puras 7'42"6 ; 2. Auriol 7'45"2 ; 3. Sainz 7'46"5 ; 4. Makinen 7'47"2 ; 5. Bugalski 7'47"9 ; Gr.N Al Wahaibi 8'19"4

SS.3 Coll de Bracons 1 (19,89 km)
1. Puras 13'02"1 ; 2. Bugalski 13'06" ; 3. Sainz 13'09" ; 4. Auriol et McRae 13'10"4 ; Gr.N Galli 13'53"1

SS.4 La Trona 1 (12,86 km)
1. Makinen 8'31"5 ; 2. McRae 8'31"6 ; 3. Sainz 8'32"5 ; 4. Auriol 8'32"8 ; 5. Bugalski 8'34"1 ; Gr.N Trellss 9'07"7

SS.5 La Fullaca – Arbuciss 1 (32,64 km)
1. Puras 20'28"4 ; 2. Bugalski 20'32" ; 3. Sainz 20'37"3 ; 4. Auriol 20'40"3 ; 5. Loix 20'49"8 ; Gr.N Trellss 21'46"7

SS.6 Cladells 1 (15,27 km)
1. Auriol 10'00"8 ; 2. Loix 10'02"5 ; 3. Bugalski 10'04"5 ; 4. Makinen 10'06"6 ; 5. Sainz 10'07"9 ; Gr.N Trellss 10'41"7

SS.7 Els Angels 2 (15,66 km)
1. Auriol 9'41"4 ; 2. Sainz 9'43"8 ; 3. Puras 9'44"4 ; 4. Makinen 9'45"1 ; 5. Bugalski 9'45"9 ; Gr.N Trellss 10'29"7

SS.8 Santa Pellaia 2 (11,66 km)
1. Puras 7'43"7 ; 2. Bugalski 7'45"3 ; 3. Auriol 7'48"1 ; 4. Sainz 7'49"1 ; 5. Lopss 7'49"8 ; Gr.N Al Wahaibi 8'22"3

SS.9 Pradss (13,77 km)
1. Bugalski 8'17"1 ; 2. Makinen 8'21"5 ; 3. Sainz 8'21"7 ; 4. Loix 8'22"1 ; 5. Thiry 8'23"7; Gr.N Trellss 9'06"5

SS.10 La Riba 1 (32,86 km)
1. McRae 20'33"4 ; 2. Makinen 20'35"6 ; 3. Bugalski 20'37" ; 4. Auriol 20'43"7 ; 5. Loix 20'44"7 ; Gr.N Trellss 22'02"

SS.11 Riudecanyss (12,68 km)
1. Auriol 8'52"8 ; 2. McRae 8'53"6 ; 3. Sainz 8'56"5 ; 4. Makinen 8'56"6 ; 5. Bugalski 8'57"8 ; Gr.N Galli 9'27"6

SS.12 Santa Marina (31,38 km)
1. Bugalski 19'18"2 ; 2. Auriol 19'24"1 ; 3. Makinen 19'26"4 ; 4. McRae 19'26"9 ; 5. Lopss 19'31"5 ; Gr.N Manfrinato 20'59"1

SS.13 Gratallops – Sscaladei (45,88 km)
1. Bugalski 29'08"9 ; 2. Auriol 29'11"7 ; 3. Burns 29'29"1 ; 4. Loix 29'33"7 ; 5. Kankkunen 29'39"7 ; Gr.N Al Wahaibi 31'51"4

SS.14 La Riba 2 (32,86 km)
1. McRae 20'37"8 ; 2. Makinen 20'38"5 ; 3. Sainz 20'40"3 ; 4. Auriol 20'43"2 ; 5. Loix 20'45"6 ; Gr.N Trellss 22'11"8

SS.15 Coll de Santigosa (10,62 km)
1. Makinen 6'49"2 ; 2. Sainz 6'52"6 ; 3. Bugalski 6'52"6 ; 4. Burns 6'54"1 ; 5. Auriol 6'54"6 ; Gr.N Trellss 7'24"1

SS.16 Coll de Bracons 2 (19,89 km)
1. Makinen 13'08"8 ; 2. Auriol 13'11"7 ; 3. Sainz 13'13"2 ; 4. Bugalski 13'13"7 ; 5. Gomez 13'17" ; Gr.N Trellss 14'05"5

SS.17 La Trona 2 (12,86 km)
1. Bugalski 8'31"3 ; 2. Makinen 8'32"7 ; 3. Auriol 8'33"6 ; 4. Kankkunen 8'37"1 ; 5. Loix 8'38"1 ; Gr.N Trellss 9'10"6

SS.18 La Fullaca – Arbuciss 2 (32,64 km)
1. Bugalski 20'24"9 ; 2. Makinen 20'31"1 ; 3. Auriol 20'38"4 ; 4. Loix 20'46"8 ; 5. Kankkunen 20'48"1 ; Gr.N Trellss 21'49"1

SS.19 Cladells 2 (15,27 km)
1. Auriol 10'08"3 ; 2. Burns 10'09"1 ; 3. Bugalski 10'10" ; 4. Kankkunen 10'10"5 ; 5. Loix 10'19"1 ; Gr.N Trellss 10'40"9

RESULTS AND RETIREMENTS

	Driver/Co-Driver	Car	Gr	Total Time
1	**Philippe Bugalski - Jean-Paul Chiaroni**	**Citroen Xsara Kit Car**	**A**	**4h13m45,6s**
2	**Didier Auriol - Denis Giraudet**	**Toyota Corolla WRC**	**A**	**4h14m17,4s**
3	Tommi Makinen - Risto Manisenmaki	Mitsubishi Lancer Ev.6	A	4h16m06,7s
4	Freddy Loix - Sven Smeets	Mitsubishi Carisma GT	A	4h16m21s
5	Richard Burns - Robert Reid	Subaru Impreza WRC	A	4h17m47,5s
6	Juha Kankkunen - Juha Repo	Subaru Impreza WRC	A	4h18m32,9s
7	Bruno Thiry - Stephane Prevot	Subaru Impreza WRC	A	4h18m46,9s
8	Oriol Gomez - Oriol Julia	Renault Maxi Megane	A	4h19m34,3s
9	**Luis Climent - Alex Romani**	**Subaru Impreza WRC**	**A**	**4h20m14,4s**
10	Piero Liatti - Carlo Cassina	Seat Cordoba WRC	A	4h20m53s
18	**Hamed Al Wahaibi - Tony Sircombe**	**Mitsubishi Lancer Ev.5**	**N**	**4h36m18,3s**
SS.5	Manfred Stohl - Kay Gerlach	Mitsubishi Lancer Ev.5	N	Gearbox
SS.9	Jesus Puras - Marc Marti	Citroen Xsara Kit Car	A	Moving off
SS.12	Pavel Sibera - Petr Gross	Skoda Octavia WRC	A	Engine
SS.13	Simon Jean-Joseph - Fred Gallagher	Ford Focus WRC	A	Electrique
SS.13	Adruzillo Lopes - Luis Lisboa	Peugeot 306 Maxi	A	Accident
SS.14	Armin Schwarz - Manfred Hiemer	Skoda Octavia WRC	A	Alternator
SS.15	Colin McRae - Nicky Grist	Ford Focus WRC	A	Retired
Finish	Carlos Sainz - Luis Moya	Toyota Corolla WRC	A	Alternator

At the end of the second leg, Simon Jean-Joseph had to retire with electrical problems, having proved little.

BEST PERFORMANCES

	1	2	3	4	5	6
Makinen	9	5	2	3	-	-
Sainz	7	3	6	2	-	-
Auriol	2	3	9	3	2	-
Radstrom	1	8	1	9	-	-
McRae	-	1	1	1	4	-
Burns	-	-	-	-	5	7
Hagstrom	-	-	-	-	5	1
Kankkunen	-	-	-	-	-	4
Lindholm	-	-	-	-	-	2
Rovanpera	-	-	-	-	-	1
Loix	-	-	-	-	-	1
Martin	-	-	-	-	-	1
Solberg	-	-	-	-	-	1

GOSSIP

• FORD MISSED THE PARTY

After two wins, in Kenya and Portugal, the Fords had nothing to celebrate at the end of the first rally appearance of the Focus WRC on dry tarmac. Right from day one McRae was badly delayed with turbo problems. The team turned this event into one big test session for the forthcoming Tour of Corsica, the Scotsman setting two fastest times before giving up, so that the team could get back to work in the UK as soon as possible. Jean-Joseph was not helped much by his team and retired with numerous diff problems followed by trouble with the power steering. In the end it was electrical problems with put him out at the end of the second leg.

• BERNIE'S LATEST MAD IDEA

Formula 1's Mr. Fixit, Bernie Ecclestone let it be known at the time of this rally that he had decided to invest around 75 million pounds on increasing media coverage of the World Rally Championship as from the middle of the 1999 season. The news broke in the Sunday Times, stating that the money would be used to provide intensive television coverage starting in 2000. Wait and see...

• THIRY WAS NOT CONVINCING

For the first time this season, Bruno Thiry had been nominated by his team as one of the drivers eligible to score points towards the constructors' championship. This he did, but finishing seventh, Subaru's tarmac specialist was beaten by his two "loose surface" team-mates, Burns and Kankkunen. Thiry certainly encountered more than his fair share of technical problems, but the biggest difficulty seemed to be a question mark over his state of mind.

• LOIX AND HIS BIG MOUTH

Freddy Loix made an acidic little comment on the subject of Carlos Sainz's constant desire to reduce the length of recces. "If we were restricted to two runs on the Tour of Ypres, I would have time to finish my bag of chips before he came off the stages!"

• STATISTICS, FRENCH STYLE

This French one-two finish with Bugalski and Auriol was the first since 1995. Back then, Didier Auriol had won the Tour of Corsica ahead of François Delecour. Since the creation of the Drivers' World Champion, this was the 57thwin by a French driver, the previous one dating back to Catalunya 1998 and another Auriol win. It was ten years since a French car had won a world championship rally, the last one dating back to 1989, when Alain Oreille won in the Ivory Coast at the wheel of a Renault 5 GT Turbo.

CHAMPIONSHIP CLASSIFICATIONS

Drivers

1. Tommi Makinen	26
2. Didier Auriol	23
3. Colin McRae	20
4. Carlos Sainz	16
5. Philippe Bugalski	10

Constructors

1. Toyota	43
2. Mitsubishi	32
3. Ford	28
4. Subaru	18
5. Seat	8

Group N

1. Hamed Al Wahaibi	26
2. Gustavo Trelles	22
3. Marc Duez	13
3. Jouko Puhakka	13
3. Miguel Campos	13

Two Litres

1. Renault	37
2. Hyundai	26
3. Volkswagen	16

Team's Cup

1. Valencia Terra Mar Team Luis Climent	20
2. Toyota Mobil Team Turkey Volkan Isik	16
3. F.Dor Rally Team Frederic Dor	14

EVENT LEADERS

SS.1 – SS.7	Puras
SS.8 – SS.19	Bugalski

PREVIOUS WINNERS

1991	Schwarz - Hertz Toyota Celica GT-Four
1992	Sainz - Moya Toyota Celica Turbo 4WD
1993	Delecour - Grataloup Ford Escort RS Cosworth
1994	Bertone - Chiapponi Toyota Celica Turbo 4WD
1995	Sainz - Moya Subaru Impreza
1996	McRae - Ringer Subaru Impreza
1997	Makinen - Harjanne Mitsubishi Lancer Ev.4
1998	Auriol - Giraudet Toyota Corolla WRC

"Typically Corsica..."

FRANCE

As the first rally for the 206 WRC, the Tour of Corsica was characterised by the excellent and promising performance of the two Peugeots with Delecour actually leading for a while. It will be remembered also for the second consecutive win for Citroen with Bugalski ahead of Puras. In fact, if reliability had not been the curse of the Lions, there is little doubt that they would have knocked the two Chevrons off their perch. The Rally of France

ended with confusion surrounding its final special stage which came with the added bonus of television coverage, so all could see. It was all to the benefit of Didier Auriol who was quickest here, even though he was the most outspoken critic of this idea, which, in the end, was more non-sporting than stupid.

The two Citroen team drivers were even more dominant here than they had been in the Catalunya rally. Jesus Puras showed amazing adaptability on his third outing on the island.

"I am really happy all the same. We now know the answer to the question, is she quick

IN THE MEANTIME it's the Xsaras, while waiting for the 206... It only lasted for one stage; an average one at just over 26 kilometres up the cruel old road from Chavira, with its sun-bleached white stones, a testament to their age, to Pietra-Rossa, past the olive trees, the sun and the hairpins that bend around the old eucalyptus trees. It was typical Corsica and the stage result was typical down to the last wheel rim with McRae, Sainz and Auriol in that order. The first stage of the 1999 Tour of Corsica finished in much the same way as so many others on the world championship trail. Apart from the unusual absence of Makinen that is. The Finn was off the pace with an overheating brake cooling system on his Mitsu, but other than that, it looked like being the same old story. But then on the famous Orzu section, it seemed this dominance was only a flash in the pan. Delecour set a remarkable fourth fastest time, proving that the new- born 206 WRC was about to get into gear. Peugeot thought they could not have dreamed of anything better. They were wrong.

The old adage goes that history has a habit of repeating itself and now it was beginning to stutter into life. It was fifteen years ago that Vatanen set the fastest time right from the second ever stage in the competition history of the 205 T16. Now, at the end of the first leg of the 99 event, Delecour was heading the field with the little lady who looked as though she was pumped up on steroids, even if he had yet to set a fastest time. In 1984, it had taken Vatanen eight stages to capture the lead. The 206s had not actually won the first leg; delayed with some minor bothers with the rear end and brake pads but as Panizzi put it so succinctly, "I am really happy all the same. We now know the answer to the question, is she quick? We must wait and see how she copes with question two; is she reliable?"

While the 206 did everything expected of it and more, the Xsaras still ruled the roost on tarmac. As in Catalunya, the Citroens were flying on the island. Out of five stages, they won four, three to Bugalski and the final one for his teammate Puras. Citroen and Peugeot had a stranglehold on the top three places and the inevitable rumblings could be heard running down the Corsican mountains from the rest of the field. The Anglo-Japanese teams were used to fighting it out between themselves and did not like this French interruption to their supremacy. They were pulling faces, they showed signs of incredulity and Makinen, Sainz and McRae and the rest were powerless and totally out-classed!

Heaven itself tried to intercede on their behalf on the second leg. It was dominated yet again by the Citroens, but then on the penultimate but especially the last stage, the rain arrived. The damp, slimy, slippery conditions should have been manna for the four wheel drive boys, but Puras put on a scintillating display to claim fastest time on the last stage of the day, which came with the added excitement of a little fog. And to ram it home, the tenacious Bugalski held onto the lead. The Red Army could be pleased with their day's work, because they were certainly up against it, even if they looked to have Corsica under their control. There was certainly no shortage of opposition, charging after them like a herd of wild boar. Delecour set the 206's first ever fastest stage time right from the first one of the day. Then came McRae and Sainz, locked in a personal mano a mano and hoping the rain would baptise their efforts. Then there was the weather itself of course. The rain should not have played a part as it arrived at the end of the day, when the rallymen should have already hung up their helmets for the day. But the organisers slipped up and underestimated the volume of traffic, which caused a massive jam on the main road linking Ajaccio and Bastia. It meant the final stage had to be delayed by an hour. But for that, the competition day would have ended in the dry. It did add a certain element of suspense though.

On the subject of suspense, there was none whatsoever on the final leg. The leader notched up another three fastest times to Puras' one and another went to Auriol. In Corsica, on a rally he had won three years back, but in different conditions, when it did not count towards the championship, "little Bug" was peerless. "It's great," he said, overcome with the joy of it all. "It's a major moment for me." All the more so as it meant he had scored two consecutive world championship wins. It was a great break, but something of an anomaly, as his main target this season had been the defence of his national title!

CITROEN WINS, but mission impossible beckons. Two world championship rallies for the Xsara and two wins. The rally folk choked on the indignity of having their limelight, not to mention wins, stolen by an outfit which was not even competing in the whole series. The Xsara is built specifically for tarmac events and its target is the French Championship, which is run exclusively on sealed surfaces, never going near any gravel. Then, as the world rally championship turns up for its little outings on tarmac, Frequelin and his merry little band, pack their knapsacks and head off to defy all of them, in Catalunya in April, in Corsica in May and then in San Remo in October. It's good to see how you stack up against the stars and it's even better when you beat them. It certainly does no harm to the sales of the Saxo and the Xsara when these victories take place in markets as important to Citroen as Spain and France. Light, almost as powerful as a WRC and wide; the Xsara is a made for tarmac winning machine. Up against

The last time Citroen took the top two places in Corsica dated back to 1961 with Trautmann and Bianchi. A good reason for Guy Frequelin to be proud of his team.

Ve must wait and see how she copes with question two; is she reliable?" Gilles Panizzi

it, the WRC cars are heavy with their four wheel drive systems, but they are built to do the whole season. They must be good enough to work in Swedish snow one day and British mud the next, or on the loose in Finland and then the tarmac in Corsica. It was a case of jack-of-all- trades against master of one.

So Citroen made hay while the sun shone, as did Bugalski. They would be stupid not to make the most of the regulations. And after all, this won't happen again. 2000 will see the Kit-Car killed off thanks to having to cart around an extra 40 kilos, while one year later their power will be knocked back. They are already on a difficult mission but it will soon become mission impossible. The call of the Xsara will be as brief as that of a swan. The biggest shame is that Citroen revealed a WRC car on the day after the Tour of Corsica, but politics in the PSA Group means it will never go near the world championship. What a shame for Frequelin's merry men, but a big relief for the opposition.

PEUGEOT WITH HONOURS. They were expected to stumble on the rally of 10,000 corners, but instead their baptism was a brilliant one. The 206 WRC was the star at its own Debs Ball. A fastest time and a brief moment which lasted for the length of one stage during which it led the rally thanks to the efforts of Delecour. For a first outing, the Lion lads could not have expected more, given how worried they were about the reliability of their baby as they had burnt plenty of midnight oil fixing myriad problems. In the end, neither car made it to the finish line; Panizzi's run halted by blocked air filters, which stopped the engine during the second leg. Delecour had major handling problems, apparently caused by problems with the central differential, before the front end was destroyed by stones (see Snippets.) "The 206 is well born," explained the team manager, Xavier Carlotti. "Now it is up to us to bring it up properly. And that was certainly the intention of Jean-Pierre Nicolas and his entire team, galvanised by its promising performance. One only had to look at the way the mechanics set about their tasks, changing a transmission or a gearbox or a differential, with great faith backing up their efficiency. Most of the workers came from the clinically clean environment of the German Touring Car series. The pits at Hockenheim have little in common with the service area at Propriano. Literally dropping off their axle stands to get to the Island of Beauty, the 206 arrived at its first major test a touch on the early side, having only really run properly at the very last three day test at the end of April, before heading for the island of Corsica. They were still far from ready or in their final form. "We have the post combustion, but we have not yet fitted the water injection," explained engine specialist Jean-Pierre Fleur. We can improve the cooling further and also the fuel consumption, so that we can tackle the stages with less fuel on board. As for the electronics, our present system is pretty prehistoric and we can improve the engine and chassis management." Another key element is that for the time being, only the central differential is controlled, while the front and rear one are mechanical. All this was linked to the fragility of the gearbox, built by the English specialist X-Trac, which had also given a painful birth to the unit in the Ford Focus WRC, although it was now running just fine in this car. Bit by bit, as the 206 made a further five appearances on the world stage, these elements were added and tweaked, transforming the car from a bomb into a little rocket. Anyway, the message had been received loud and clear by the other teams entered in the world championship: Peugeot was back and would not settle for just taking part. That much was clear.

THE RULES AND OPINIONS THEREON. "Just because I've picked up three extra points in the world championship thanks to the last stage that I'm going to change my mind. Quickest on the final stage of the Tour of Corsica, Didier Auriol stood firm at the end of the event. He was disgusted by the system which gave an inappropriately large reward for fastest time on the final stage; a reward which was handed out here in Corsica and then in Finland in August. It bothered him every time he stepped out of the car. Because in the space of ten minutes and two seconds, he had picked up three points, as many as Colin McRae was given for coming fourth after three days of competition. Makinen only hung onto his championship lead thanks to his valuable two points for coming second, while Sainz also picked up an extra point for coming third on the final stage. "I keep worrying about the fact that this system can alter the outcome of a world championship," warned the Spaniard. Going against all the principles of rallying, this FIA invention of handing out 3-2-1 points to the top three on the final televised stage, was not well received and convinced no one in Corsica, particularly Auriol who was on his high horse over it. What would television viewers who knew little of rallying make of the spectacle. To start with, they would see two cars which had retired from the event; Jean-Joseph and his Ford and Panizzi and his 206, drive the stage as they had been allowed to by the others. Then the rest of the field ran in reverse order of classification, which meant the spectator could see the two Xsaras tiptoeing around to make sure of their one-two finish. Where was the extra excitement supposedly generated according to the creators of this system?

FRANCE

"Typically Corsica..."

90.1
On his 100th participation on a world championship rally, Didier Auriol did not have an easy ride.

90.2 - 91.1
Delecour delivered the first fastest stage time the Peugeot 206 WRC.

90.3
Once again, Richard Burns was not able to fight for the lead.

90.4
First of the WRCs, Carlos Sainz was furious to find himself behind Jesus Puras.

90.1

90.2

90.3

90.4

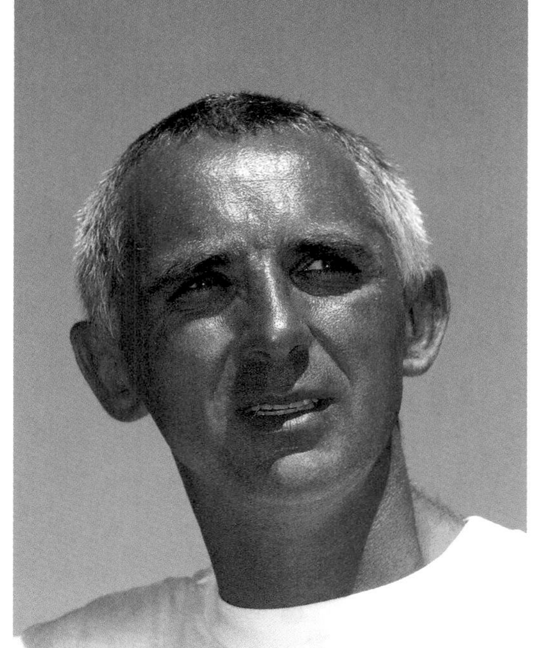

91.1

91.2

91.2
With the help of possibly the best car, Philippe Bugalski was exemplary.

91.3
Colin McRae lost his duel with Sainz after a knock.

91.4
Jean-Pierre Nicolas and Gilles Panizzi radiate happiness at the end of the first leg.

91.5
The Seat Cordoba and Pirelli tyres did not let Liatti shine, except in the wet.

91.3

91.5

43RD RALLY OF FRANCE

TOP ENTRIES

1 Tommi Makinen - Risto Mannisenmaki
MITSUBISHI LANCER EV.6

2 Freddy Loix - Sven Smeets
MITSUBISHI CARISMA GT

3 Carlos Sainz - Luis Moya
TOYOTA COROLLA WRC

4 Didier Auriol - Denis Giraudet
TOYOTA COROLLA WRC

5 Richard Burns - Robert Reid
SUBARU IMPREZA WRC

6 Bruno Thiry - Stephane Prevot
SUBARU IMPREZA WRC

7 Colin McRae - Nicky Grist
FORD FOCUS WRC

8 Simon Jean-Joseph - Fred Gallagher
FORD FOCUS WRC

9 Harri Rovanpera - Risto Pietilainen
SEAT CORDOBA WRC

10 Piero Liatti - Carlo Cassina
SEAT CORDOBA WRC

14 François Delecour - Daniel Grataloup
PEUGEOT 206 WRC

15 Gilles Panizzi - Herve Panizzi
PEUGEOT 206 WRC

16 Philippe Bugalski - Jean-Paul Chiaroni
CITROEN XSARA KIT CAR

17 Jesus Puras - Marc Marti
CITROEN XSARA KIT CAR

18 Luis Climent - Alex Romani
SUBARU IMPREZA

19 Abdullah Bakashab - Michael Park
TOYOTA COROLLA WRC

20 Henrik Lundgaard - Freddy Pedersen
TOYOTA COROLLA WRC

21 Isolde Holderied - Catherine François
TOYOTA COROLLA WRC

23 Tapio Laukkanen - Kaj Lindstrom
RENAULT MEGANE MAXI

24 Martin Rowe - Derek Ringer
RENAULT MEGANE MAXI

26 Gustavo Trelles - Martin Christie
MITSUBISHI LANCER EV.5

27 Manfred Stohl - Peter Muller
MITSUBISHI LANCER EV.5

28 Jouko Puhakka - Jakke Honkanen
MITSUBISHI LANCER EV.5

29 Hamed Al Wahaibi - Tony Sircombe
MITSUBUSHI LANCER EV.5

31 Benoit Rousselot - Jack Boyere
RENAULT MEGANE MAXI

32 Fabien Vericel - Vincent Ducher
CITROEN SAXO KIT CAR

49 Sebastien Loeb - Daniel Elena
CITROEN SAXO KIT CAR

111 Cedric Robert - Lionel Currat
PEUGEOT 306 S16

6th leg of the 1999 world rally championships for constructors and drivers
6th leg of the constructors' «2 litre», production car drivers' and teams'world cups

Date: *7 - 9 May 1999*

Route: *1073,61 km divided into 3 legs, 17 stages on tarmac roads (375,47 km)*
1st leg : Friday 7th May, Ajaccio – Propriano – Ajaccio, 6 stages (139,35 km)
2nd leg : Saturday 8th May, Ajaccio – Corte – Ajaccio, 6 stages (125,22 km)
3rd leg : Sunday 9th May, Ajaccio – Campo dell'Oro – Ajaccio, 5 stages (110,90 km)

Starters/Finishers: *138/85*

Gustavo Trelles picked up an easy win after Manfred Stohl broke his suspension in the penultimate stage.

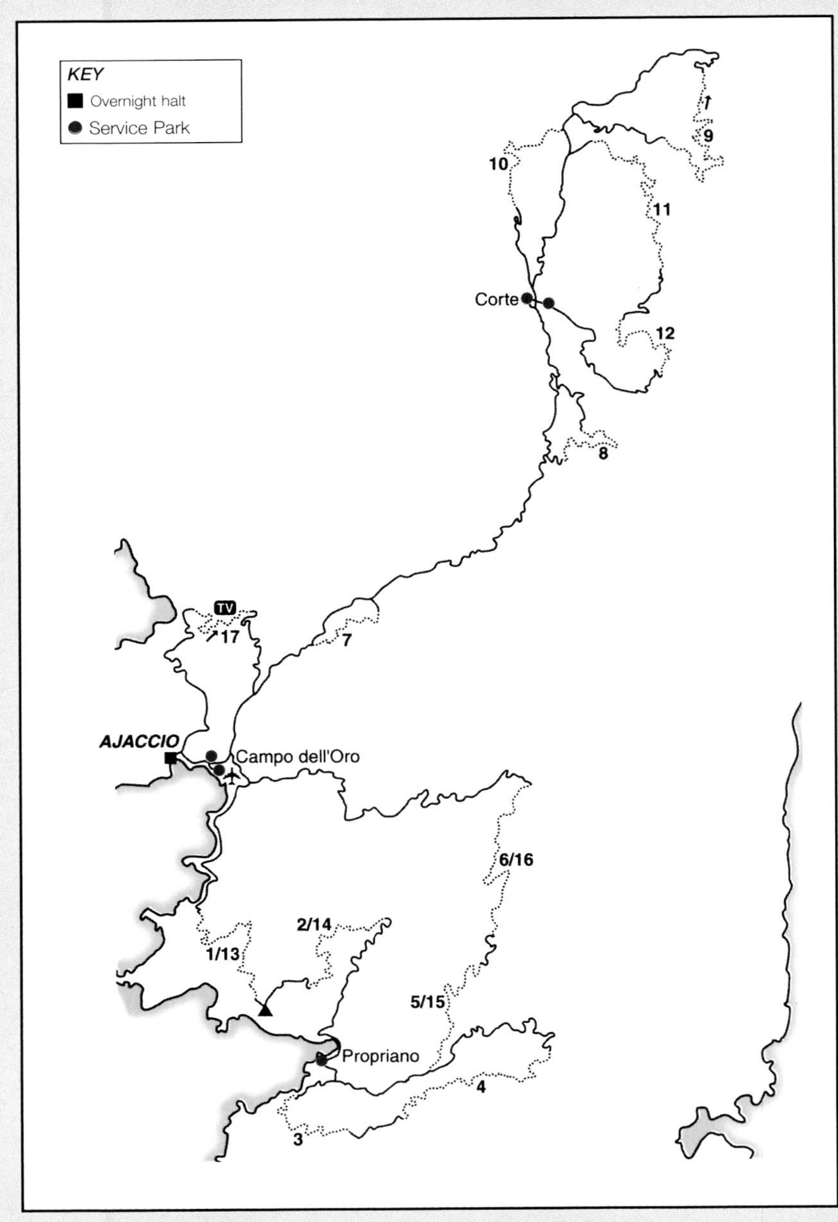

SPECIAL STAGE TIMES

SS.1 Verghia – Pietra Rossa 1 (26,55 km)
1. McRae 16'53"6 ; 2. Sainz 16'55"2 ; 3. Auriol 16'55"3 ; 4. Delecour 16'57"7 ; 5. Puras 16'59"4 ; Gr.N Stohl 18'20"

SS.2 Filitosa – Bicchisano 2 (22,63 km)
1. Bugalski 14'21" ; 2. Delecour 14'23"4 ; 3. Puras 14'24"4 ; 4. Panizzi 14'27"7 ; 5. Sainz 14'29"7 ; Gr.N Santoni 15'34"9

SS.3 Portigliolo – Boca Albitrina (16,54 km)
1. Bugalski 9'46" ; 2. Delecour 9'46"5 ; 3. Sainz 9'48"5 ; 4. Panizzi 9'50" ; 5. Puras 9'51"3 ; Gr.N Galli 10'37"9

SS.4 Sartene – Carbini (27,21 km)
1. Bugalski 16'27"8 ; 2. Delecour 16'28"8 ; 3. Sainz 16'30"8 ; 4. Panizzi 16'32"2 ; 5. Puras 16'33"6 ; Gr.N Galli 17'55"3

SS.5 Pont d'Arcoravo – Zérubia 1 (20,94 km)
Cancelled

SS.6 Aullene – Zicavo 1 (25,48 km)
1. Puras 16'05"3 ; 2. Bugalski 16'06"4 ; 3. Delecour 16'16"6 ; 4. Sainz 16'18"6 ; 5. Panizzi 16'20" ; Gr.N Santoni 17'28"

SS.7 Gare de Carbuccia – Gare D'Ucciani (11,11 km)
1. Delecour 7'44" ; 2. Puras 7'44'4 ; 3. McRae 7'45" ; 4. Bugalski 7'45"1 ; 5. Sainz 7'45"4 ; Gr.N Santoni 8'16"7

SS.8 Muracciole – Noceta (16,48 km)
1. Bugalski 10'01"2 ; 2. Puras 10'05"5 ; 3. McRae 10'06" ; 4. Sainz 10'08"8 ; 5. Delecour 10'09"6 ; Gr.N Galli 10'57"9

SS.9 Morasaglia – Campile (31,91 km)
1. Puras 20'04"3 ; 2. Bugalski 20'04"5 ; 3. Auriol 20'04"9 ; 4. McRae 20'07"7 ; 5. Sainz 20'11"1 ; Gr.N Galli 21'40"7

SS.10 Taverna – Pont de Castiria (16,08 km)
1. Bugalski 9'30"1 ; 2. Puras 9'31" ; 3. McRae 9'34"2 ; 4. Auriol 9'34"4 ; 5. Panizzi 9'34"9 ; Gr.N Galli 10'18"4

SS.11 Pont St Laurent – Bustanico (33,12 km)
1. Bugalski 22'20"8 ; 2. McRae 22'28"5 ; 3. Sainz 22'35"8 ; 4. Puras 22'40"2 ; 5. Panizzi 22'46"5 ; Gr.N Galli 24'41"3

SS.12 Feo – Altiani (16,52 km)
1. Puras 11'13"9 ; 2. Sainz 11'15" ; 3. McRae 11'22" ; 4. Liatti 11'24"8 ; 5. Auriol 11'25"8 ; Gr.N Trellss 12'05"4

SS.13 Verghia – Pietra Rossa 2 (26,55 km)
1. Bugalski 16'35"9 ; 2. Puras 16'36"4 ; 3. Auriol 16'39"8 ; 4. McRae 16'44"5 ; 5. Sainz 16'49"8 ; Gr.N Trellss 18'04"6

SS.14 Filitosa – Bicchisano 2 (22,63 km)
1. Puras 14'06"2 ; 2. Bugalski 14'06"6 ; 3. Auriol 14'13"6 ; 4. Delecour 14'17"9 ; 5. Makinen 14'18"5 ; Gr.N Trellss 15'21"4

SS.15 Pont d'Acoravo – Zérubia 2 (20,94 km)
1. Bugalski 12'29"8 ; 2. Auriol 12'31"3 ; 3. Delecour 12'33"3 ; 4. Makinen 12'35"5 ; 5. McRae 12'36"3 ; Gr.N Trellss 13'32"6

SS.16 Aullene – Zicavo 2 (25,48 km)
1. Bugalski 16'01"4 ; 2. McRae 16'12"5 ; 3. Auriol et Makinen 16'12"7 ; 5. Puras 16'13"6 ; Gr.N Santoni 17'41"

SS.17 Cannelle d'Orcino – La Liscia (13,82 km)
1. Auriol 10'02"6 ; 2. Makinen 10'04"7 ; 3. Sainz 10'05"2 ; 4. Burns 10'05"4 ; 5. Panizzi 10'06" ; Gr.N Al Wahaibi 10'48"8

RESULTS AND RETIREMENTS

	Driver/Co-Driver	Car	Gr	Total Time
1	**Philippe Bugalski – Jean-Paul Chiaroni**	**Citroen Xsara Kit Car**	**A**	**3h44m35,7s**
2	Jesus Puras – Marc Marti	Citroen Xsara Kit Car	A	3h45m10,4s
3	**Carlos Sainz – Luis Moya**	**Toyota Corolla WRC**	**A**	**3h45m45s**
4	Colin McRae – Nicky Grist	Ford Focus WRC	A	3h45m53,8s
5	Didier Auriol – Denis Giraudet	Toyota Corolla WRC	A	3h46m08,3s
6	Tommi Makinen – Risto Mannisenmaki	Mitsubishi Lancer Ev.6	A	3h47m26,1s
7	Richard Burns – Robert Reid	Subaru Impreza WRC	A	3h47m42,6s
8	Freddy Loix – Sven Smeets	Mitsubishi Carisma GT	A	3h50m27,3s
9	Piero Liatti – Carlo Cassina	Seat Cordoba WRC	A	3h51m41,6s
10	Tapio Laukkkanen – Kaj Lindstrom	Renault Megane Maxi	A	3h54m32,8s
12	**Luis Climent – Alex Romani**	**Subaru Impreza WRC**	**A**	**3h55m27,7s**
20	**Gustavo Trelles – Martin Christie**	**Mitsubishi Lancer Ev.5**	**N**	**4h04m52,2s**
SS.1	Simon Jean-Joseph – Fred Gallagher	Ford Focus WRC	A	Electonics
SS.3	Abdullah Bakashab – Michael Park	Toyota Corolla WRC	A	Accident
SS.12	Gilles Panizzi – Herve Panizzi	Peugeot 206 WRC	A	Fuel presssure
SS.16	Martin Rowe – Derek Ringer	Renault Megane Maxi	A	Gearbox
SS.16	Bruno Thiry – Stephane Prevot	Subaru Impreza	A	Suspension
SS.17	François Delecour – Daniel Grataloup	Peugeot 206 WRC	A	Electronics

EVENT LEADERS

SS.1	McRae
SS.2	Delecour
SS.3 – SS.17	Bugalski

BEST PERFORMANCES

	1	2	3	4	5	6
Bugalski	9	3	-	1	-	-
Puras	4	4	1	1	4	-
Delecour	1	3	2	2	1	1
McRae	1	2	4	2	1	5
Auriol	1	1	4	2	1	1
Sainz	-	2	4	2	4	3
Makinen	-	1	1	1	1	3
Panizzi	-	-	-	4	1	
Burns	-	-	-	1	-	
Liatti	-	-	-	1	-	

CHAMPIONSHIP CLASSIFICATIONS

Drivers

1. Tommi Makinen	29
2. Didier Auriol	28
3. Colin McRae	23
4. Carlos Sainz	21
5. Philippe Bugalski	20

Constructors

1. Toyota	61
2. Mitsubishi	38
3. Ford	34
4. Subaru	20
5. Seat	8

Group N

1. Gustavo Trelles	35
2. Hamed Al Wahaibi	31
3. Manfred Stohl	14

Two Litres

1. Renault	52
2. Hyundai	26
3. Volkswagen	16

Team's Cup

1. Valencia Terra Mar Team Luis Climent	30
2. Toyota Mobil Team Turkey Volkan Isik	16
3. F.Dor Rally Team Frederic Dor	14

PREVIOUS WINNERS

1973	Nicolas - Vial Alpine Renault A 110
1974	Andruet - "Biche" Lancia Stratos
1975	Darniche - Mahe Lancia Stratos
1976	Munari - Maiga Lancia Stratos
1977	Darniche - Mahe Fiat 131 Abarth
1978	Darniche Mahe Fiat 131 Abarth
1979	Darniche - Mahe Lancia Stratos
1980	Therier - Vial Porsche 911SC
1981	Darniche - Mahe Lancia Stratos
1982	Ragnotti - Andrie Renault 5 Turbo
1983	Alen - Kivimaki Lancia Rally 037
1984	Alen - Kivimaki Lancia Rally 037
1985	Ragnotti - Andrie Renault 5 Turbo
1986	Saby - Fauchille Peugeot 205 T16
1987	Beguin - Lenne Bmw m3
1988	Auriol - Occelli Ford Sierra RS Cosworth
1989	Auriol - Occelli Lancia Delta Integrale
1990	Auriol - Occelli Lancia Delta Integrale
1991	Sainz - Moya Toyota Celica GT-Four
1992	Auriol - Occelli Lancia Delta HF Integrale
1993	Delecour - Grataloup Ford Escort RS Cosworth
1994	Auriol - Occelli Toyota Celica Turbo 4WD
1995	Auriol - Giraudet Toyota Celica GT-Four
1996	Bugalski - Chiaroní Renault Maxi Megane
1997	McRae - Grist Subaru Impreza WRC
1998	McRae - Grist Subaru Impreza WRC

GOSSIP

• DELECOUR STONED

It is the penultimate stage and Delecour has the finish in his sights. But he hits two big rocks on the road which had been placed there intentionally. Burns had been through minutes earlier and had climbed the Col de la Vaccia without seeing them. Two days earlier, in the same spot, a member of the Peugeot team had seen a man place some rocks there and then remove them shortly before the first of the 206 WRC came through. It was genuine sabotage which prevented Delecour and his badly wounded beast from making it back to Ajaccio.

• FORD TAKES THE MICKEY OUT OF JEAN-JOSEPH

Having supplied him with a less than perfect Focus for his trip to Catalunya, Ford did not have anything better for Jean-Joseph in Corsica. His car was 60 kilos heavier than McRae's. What is more, after just 4.5 kilometres of the rally, it stopped with an electrical problem. Thanks Mr. Ford, especially as with a competitive car, McRae finished fourth.

• AURIOL'S CENTURY

Corsica marked Didier Auriol's one hundredth world championship rally. On the way, the 1994 world champion had won eighteen events and there was more to come.

• THE LOGIC OF THE "LITTLE CLASSES"

Gustavo Trelles took an untroubled win in the Group N category, helped by a mistake on the final day from Austria's Stohl, who bent his front suspension when leading. Despite coming third in the category, Oman's Al-Wahaibi was never on the pace. In the two litre class, with Citroen not officially entered for the World Cup, victory went to the Megane of Finland's Laukkanen.

• SUBARU EXTENDS ITS LEASE

After a calamitous start to the season for the Impreza WRC, rumours were doing the rounds that Subaru, now without its tobacco money since BAT decided to dabble in Formula 1 with BAR this season, would pull out at the end of 2000. David Richards simply smiled as he announced in Corsica that the Japanese manufacturer had actually extended its contract to 2002. Rallying had proved fantastically beneficial since it claimed three constructors championships in 1995, 96 and 97 and the drivers crown with McRae in 1995. Sales had increased by 51 percent.

“The old lion listened an

smiled..."

ARGENTINA

Subaru lives again! Juha Kankkunen chose to ignore team orders called up to favour his young team-mate Richard Burns and fought hard to win his first rally since 1994. It was also the first world championship win for co-driver Juha Repo. You don't tell old Juha what to do. He thus managed to put Subaru back on the road to victory at a time when everyone thought it was on a downward spiral to obscurity. Thanks to a pugnacious then prudent third place, Didier Auriol found himself leading the championship as it reached the halfway point of the season, albeit joint equal with Tommi Makinen. The Finn came home fourth, out of the running thanks to a Mitsubishi whose reliability seemed to be called into question. Kankkunen and Subaru: the Argentine Rally had witnessed two remarkable returns to form.

96.1

KANKKUNEN AGAINST THE REST. The long run without one was becoming worrying. Nine rallies Colin McRae had gone without a spectacular or retirement inducing accident. Had he definitely exorcised his old demons? The tenth rally proved to be the good one. No doubt he was inspired by a fastest time on stage two. No doubt he had wanted to do something extra special for those enthusiastic Argentinian rally fans whose heated exuberance was in direct contrast to the autumnal weather. More likely, he knew that the stages here would not suit the Ford very well, so he would have wanted to build up a sizeable lead as soon as possible. It was fate really, but for the first time in its history, the Giulio Cesare stage was run downhill instead of up. Whatever the reason, the result was the same for Colin McRae. In 1998, he had destroyed the rear suspension on his Subaru and this time he hit a rock and flew off the road.

McRae's devilish tango in the rockery was a prelude to a crazy first leg. Tommi Makinen and Carlos Sainz were the next two victims. At the end of stage five, the world champion, who had set a fastest time and had been going well up until then, jumped out of his Lancer and started attacking his door with his foot in a blind rage. His failing gearbox had left him without fourth gear and he would have to live with that for the rest of the day and was never in the rally after that. Then, at the start of the next stage, Sainz threw away 40 seconds and it was all his fault. "Because of a deep ford coming up we had to modify the air filter," explained the Spanish driver's co-pilot, Luis Moya. They did this but made a dogs dinner of shutting down the bonnet. Four hundred metres into the stage, it flew up obscuring their vision.

All this drama played into the hands of Auriol. Taking it steadily on these killer roads, the Frenchman drove quickly enough all the same, without setting any fastest times and found himself leading after three stages. Not for long however, because just like a condor, the two Subarus were circling in the rally skies before diving on their prey. The pretty Impreza coupes were on form again, because thanks partly to their Pirelli tyres the drivers were prepared to take incredible risks. By the middle of the leg, Burns was in the lead, but he would end up handing it over to Mr. K.

The second leg wound its way around the outskirts of La Cumbre, a pretty little town to the north of Cordoba which the Argentinians think is "so British." While it bears no resemblance to Oxford, Burns, a resident of Oxfordshire must have felt some sort of affinity for the place. It had to explain why the lanky red head with the face of a llama was more than inspired. Very soon and despite a recalcitrant gearbox in the morning, he took the lead. "I am running on wide rims and tyres," explained Kankkunen, now second. "In some places, on the gravel, it is very slippery." At first, Burns' only rival was Auriol, but after a while the Frenchman seemed to lose heart. "I cannot match the Impreza's times," he cursed at the end of the leg. "I don't know why. At one point I was giving it some opposite lock, first one way then the other and I heard a loud "clong" in the steering and the car started to understeer." The only visible sign being the off- centre steering wheel on the Toyota.
Nevertheless, to finish second, 15 seconds down on Burns meant that, prior to the final leg, he had good reason to be very optimistic. But those hopes would soon be dashed. "We really pushed hard," he explained in the middle of the third leg. I am taking some big risks, but I have no alternative." He could watch the deadly duel being fought out between the Englishman and the Finn in the Subaru team. On the face of it, the team orders between the two of them seemed pretty clear: "stay on the road!" according to David Richards, who was rather stressed out. Stay on the road of course, but Mister K continued to swallow up the Sierras Chicas at a healthy pace, so that little by little, he was beginning to menace Burns who had stopped fighting. Before the final stage they were separated by 1.2 seconds. Kankkunen, the old lion, whose last win was almost lost in the mists of time back in Portugal in 1994 was not going to be done up like a kipper. He listened to Richards. He listened for a long time, with a smile on his lips without saying a word. Then...fastest time on the final stage and victory, the 22nd of his career, thus equalling the record holder Sainz. The Subaru boss, who had told us, "Burns is going to win!" was trying to make his laugh seem natural, without much success. Since then, the two Subaru driver have hardly exchanged a word.

SUBARU, MORE PHOENIX THAN CONDOR. This was the Japanese team's first win since the 1998 Acropolis and it was a great shot in the arm for this regenerated team. They seemed to be at the bottom of an abyss after a catastrophic start to the season. But they were not dead yet. "I never doubted our ability to get back to the top," sighed David Richards on the night of the win. It remained to be seen why the little blue coupes had lost their form. The boss answered this with a typical reply which was situated somewhere between diplomacy, silence and hypocrisy.
Piece of dialogue:
"I think Pirelli has done a lot of work on the tyres," explained

the Subaru boss.
* So the tyres were the biggest handicap for your team?
* "I didn't say that."
Another important factor was the departure of Colin McRae. The genial and mercurial Scotsman not only had a team built around him with the car made to suit his particular needs, but on top of that there was the matter of his talent, a driving jewel which made up for the weaknesses of the Impreza WRC, just as much as the tyres. "It's true that with new drivers, you have to give it time to gel," admitted Richards. "It is not easy and it does not work straightaway." It was true that, although another Brit, Burns was taking a while to get the team on his side. But improvements were not long in coming; to the engine and to the new transmission, although their effect was masked by organisational difficulties. So the changes in the driving seats and the Pirelli shortcomings, which were not, with the exception of Kenya, up to the Michelin level until Argentina. However, now at the mid-point of the season, Subaru was back. The stars in its badge were shining once again. "One has to get drunk looking at a star," said the Argentinian navigator-poet Vito Dumas. "And move on to another when one gets dizzy." A premonition perhaps?

ARGENTINE PROMISES. The sierras, the pampas, the rios... the extraordinary backdrop to the Argentinian Rally was the scene of one of the toughest tussles that the world championship had to offer. Judge for yourself: four different leaders and seven changes of lead before Kankkunen walked off with it at the end of the very last stage which was tinged with controversy and conflict. The 1999 Championship had reached its halfway mark in the land of the condor and it was throwing more drama than even the surroundings of the Sierra de Los Gigantes, and that's saying something.
In the drivers' category, Auriol was now joint leader with Makinen, who seemed more determined than ever to retain his crown, despite the fact his team was going through a bad patch, floundering in the water. He and the Frenchman had pulled out a small nine point lead over McRae and Sainz and were 14 points clear of Kankkunen. The two Toyota driver had put their team into a strong but at the same time, difficult position. First in the constructors' championship on 67 points, Toyota had not actually won a rally, unlike their traditional rivals, Mitsubishi (Monte Carlo and Sweden, 41 points,) Ford (Kenya then Portugal, 35) and now the Subarus (36) who, in Argentina, had suddenly come back to life after a bad start. There were now seven rallies to go, all on the loose with the exception of San Remo and it was far too close to call. Argentina had become the land of beautiful promise.

THE PROMISES OF AGE. One does not give out orders to Juha Kankkunen. Subaru hoped for, wanted even a victory for its new little British prot?g?, Richard Burns. They did not get it. Richard Burns felt protected from the antics of the old lion, but he was not. Flash back to the service point at Santa Rosa de Calamuchita during the third leg to the south of Cordoba. Kneeling at the door of Mister K's Subaru, team boss David Richards tries to sweet talk his driver. Little snippets of conversation drift on the air: "second...not so bad... one-two finish." The old mercenary's face never flinches, never moves, never shows emotion. Then he decides to find out something. Before getting back on route for the last stage, he makes a detour via the Toyota motorhome to find out what Didier Auriol, currently third, has in mind. For the past few stages, the Frenchman has slowed his pace as he is incapable of posing a real threat to the Subarus. He just wants to make sure of his podium finish. From now on, only Burns or Kankkunen can win. The slight twist comes from the fact Burns thinks his boss has fixed the positions with the Finn currently 1.2 seconds down, pledged not to push for the lead. He is wrong. 21.33 kilometres later, the mustachioed one goes around 4 seconds quicker. He gave it his best shot and he has won. Tough luck for David Richards, tough luck too for Richard Burns. "If I had known Juha was going to attack, I would have done the same," lamented the read head. The old hand at Subaru had not respected the team orders and he was right not to do so. Unlike the Englishman, his best days are behind him and there will not be too many more chances like this. His last win dated back to Portugal 1994 and his current co-driver, Juha Repo had never actually won a world championship event. Then, there was that long gap from the start of 96, when he found himself without a drive, after Toyota had been kicked out for cheating. He returned to grace and Greece in fact, in 1997 when he called back by Malcolm Wilson to drive the second Ford Escort WRC alongside Sainz, before he bought a new and winning ticket with Subaru. What is more, the win for this proud man in Argentina who already held the record for the number of titles - four - now joined Sainz as the winner of the most rallies - 22. The rumour mill reckoned the old man would pack it in at the end of the year, which meant he had just seven more opportunities to improve his score. Juha Kankkunen and indeed Didier Auriol could both prove that just like a good wine, old age sometimes held a lot of promise.

"I never doubted our ability to get back to the top" David Richards

.1

96.1
Juha Kankkunen's last victory dated back to the 1994 Portuguese Rally.

97.1
Richard Burns was clear: "There will be no team orders."

97.2
Juha Kankkunen offered his co-driver Juha Repo his first world championship win in fine style.

97.2

ARGENTINA

"The old lion listened and smiled..."

98.1
Unlucky Carlos Sainz was the first to fall by the wayside.

98.2
Before going off on stage three, Colin McRae looked like repeating his Portuguese success.

98.3
Throughout the three legs, the Argentine spectators witnessed the Richard Burns festival.

99.1
Just as in Corsica, there was no holding back for Tommi Makinen in the third leg.

99.2
For much of the event, Didier Auriol was the only one who could live with the dominant Subarus.

98.1

98.2

98.3

99.1

99.2

19th Rally of Argentina

TOP ENTRIES

1 Tommi Makinen - Risto Mannisenmaki
MITSUBISHI LANCER EV.6

2 Freddy Loix - Sven Smeets
MITSUBISHI CARISMA GT

3 Carlos Sainz - Luis Moya
TOYOTA COROLLA WRC

4 Didier Auriol - Denis Giraudet
TOYOTA COROLLA WRC

5 Richard Burns - Robert Reid
SUBARU IMPREZA WRC

6 Juha Kankkunen - Juha Repo
SUBARU IMPREZA WRC

7 Colin McRae - Nicky Grist
FORD FOCUS WRC

8 Thomas Radstrom - Fred Gallagher
FORD FOCUS WRC

9 Harri Rovanpera - Risto Pietilainen
SEAT CORDOBA WRC

10 Piero Liatti - Carlo Cassina
SEAT CORDOBA WRC

11 Volkan Isik - Erkan Bodur
TOYOTA COROLLA WRC

12 Frederic Dor - Didier Breton
SUBARU IMPREZA WRC

14 Marco Galanti - Victor Zucchini
TOYOTA COROLLA WRC

15 Gustavo Trelles - Martin Christie
MITSUBISHI LANCER EV.5

16 Manfred Stohl - Kay Gerlach
MITSUBISHI LANCER EV.5

18 Hamed Al Wahaibi - Tony Sircombe
MITSUBUSHI LANCER EV.5

19 Jorge Recalde - Jose Garcia
MITSUBISHI LANCER EV.5

21 Gwyndaf Evans - Howard Davies
SEAT IBIZA KIT CAR

22 Walter Suriani - Juan Carbonari
RENAULT MEGANE MAXI

7th leg of the 1999 world rally championships for constructors and drivers
7th leg of the constructors' «2 litre», production car drivers' and teams'world cups

Date: *20 - 23 May 1999*

Route: *1528,15 km divided into 3 legs, 22 stages on loose surface roads (396,63 km)*
1st leg : Saturday 22nd and Sunday 23rd May, Villa Carlos Paz – Mina Clavero - Cordoba 9 stages (136,71 km)
2nd leg : Monday 24th May, Cordoba – La Cumbre – Cordoba, 7 stages (127,50 km)
3rd leg : Tuesday 25th May, Cordoba – Santa Rosa de Calamuchita – Cordoba, 6 stages (132,42 km)

Starters/Finishers: *71/25*

Gwyndaf Evans had a fruitless journey in the 2 litre category.

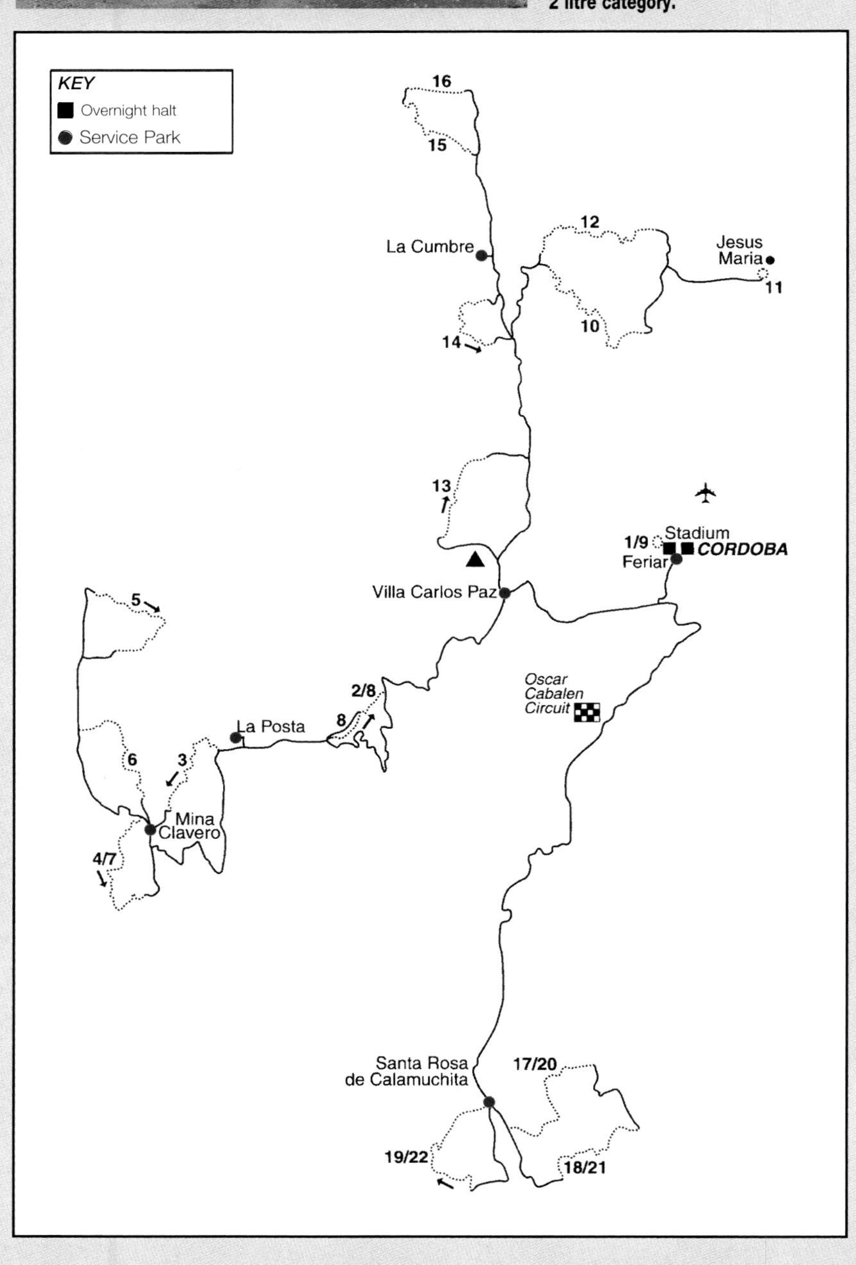

SPECIAL STAGE TIMES

SS.1 Super Spéciale (3,97 km)
1. Sainz 3'02"8 ; 2. Makinen 3'03"9 ; 3. Burns 3'04"3 ; 4. Radstrom 3'04"6 ; 5. Kankkunen 3'05"1; Gr.N Al Wahaibi 3'12"6; F2 Evans 3'22"9

SS.2 El Condor – Copina (8,39 km)
1. McRae 6'49"9 ; 2. Auriol 6'50"4 ; 3. Sainz 6'51"8 ; 4. Kankkunen 6'52"1 ; 5. Thomas Radstrom 6'53"2 ; Gr.N Trellss 7'10"7 ; F2 Evans 7'23"2

SS.3 Giulio – Mina Clavero (19,23 km)
1. Makinen 16'42"3 ; 2. Auriol 16'43"5 ; 3. Burns 16'47"9 ; 4. Sainz 16'54" ; 5. Kankkunen 16'54"1 ; Gr.N Al Wahaibi 17'57"8 ; F2 Evans 18'30"9

SS.4 Cura Brochero – Nono 1 (19,26 km)
1. Burns 9'41"6 ; 2. Kankkunen 9'43"7 ; 3. Sainz 9'44"5 ; 4. Auriol 9'47"4 ; 5. Makinen 9'51"8 ; Gr.N Menzi 10'37"2 ; F2 Suriani 11'00"3

SS.5 Chamico – Ambul (24,82 km)
1. Burns 18'16"4 ; 2. Sainz 18'17"7 ; 3. Kankkunen 18'19"3 ; 4. Auriol 18'23"1 ; 5. Liatti 18'38"1 ; Gr.N Preto 19'42"6 ; F2 Suriani 20'18"7

SS.6 El Mirador – San Lorenzo (20,70 km)
1. Kankkunen 11'38"2 ; 2. Burns 11'38"9 ; 3. Auriol 11'42"9 ; 4. Liatti 11'50"1 ; 5. Makinen 11'51"4 ; Gr.N Trellss 12'26"7 ; F2 Suriani 12'46"8

SS.7 Cura Brochero – Nono 2 (19,26 km)
1. Kankkunen 9'33"9 ; 2. Auriol 9'36"7 ; 3. Burns 9'39"1 ; 4. Sainz 9'41"5 ; 5. Loix 9'48"1 ; Gr.N Menzi 10'34"9 ; F2 Suriani 10'48"8

SS.8 El Condor – Copina (16,98 km)
1. Kankkunen 13'44"2 ; 2. Auriol 13'45"8 ; 3. Sainz 13'49"3 ; 4. Burns 13'50"8 ; 5. Radstrom 13'53" ; Gr.N Trellss 14'35"2 ; F2 Suriani 15'07"

SS.9 Camping Gral. San Martin (4,10 km)
1. Burns 2'41"9 ; 2. Sainz 2'42"2 ; 3. Auriol 2'42"3 ; 4. Liatti 2'42"4 ; 5. Rovanpera 2'43"6 ; Gr.N Al Wahaibi 2'49"6 ; F2 Suriani 2'56"4

SS.10 La Cumbre – Agua de Oro (23,67 km)
1. Burns 20'11"6 ; 2. Auriol 20'17" ; 3. Makinen 20'22"5 ; 4. Kankkunen 20'24"6 ; 5. Sainz 20'34"9; Gr.N Al Wahaibi 21'26"3 ; F2 Evans 22'18"2

SS.11 Colonia Caroya (3,40 km)
1. Auriol 2'22"9 ; 2. Burns 2'23"1 ; 3. Makinen 2'23"5 ; 4. Kankkunen 2'23"6 ; 5. Sainz et Radstrom 2'23"8 ; Gr.N Al Wahaibi 2'30"4 ; F2 Suriani 2'31"7

SS.12 Ascochinga – La Cumbre (28,93 km)
1. Burns 18'51"7 ; 2. Auriol 18'53"2 ; 3. Sainz 18'53"9 ; 4. Kankkunen 19'00" ; 5. Makinen 19'04"9 ; Gr.N Menzi 19'56"3 ; F2 Evans 20'12"4

SS.13 Tanti – Cosquin (16,14 km)
1. Sainz 8'36"6 ; 2. Makinen 8'36"8 ; 3. Kankkunen 8'37"6 ; 4. Burns 8'37"9 ; 5. Auriol 8'39"3 ; Gr.N Menzi 9'16"6 ; F2 Suriani 9'19"1

SS.14 Villa Giardino – La Falda (22,53 km)
1. Kankkunen 16'28"7 ; 2. Makinen 16'29"8 ; 3. Burns 16'34"6 ; 4. Sainz 16'39"1 ; 5. Auriol 16'42"9; Gr.N Recalde 18'10"5 ; F2 Suriani 18'46"1

SS.15 Capilla del Monte – San Marcos Sierra (23,03 km)
1. Sainz 17'35"6 ; 2. Makinen 17'37"3 ; 3. Burns 17'38"2 ; 4. Auriol 17'38"5 ; 5. Liatti 17'43"5 ; Gr.N Trellss 18'47"1 ; F2 Suriani 19'35"6

SS.16 San Marcos Sierra – Charbonier (9,80 km)
1. Burns 6'38"3 ; 2. Makinen 6'41"6 ; 3. Kankkunen 6'41"9 ; 4. Sainz 6'43"8 ; 5. Auriol 6'44" ; Gr.N Sanchez 7'24"8 ; F2 Suriani 7'49"6

SS.17 Santa Rosa de Calamuchita – San Augustin 1 (26,16 km)
1. Burns 15'24"7 ; 2. Kankkunen 15'25'5 ; 3. Auriol 15'27" ; 4. Makinen 15'30" ; 5. Sainz 15'30"3 ; Gr.N Trellss 16'44" ; F2 Goldenhersch 18'41"7

SS.18 Las Bajadas – Villa Del Dique 1 (18,72 km)
1. Kankkunen 9'56"3 ; 2. Makinen 9'57"4 ; 3. Burns 10'00'5 ; 4. Sainz 10'01"3 ; 5. Auriol 10'02"2 ; Gr.N Menzi 10'50"5 ; F2 Goldenhersch 12'21"5

SS.19 Amboy – Santa Rosa de Calamuchita 1 (21,33 km)
1. Kankkunen 11'18"8 ; 2. Burns 11'21"6 ; 3. Makinen 11'22" ; 4. Auriol 11'25"9 ; 5. Sainz 11'27"5 ; Gr.N Menzi 12'35"3 ; F2 Hubmann 15'12"

SS.20 Santa Rosa de Calamuchita – San Augustin 2 (26,16 km)
1. Makinen 15'12"9 ; 2. Sainz 15'19"7 ; 3. Kankkunen 15'22"6 ; 4. Auriol 15'24"4 ; 5. Burns 15'28"5 ; Gr.N Trellss 16'40"2 ; F2 Quatroccio 19'52"7

SS.21 Las Bajadas – Villa Del Dique 2 (18,72 km)
1. Kankkunen 9'58" ; 2. Auriol 10'01"6 ; 3. Burns 10'03"1 ; 4. Makinen 10'08"4 ; 5. Radstrom 10'10"4 ; Gr.N Recalde 10'57"2 ; F2 Quatroccio 12'44"6

SS.22 Amboy – Santa Rosa de Calamuchita 2 (21,33 km)
1. Kankkunen 11'16"9 ; 2. Burns 11'20"5 ; 3. Makinen 11'24"3 ; 4. Sainz 11'32"8 ; 5. Auriol 11'38"2 ; Gr.N Menzi 12'37"2 ; F2 Hubmann 14'55"2

RESULTS AND RETIREMENTS

	Driver/Co-Driver	Car	Gr	Total Time
1	**Juha Kankkunen – Juha Repo**	**Subaru Impreza WRC**	**A**	**4h17m15,4s**
2	Richard Burns – Robert Reid	Subaru Impreza WRC	A	4h17m17,8s
3	Didier Auriol – Denis Giraudet	Toyota Corolla WRC	A	4h17m55s
4	Tommi Makinen – Risto Mannisenmaki	Mitsubishi Lancer Ev.5	A	4h18m40,6s
5	Carlos Sainz – Luis Moya	Toyota Corolla WRC	A	4h19m43,5s
6	Thomas Radstrom – Fred Gallagher	Ford Focus WRC	A	4h22m07,3s
7	**Gustavo Trelles – Martin Christie**	**Mitsubishi Lancer Ev.5**	**N**	**4h39m46,2s**
8	Jorge Recalde – Jose Garcia	Mitsubishi Lancer Ev.5	N	4h41m09s
9	Claudio Menzi – Rodolfo Ortiz	Subaru Impreza WRX	N	4h41m33s
10	**Frederic Dor – Kevin Gormley**	**Subaru Impreza WRC**	**A**	**4h45m18,2s**
15	**SSteban Goldenhersch – Nestor Juarez**	**Seat Ibiza 2L**	**N**	**5h31m39,9s**
SS.3	Colin McRae – Nicky Grist	Ford Focus WRC	A	Accident
SS.8	Volkan Isik – Erkan Bodur	Toyota Corolla WRC	A	Engine
SS.12	Hamed Al Wahaibi – Tony Sircombe	Mitsubishi Lancer Ev.5	N	Accident
SS.14	Harri Rovanpera – Risto Pietilainen	Seat Cordoba WRC	A	Engine
SS.16	Gwyndaf Evans – Howard Davies	Seat Ibiza Kit Car	A	Engine
SS.17	Walter Suriani – Juan Carbonari	Renault Megane Maxi	A	Accident
SS.17	Freddy Loix – Sven Smeets	Mitsubishi Carisma GT	A	Accident
SS.22	Pierro Liatti – Carlo Cassina	Seat Cordoba WRC	A	Accident

EVENT LEADERS

SS.1 – SS.2	Sainz
SS.3 – SS.4	Auriol
SS.5 – SS.7	Burns
SS.8 – SS.9	Kankkunen
SS.10 – SS.12	Auriol
SS.13 – SS.21	Burns
SS.22	Kankkunen

BEST PERFORMANCES

	1	2	3	4	5	6
Makinen	9	5	2	3	-	-
Kankkunen	8	2	4	4	2	2
Burns	7	4	7	2	1	-
Sainz	3	3	4	6	4	1
Makinen	2	6	4	2	3	-
Auriol	1	7	3	5	5	-
McRae	1	-	-	-	-	1
Liatti	-	-	-	2	2	5
Radstrom	-	-	-	1	4	11
Rovanpera	-	-	-	-	1	1
Loix	-	-	-	-	1	-

PREVIOUS WINNERS

1980	Rohrl - Geistdorfer Fiat 131 Abarth
1981	Frequelin - Todt Talbot Sunbeam Lotus
1983	Mikkola - Hertz Audi Quattro
1984	Blomqvist - Cederberg Audi Quattro
1985	Salonen - Harjanne Peugeot 205 T16
1986	Biasion - Siviero Lancia Delta S4
1987	Biasion - Siviero Lancia Delta HF Turbo
1988	Recalde - Del Buono Lancia Delta Integrale
1989	Ericsson - Billstam Lancia Delta Integrale
1990	Biasion - Siviero Lancia Delta Integrale 16v
1991	Sainz - Moya Toyota Celica GT4
1992	Auriol - Occelli Lancia Delta HF Integrale
1993	Kankkunen - Grist Toyota Celica Turbo 4WD
1994	Auriol - Occelli Toyota Celica Turbo 4WD
1995	Recalde - Christie Lancia Delta HF Integrale
1996	Makinen - Harjanne Mitsubishi Lancer Ev.3
1997	Makinen - Harjanne Mitsubishi Lancer Ev.4
1998	Makinen - Mannisenmaki Mitsubishi Lancer Ev.5

GOSSIP

• AUTUMN HAS ARRIVED

Recceing for the Rally of Argentina took place in the fog and the mud. "Incredible! I have never seen that here, " commented a surprised Didier Auriol before the event, even though he had been on several previous occasions. In temperatures hovering around a chilly ten degrees and clouds lower than a stealth bomber's flight path, autumn was well installed and only made way for the sun on the very last leg.

• THE HONESTY OF AL-WAHAIBI

The fight for Group N was a short one, won by a consistent Trelles. Definitely quickest in the first part of the rally, Al-Wahaibi went off the road at the start of the second leg shortly after the class leader Preto went out with a blown turbo. Very honest, the man from Oman explained: "there are two explanations for this incident: the truth and the excuse. The truth is that I made a mistake and I had my first ever rally accident. The excuse? At this point there was a bump that we had not noticed on our recce in a hire car. What's more, I went off where I had a puncture during the recce" "With Al-Wahaibi out of the way, the Uruguayan triumphed and increased his lead in the championship with 48 points against 31 for his Arab opponent.

• THE SHADOW OF FAST FREDDY

Belgium's Freddy Loix had a terrible time in Argentina and it will be hard to nickname him "Fast Freddy" from now on. Never on the pace, he had to submit to comparisons with Thomas Radstrom, who like him, was tackling this event for the first time. Finally, in a quick section, he had a huge off in the first stage of the third and final leg. He had nothing to reproach himself for, as the front right wheel of his Mitsubishi had decided to go its own way.

CHAMPIONSHIP CLASSIFICATIONS

Drivers

1. Tommi Makinen	32
1. Didier Auriol	32
3. Colin McRae	23
3. Carlos Sainz	23
5. Philippe Bugalski	20

Constructors

1. Toyota	67
2. Mitsubishi	41
3. Subaru	36
4. Ford	35
5. Seat	8

Group N

1. Gustavo Trelles	48
2. Hamed Al Wahaibi	31
3. Manfred Stohl	14

Two Litres

1. Renault	62
2. Hyundai	26
3. Volkswagen	16

Team's Cup

1. Valencia Terra Mar Team Luis Climent	30
2. F.Dor Rally Team Frederic Dor	24
3. Toyota Mobil Team Turkey Volkan Isik	16

“Cars that matched the ancient

ruins..."

ACROPOLIS

Not for a long time had the Acropolis Rally route been such a car breaker. Kicking off at an incredible pace, victory eventually went to a hard charging Richard Burns. He also played the strategy well and was able to rely on the strength of his Subaru which survived the mechanical mayhem which befell much of the opposition, or at least the ones that did not fly off the road. It was an important win for the young Englishman, coming just after he was denied victory in Argentina by Juha Kankkunen. Makinen finished third and that was good enough to leave him alone in the championship lead after Didier Auriol, whose reliability so far this season had been exceptional, had an impromptu coming together with a rock.

104.1

104.2

104.1 - 105.1
Crippled with mechanical problems, Tommi Makinen saved his bacon and hung onto the championship lead.

104.2
Didier Auriol posted his first 1999 retirement after colliding with a rock.

"I was never able to let up and on these car breaking roads I scared myself

BURNS TAKES HIS REVENGE. On Sundays in June around Athens, there are several ways to spend one's leisure time. One can lend an attentive ear to the song of the sirens and unlike Ulysses, slip gently into a welcoming wave, lightly rippled by the passing breeze. Or one can head for the dust bowl that is Anavissos, to the south of the capital to watch the opening moments of the eighth round of the World Rally Championship; the appropriately named Acropolis rally where the ruins, faded by the weight of history, watch from its columns as the 1999 event gets underway. And all those who chose the dust bath in preference to a cooling dip in the sea were rewarded with watching a small piece of modern history. Well, it's all relative! This was Marcus Gronholm's first visit to the Greek event and a first start for the thin Finn at the wheel of the 206 WRC. It was also the Peugeot's first ever start on a loose surface event, its first fastest time and the first time it led. There was plenty for the white team to smile about. Never before had a lion tamer managed to get to the top of the time sheet on his very first outing. It was worth witnessing because the next day, for the rest of the leg, it was not quite the same picture.

The state of the cars, as they straggled into the last service point, bore easy comparison to the ancient ruins that surrounded the area. The sills were dented, the paint scratched and scarred by the rocks, boiling oil bubbled from under the bonnets of some cars and the smell of burnt rubber and hot metal permeated the air. The mechanicals were sweating after their exertions as were the drivers who crawled out of the cockpits. Rivers of sweat poured over Makinen's tired wrinkles and clouded Delecour's face, just as it matted Sainz's hair. Of them all, Richard Burns looked the freshest. The unflappable Brit was in fine form. The first leg had displayed all his talents on his way to take the lead in spectacular style. But he did not keep the lead for long as a few minutes later, he was about to make a tactical decision to go into parc ferme after the final service point three minutes late, in order to incur a decisive thirty second penalty. The result of this ruse was that he was classified fourth in a leg which was therefore won by McRae. All this meant that Burns would not have the problem of opening the road on the second leg. He would not have the honour of blowing away the dust so that the others, coming along behind, would have an easier time of it. It was certainly a sign that Burns felt very confident about the outcome. What is more, he was at the wheel of a Subaru which had been completely trouble free all day long. Another element in his favour was the carnage taking place in his wake. The first to go was Gronholm, who drowned the engine, his hopes and his rally in the first ford on the route. Then Radstrom was sidelined with mechanical failure on the same stage as Auriol. A bump, a bend, a bang with a big rock and the Corolla's suspension was spaghetti. The accident stopped Didier from scoring on eight consecutive events.

Right from the outset the next morning, Burns proved his clever ruse had been the right one. In the space of just one stage, the Subaru driver had reestablished his lead. "That's perfect as I am back where I started," he said. "I think we did the right thing." Behind him, all or almost all the others were scaring themselves silly. McRae only just missed out on yet another huge accident, before he was forced out with a broken gearbox. Delecour ran for a while with an errant steering arm, Loix threw his Mitsubishi into a tree and Makinen modified the front left corner of his when he hit a rock. Kankkunen destroyed the rear suspension of his Subaru and Liatti, who had been going really well, ended his rally with a huge off on the final stage of the day. It happened at exactly the same place where team-mate Rovanpera had destroyed his own Cordoba the previous day.

Despite the small gap between the first three at the start of the final leg, with just 35.1 seconds separating Burns from Makinen, with Sainz in the middle, the mechanical decimation continued unabated once again. Delecour's 206 gearbox was a flat-liner. Makinen was determined to worry Burns and attacked hard from the word go. He managed to make up ten seconds of his deficit in just a few kilometres, but then a big rock chose to destroy the back end of the Lancer. From that point on, the Finn decided that third place was the better part of valour as it would ensure he would keep the lead in the championship ahead of the poor unfortunate Auriol. Sainz was bothered by a string of punctures and dodgy dampers and the Spaniard was therefore unable to pose a threat to Burns. It was enough for Burns to take the win, which made up for the one Kankkunen took off him two weeks earlier in South America. "To be honest, of course I would have preferred to win there as well," he admitted. "But this makes Argentina easier to swallow."

THE ACROPOLIS ENTERTAINS THE VISITORS. Who said rallying only interested a handful of specialist constructors, a sub- species almost of car builders incapable of shining in the circuit racing disciplines? Those who bad mouthed the sport and there were a few, will have to eat their words, because the opposite is becoming more and more true with each passing event. Look at the Acropolis; no less than fourteen works cars sporting the colours of seven major constructors lined up for the start. Never in its long history, had rallying been able to make a similar

ew times.." Richard Burns

boast. Ploughing through the record books shows the current era to be without compare. Since 1973, the championship had often been a simple three way fight. When Peugeot won it in 1985 and again in 1986, it only really had to beat Audi and Lancia. Today the sport is played out on a very different ball park. To start with, in order to score points, it is compulsory for teams to take part in all the events, that is to say fourteen rallies. Along with the familiar names like Ford, Mitsubishi, Subaru and Toyota, loyal supporters of the series this past decade, one can add the name of Seat, who arrived in 1998, along with Skoda and Peugeot, while Hyundai is expected in 2000. By comparison, that most glamorous of disciplines, Formula 1, can only boast four major constructors: Mercedes, Fiat under the guise of Ferrari, Peugeot and Ford. From his position as a holder of no less than thirteen campaign medals, his four titles and his twenty two wins, the master Juha Kankkunen summed it up thus and better than anyone else: It has never been so hard to win."

THE TRIPLE CROWN OF KING RICHARD. Richard Burns triumphed in timid fashion. When he reached the final service area and his team after the last stage, with victory in his pocket, the Englishman wore a look of someone who had not quite understood. Words were not enough, so nobody spoke. There was plenty of laughter and congratulations , back slapping and an improvised podium on the shoulders of the sweating mechanics. The sun beat down on the plain of Inoi. It dessicated the retzina vines and a haze of heat enveloped the peaceful summit of Patra. Burns didn't care, he just laughed. He had now won his third world championship event, with a well put together win, his first of the season. Out of twenty one stages, he was quickest on twelve, which proved beyond doubt that he was the quickest man out there. In addition to skill and power, he also proved adept at playing the tactics game, jiggling around the starting order with malicious control. No one could do any better. Only Kankkunen, at the wheel of the same type of Subaru until his rear end gave way and especially Makinen were capable of mounting any sort of attack, although they both failed. "I wasn't able to let up for a moment," he explained when he finally managed to find his voice again after overcoming the emotion of it all. "And on such tough going, that was a bit nerve wracking." Twenty eight years old, the Subaru driver had proved himself capable of winning the toughest rallies: Safari, RAC and Acropolis was an impressive trio.

FRAGILE PEUGEOT. The Acropolis marked the second appearance of the Peugeots on the world championship stage and yet again they surprised everyone, except the men who built them. They had been quick in Corsica, but after all this was Peugeot's favourite stomping ground with the extraordinary 306 Maxi and so everyone had expected them to trip up in Greece on their first loose surface rally. "In terms of outright performance, we are not too bad," prognosticated chief engineer Michel Nandan just before the start, "but we need to see if the car will hold together. On this very tough terrain, we will have to find the right compromise between speed and the minimum amount of breakages. From now on, we have to tackle the reliability issue." To this end, both cars had been considerably strengthened. Of course, the gearbox which had proved frail in Corsica was still a source of concern in Greece, aggravated by the much higher temperatures. "My only worry," admitted Delecour, "is that we did not come testing here. We have done a lot of kilometres in France, at Chateau Lastours, but in conditions where the maximum temperature was 17 degrees. Here it is around 35 degrees. It's not the same." Notwithstanding these misgivings, Marcus Gronholm went into the lead right from the start with the super special which kicked off the event, not far from the centre of Athens. Unfortunately, on the first real stage of the rally, the giant Finn drowned out his little baby lion cub in a ford right under the eyes of an unbelieving Gilles Panizzi, who had chose to watch at this particularly spectacular viewing point. Full of water, the engine coughed and spluttered and then, as the driver rather overdid the clutch in his efforts to get going again, the engine died completely. It was over. What a wonderful paradox. It had taken one of the driest routes to produce sufficient water to drown out an engine, a hope and a rally!

For the remaining two days, the likeable Gronholm rambled around like a man in pain, after his abortive first ever run in French colours. All the more so, because Francois Delecour was on form and proving that the little rocket seemed to have an aptitude for dealing with the difficulties of Greek terrain. He set a fastest time on of the fastest sections of the rally, before mechanical bothers interrupted his flight. He had a spectacular left front damper failure when the unit punched its way through the bonnet. The dampers failed regularly and were a definite weak point. On top of that, a rear suspension joint broke, it got through vast quantities of oil, the power steering played up, before the gearbox finally called it a day on the third leg, preventing the car making it to the finish and to the points zone. Despite this avalanche of irritants, the team was all smiles at the end of the rally. No fundamental faults had cropped up and nothing went wrong that could not be fixed with a bit of time and experience. In Greece, it is always a good idea for things to augur well.

ACROPOLIS

"Cars that matched the ancient ruins..."

106. 1-4

But for a gearbox failure, Francois Delecour's 206 WRC would have finished in the points.

106. 2-3 - 107. 3

Outstanding the Michelin "ATS" tyres, as demonstrated by Makinen and McRae, who pushed them to the limit.

106. 5

A broken damper kept Carlos Sainz out of the winner's circle.

106.1

106.2

106.3

106.4

106.5

107.1

107.2

107.3

107.1

By mid-season, Toyota had still not won a rally and Carlos Sainz was enquiring what the opposition had in mind for the future.

107.2

Skoda achieved the rare feat of getting both its cars to the finish.

107.4

Volkan Isik was impressive before his engine broke.

46TH ACROPOLIS RALLY

TOP ENTRIES

1 Tommi Makinen - Risto Mannisenmaki
MITSUBISHI LANCER EV.6

2 Freddy Loix - Sven Smeets
MITSUBISHI CARISMA GT

3 Carlos Sainz - Luis Moya
TOYOTA COROLLA WRC

4 Didier Auriol - Denis Giraudet
TOYOTA COROLLA WRC

5 Richard Burns - Robert Reid
SUBARU IMPREZA WRC

6 Juha Kankkunen - Juha Repo
SUBARU IMPREZA WRC

7 Colin McRae - Nicky Grist
FORD FOCUS WRC

8 Thomas Radstrom - Fred Gallagher
FORD FOCUS WRC

9 Harri Rovanpera - Risto Pietilainen
SEAT CORDOBA WRC

10 Piero Liatti - Carlo Cassina
SEAT CORDOBA WRC

11 Armin Schwarz - Manfred Hiemer
SKODA OCTAVIA WRC

12 Emil Triner - Milos Hulka
SKODA OCTAVIA WRC

14 François Delecour - Daniel Grataloup
PEUGEOT 206 WRC

15 Marcus Gronholm - Timo Rautiainen
PEUGEOT 206 WRC

16 Leonidas Kirkos - John Stravopoulos
FORD ESCORT WRC

17 Matthias Kahle - Dieter Schneppenheim
TOYOTA COROLLA WRC

18 Aris Vovos - John Alvanos
TOYOTA COROLLA WRC

19 Volkan Isik - Erkan Bodur
TOYOTA COROLLA WRC

21 Abdullah Bakashab - Michael Park
TOYOTA COROLLA WRC

22 Luis Climent - Alex Romani
SUBARU IMPREZA

23 Markko Martin - Toomas Kitsing
TOYOTA COROLLA WRC

24 Frederic Dor - Didier Breton
SUBARU IMPREZA WRC

25 Toshihiro Arai - Roger Freeman
SUBARU IMPREZA WRC

26 Jean-Pierre Richelmi - Freddy Delorme
SUBARU IMPREZA WRC

27 Kenneth Eriksson - Staffan Parmander
HYUNDAI COUPE EV.2

28 Alister McRae - David Senior
HYUNDAI COUPE EV.2

30 Gustavo Trelles - Martin Christie
MITSUBISHI LANCER EV.6

31 Hamed Al Wahaibi - Tony Sircombe
MITSUBUSHI LANCER EV.5

32 Manfred Stohl - Ilka Petrasko
MITSUBISHI LANCER EV.5

39 Simon Jean-Joseph - Patrick Privato
FORD PUMA

40 Kris Princen - Dany Colebunders
RENAULT MEGANE MAXI

8th leg of the 1999 world rally championships for constructors and drivers
8th leg of the constructors' "2 litre", production car drivers' and teams'world cups

Date: *6 - 9 June 1999*

Route: *1400,91 km divided into 3 legs, 21 stages on loose surface roads (413 km)*
1st leg : Sunday 6th and Monday 7th June, Agii Theodori – Inoi – Agii Theodori, 8 stages (138,02 km)
2nd leg : Tuesday 8th June, Agii Theodori – Kouros – Agii Theodori, 8 stages (166,51 km)
3rd leg : Wednesday 9th June, Agii Theodori – Inoi – Megara, 5 stages (108,47 km)

Starters/Finishers: *104/47*

On his first visit to the event, Kris Princen set several fastest times ahead of the works Hyundais.

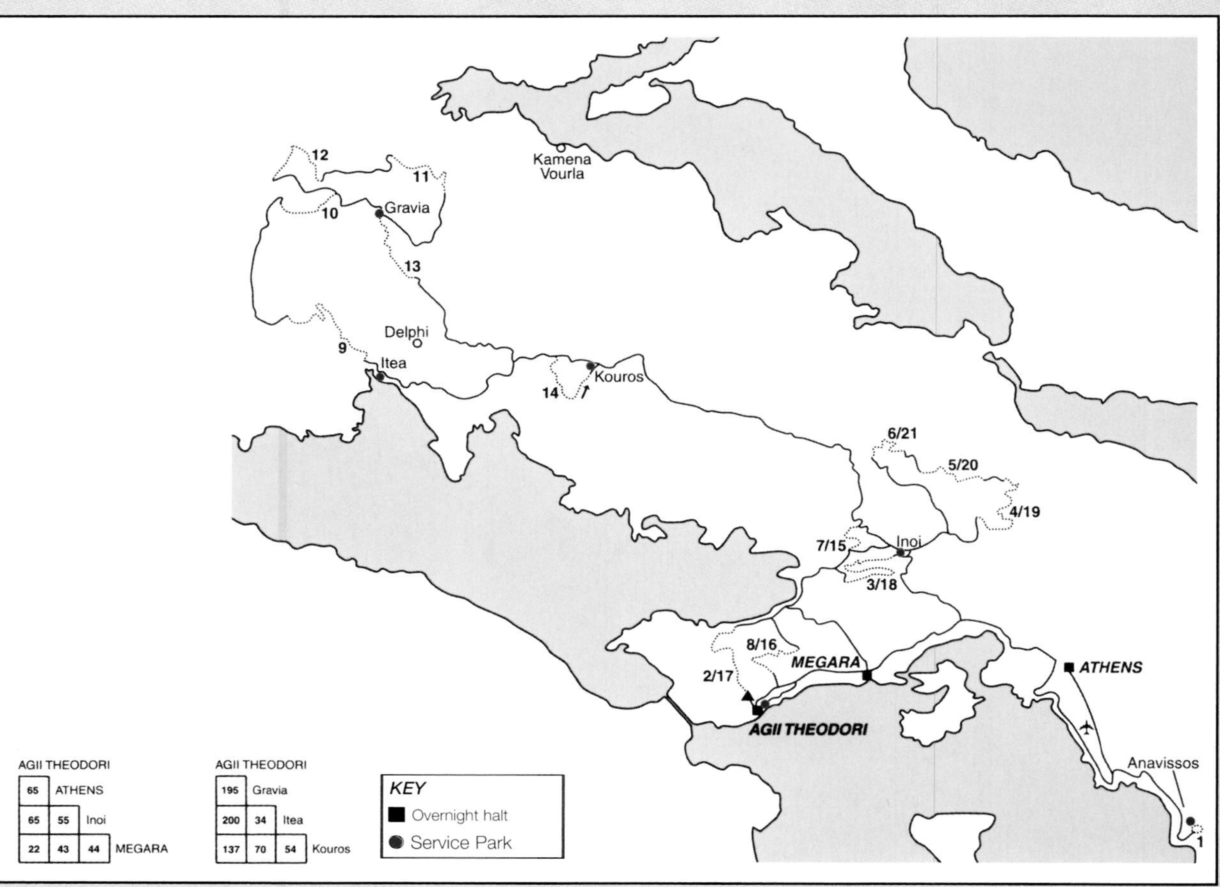

SPECIAL STAGE TIMES

SS.1 Super Spéciale (2,40 km)
1. Gronholm 2'15"6 ; 2. Loix 2'15"7 ; 3. Sainz 2'16" ; 4. Auriol 2'16" ; 5. McRae 2'16"3 ; Gr.N Al Wahaibi 2'18"2 ; F2 McRae 2'22"5

SS.2 Agii Theodori 1 (26,25 km)
1. McRae 20'38" ; 2. Delecour 20'41"2 ; 3. Radstrom 20'41"6 ; 4. Sainz 20'43"7 ; 5. Makinen 20'47"3 ; Gr.N Stohl 22'13"3 ; F2 McRae 23'10"6

SS.3 Pateras 1 (7,46 km)
1. Burns 4'10"1 ; 2. Kankkunen 4'11"2 ; 3. Makinen 4'13"5 ; 4. Radstrom 4'16"8 ; 5. Sainz 4'17" ; Gr.N Stohl 4'39"6 ; F2 McRae 4'57"

SS.4 Skourta 1 (18,95 km)
1. Burns 10'31" ; 2. Kankkunen 10'36"7 ; 3. Delecour 10'39"1 ; 4. Makinen 10'39"3 ; 5. Loix 10'42"3 ; Gr.N Al Wahaibi 11'30"4 ; F2 11'59"6

SS.5 Klidi 1 (15,48 km)
1. Burns 10'14"4 ; 2. Kankkunen 10'20"5 ; 3. Makinen 10'24"9 ; 4. McRae 10'26"5 ; 5. Loix 10'26"5 ; Gr.N Al Wahaibi 11'04"7 ; F2 Eriksson 11'30"3

SS.6 Thiva 1 (20,12 km)
1. Burns 16'10" ; 2. McRae, Sainz et Loix 16'18"; 5. Makinen et Liatti 16'20" ; Gr.N Al Wahaibi 16'58" ; F2 McRae 17'38"

SS.7 Kitheronas 1 (10,77 km)
1. Kankkunen 6'31"4 ; 2. Loix 6'32"6 ; 3. Sainz 6'33"4 ; 4. Liatti 6'33"7 ; 5. Makinen 6'34"8 ; Gr.N Stohl 7'09"7 ; F2 Eriksson 7'27"1

SS.8 Kineta 1 (15,44 km)
1. Delecour 8'38"6 ; 2. Kankkunen 8'39"3 ; 3. Liatti 8'40" ; 4. McRae 8'42"5 ; 5. Burns 8'44"2; Gr.N Stohl 9'35"9 ; F2 Eriksson 9'44"1

SS.9 Bauxitss – Karoutss (28,85 km)
1. Burns 18'00"3 ; 2. Kankkunen 18'02"4 ; 3. Sainz 18'04"7 ; 4. Liatti 18'06"4 ; 5. Delecour 18'10"1 ; Gr.N Al Wahaibi 19'17"4 ; F2 Eriksson 20'18"1

SS.10 Stromi – Inohori (22,89 km)
1. Burns 18'27"5 ; 2. Kankkunen 18'29" ; 3. Loix 18'30"8 ; 4. Liatti 18'31"6 ; 5. Makinen 18'32"1; Gr.N Stohl 19'25"4 ; F2 Princen 20'24"5

SS.11 Drimea (25,29 km)
1. Makinen 17'26"5 ; 2. Sainz 17'30"8 ; 3. Loix 17'31"7 ; 4. McRae 17'36"2 ; 5. Burns 17'38"3; Gr.N Al Wahaibi 19'09"9 ; F2 Princen 20'17"2

SS.12 Pavliani (25,06 km)
1. Burns 20'59"4 ; 2. McRae 20'59"7 ; 3. Delecour 20'59"9 ; 4. Sainz 21'02"5 ; 5. Makinen 21'10"8 ; Gr.N Stohl 21'54"4 ; F2 Eriksson 23'08"2

SS.13 Gravia (25,58 km)
1. Burns 18'18"6 ; 2. Sainz 18'21"9 ; 3. Makinen 18'27"1 ; 4. McRae 18'34"5 ; 5. Delecour 18'39'9 ; Gr.N Al Wahaibi 19'34" ; F2 Eriksson 20'35"2

SS.14 Livadia (11,69 km)
1. Makinen 9'36" ; 2. Burns 9'37"3 ; 3. McRae 9'38"2 ; 4. Delecour 9'38"8 ; 5. Sainz 9'40"3 ; Gr.N Stohl 10'02"6 ; F2 Eriksson 10'35"6

SS.15 Kitheronas 2 (10,77 km)
1. Makinen 6'30"1 ; 2. Delecour 6'32"6 ; 3. Sainz 6'33"3 ; 4. Burns 6'33"6 ; 5. Loix 6'38"1 ; Gr.N Stohl 7'07"7 ; F2 Princen 7'38"1

SS.16 Kineta 2 (15,44 km)
1. Burns 8'36" ; 2. Sainz 8'38" ; 3. Makinen et Loix 8'47"7 ; 5. Arai 9'00"4 ; Gr.N Stohl 9'24"7 ; F2 Eriksson 10'07"3

SS.17 Agii Theodori 2 (26,25 km)
1. Burns 20'48"2 ; 2. Sainz 20'54"8 ; 3. Loix 21'03"4 ; 4. Arai 21'20"3 ; 5. Martin 21'33" ; Gr.N Al Wahaibi 22'19"3 ; F2 Eriksson 22'33"9

SS.18 Pateras 2 (25,93 km)
1. Burns 4'22" ; 2. Loix 4'31"4 ; 3. Arai 4'36"2 ; 4. Climent 4'40"3 ; 5. Bakashab 4'40"9 ; Gr.N Al Wahaibi 4'53"3 ; F2 Princen 5'20"8

SS.19 Skourda 2 (20,69 km)
1. Burns 10'54"9 ; 2. Makinen 10'55" ; 3. Loix 10'55"9 ; 4. Sainz 10'56"3 ; 5. Schwarz 11'15"3 ; Gr.N Stohl 11'48"5 ; F2 Princen 12'38"

SS.20 Klidi 2 (15,48 km)
1. Makinen 10'21"8 ; 2. Burns 10'26"1 ; 3. Sainz 10'29"7 ; 4. Martin 10'37"6 ; 5. Bakashab 10'43"7; Gr.N Al Wahaibi 11'17"1 ; F2 Princen 11'48"6

SS.21 Thiva 2 (20,12 km)
1. Makinen 16'21"2 ; 2. Burns 16'22"3 ; 3. Sainz 16'31"3 ; 4. Martin 16'38" ; 5. Climent 16'40"2; Gr.N Al Wahaibi 17'35"6 ; F2 Eriksson 18'01"1

RESULTS AND RETIREMENTS

	Driver/Co-Driver	Car	Gr	Total Time
1	**Richard Burns – Robert Reid**	**Subaru Impreza WRC**	A	**4h21m21,2s**
2	Carlos Sainz – Luis Moya	Toyota Corolla WRC	A	4h22m22,5s
3	Tommi Makinen – Risto Mannisenmaki	Mitsubishi Lancer Ev.6	A	4h25m01,2s
4	Freddy Loix – Sven Smeets	Mitsubishi Carisma GT	A	4h25m33,6s
5	Markko Martin – Toomas Kitsing	Toyota Corolla WRC	A	4h30m02,7s
6	Leonidas Kirkos – John Stravopoulos	Ford Escort WRC	A	4h35m17,7s
7	**Luis Climent – Alex Romani**	**Subaru Impreza**	A	**4h35m25,1s**
8	Abdullah Bakhashab – Michael Park	Toyota Corolla WRC	A	4h36m18,5s
9	Toshihiro Arai – Roger Freeman	Subaru Impreza WRC	A	4h37m05,6s
10	Frederic Dor – Didier Breton	Subaru Impreza WRC	A	4h39m16,4s
11	**Hamed Al Wahaibi – Tony Sircombe**	**Mitsubishi Lancer Ev.5**	N	**4h41m35,7s**
15	**Kenneth Eriksson – Staffan Parmander**	**Hyundai Coupe Ev.2**	A	**4h55m57,1s**
SS.2	Marcus Gronholm – Timo Rautiainen	Peugeot 206 WRC	A	Clutch
SS.6	Thomas Radstrom – Fred Gallagher	Ford Focus WRC	A	Engine
SS.6	Didier Auriol – Denis Giraudet	Toyota Corolla WRC	A	Suspension
SS.8	Alister McRae – David Senior	Hyundai Coupe Ev.2	A	Sump
SS.8	Harri Rovanpera – Risto Pietilainen	Seat Cordoba WRC	A	Accident
SS.9	Simon Jean-Joseph – Patrick Pivato	Ford Puma	A	Shock absorber
SS.11	Juha Kankkunen – Juha Repo	Subaru Impreza WRC	A	Rear strut
SS.12	Gustavo Trelles – Martin Christie	Mitsubishi Lancer Ev.6	N	Electrics
SS.13	Jean-Pierre Richelmi – Freddi Delorme	Subaru Impreza WRC	A	Turbo
SS.16	Colin McRae – Nicky Grist	Ford Focus WRC	A	Gearbox
SS.16	Piero Liatti – Carlo Cassina	Seat Cordoba WRC	A	Transmission
SS.19	François Delecour – Daniel Grataloup	Peugeot 206 WRC	A	Gearbox
SS.19	Manfred Stohl – Ilka Petrasko	Mitsubishi Lancer Ev.5	N	Engine

GOSSIP

• THE RULE OF STATISTICS

Subaru's win here, after the won in Argentina proved that in the 1999 season, one win for a team meant that it was likely to do the double immediately. This was better than the casino. Out of eight races, Mitsubishi, Ford, Citroen and now Subura had both won twice. And always or almost, ahead of a Toyota, the marque that had a clear lead in the constructors' championship, even if it was desperately chasing that elusive first win of the year.

• RELIABLE SKODA

Despite all the problems Skoda had encountered with its new Octavia, including two regal rolls from Armin Schwarz on the Tuesday, those driving for the Czech marque knew how to finish a rally, Schwarz twelfth and Triner thirteenth. The reliability of these two WRC meant that Skoda scored its first three points in this season's world championship.

• AL WAHAIBI FEARS NO ONE

Having led Group N from start to finish. Hamed Al-Wahaibi naturally and logically walked off with this category. This meant he was now in a position to menace the seemingly eternal triple world champion in the production car class, Uruguay's Gustavo Trelles. He had never been capable of taking the fight to Al-Wahaibi anyway, before retiring with electrical problems. The two men were now only four points apart with Austria's Stohl a long way back. The presence of the talented man from Oman had definitely served to renew interest in the Group N class this year.

• THANKS FREDDY!

Number Two Mitsubishi driver Freddy Loix had been scrupulous in letting his team leader Tommi Makkinen pass him, slowing down considerably in the final two stages. The Finn just did it and thus finished third instead of fourth. As for the embarrassing question of team orders, which had become a hot topic ever since the 1998 Australian Formula 1 Grand Prix, Makinen stuttered and blushed at the finish as he scrambled for the excuse box. "I don't know what to say. The position I am in now is the one I was in for quite a while." Thanks Freddy!

EVENT LEADERS

SS.1	Gronholm
SS.2	McRae
SS.3	Radstrom
SS.4	Kankkunen
SS.5 – SS.8	Burns
After SS.8	McRae
SS.9 – SS.10	Burns
SS.11	Makinen
SS.12 – SS.21	Burns

BEST PERFORMANCES

	1	2	3	4	5	6
Burns	1	2	3	-	1	2
Makinen	5	1	4	1	5	1
Kankkunen	1	6	-	-	-	1
Delecour	1	2	2	1	2	1
McRae	1	2	1	5	-	1
Gronholm	1	-	-	-	-	-
Sainz	-	5	6	3	2	3
Loix	-	4	5	-	3	2
Liatti	-	-	1	3	1	2
Arai	-	-	1	1	1	2
Radstrom	-	-	1	1	-	-
Martin	-	-	-	-	3	-
Climent	-	-	-	1	1	1
Bakashab	-	-	-	-	3	-
Schwarz	-	-	-	-	-	3
Rovanpera	-	-	-	-	-	1
Kirkos	-	-	-	-	-	1

CHAMPIONSHIP CLASSIFICATIONS

Drivers

1. Tommi Makinen	36
2. Didier Auriol	32
3. Carlos Sainz	29
4. Colin McRae	23
4. Richard Burns	23

Constructors

1. Toyota	73
2. Mitsubishi	48
3. Subaru	45
4. Ford	35
5. Seat	8

Group N

1. Gustavo Trelles	48
2. Hamed Al Wahaibi	44
3. Manfred Stohl	14

Two Litres

1. Renault	72
2. Hyundai	36
3. Volkswagen	16

Team's Cup

1. Valencia Terra Mar Team Luis Climent	40
2. F.Dor Rally Team Frederic Dor	28
3. Toyota Mobil Team Turkey Volkan Isik	16

PREVIOUS WINNERS

1973	Therier - Delferrier ALPINE RENAULT A110
1975	Rohrl - Berger OPEL ASCONA
1976	Kallstrom - Andersson DATSUN 160J
1977	Waldegaard - Thorszelius FORD ESCORT RS
1978	Rohrl - Geistdorfer FIAT 131 ABARTH
1979	Waldegaard - Thorszelius FORD ESCORT RS
1980	Vatanen - Richards FORD ESCORT RS
1981	Vatanen - Richards FORD ESCORT RS
1982	Mouton - Pons AUDI QUATTRO
1983	Rohrl - Geistdorfer LANCIA RALLY 037
1984	Blomqvist - Cederberg AUDI QUATTRO
1985	Salonen - Harjanne PEUGEOT 205 T16
1986	Kankkunen - Piironen PEUGEOT 205 T16
1987	Alen - Kivimaki LANCIA DELTA HF TURBO
1988	Biasion - Siviero LANCA DELTA INTEGRALE
1989	Biasion - Siviero LANCA DELTA INTEGRALE
1990	Sainz - Moya TOYOTA CELICA GT4
1991	Kankkunen - Piironen LANCIA DELTA INTEGRALE 16V
1992	Auriol - Occelli LANCIA DELTA INTEGRALE
1993	Biasion - Siviero FORT ESCORT RS COSWORTH
1994	Sainz - Moya SUBARU IMPREZA
1995	Vovos - Stefanis LANCIA DELTA INTEGRALE
1996	McRae - Ringer SUBARU IMPREZA
1997	Sainz - Moya FORD ESCORT WRC
1998	McRae - Grist SUBARU IMPREZA WRC

"Shame about the clouds, damn

the rain..."

NEW ZEALAND

Tommi Makinen finally renewed his acquaintance with the winner's circle at the end of a rally he had totally dominated. The result was enough to let him fly off into a healthy championship lead. Colin McRae had been the only one to threaten him until the engine in his Focus expired at the end of the first leg, for reasons which were as mysterious as they were electrical to the Ford technicians. Under the rain and in the mud, this rally also showcased the incredible talent of Toni Gardemeister at the wheel of the latest evolution of the Cordoba WRC, named

the E2 which completed a totally Finnish podium as Kankkunen helped himself to second place. Gardemeister's guts had given Seat its first world championship podium finish sine 1979.

112.1

112.2

112.3

112.4

"Little Toni is pushing me, but he is one of ours. Tommi and I can be proud of that."

Juha Kankkunen

SHAME ABOUT THE CLOUDS, damn the rain. But just like a rugby match or a regatta out at sea, no matter how disgusting the weather, sport goes on in New Zealand and never mind the rain. Spectacle, theatre, strange twists and turns, the worthy spectators saw it all, with their boots and waterproofs, their hats and brollies deployed. In the first leg they certainly got their money's worth for their five NZ dollars, which was the entry fee for the stages. Because the first leg produced an unforgettable fight; a strong arm competition, a tough guys face-off in true All Blacks style. It seemed that the strong winds and ferocious rain had inspired Makinen and McRae. Throughout the eight stages of the first leg, this pair were out on their own as they charged the misty summits. The others, all of them, could only cough and splutter and wipe their noses in their wake. The Finn struck first, setting a great scratch time right from the very first special stage. The performance owed something to his choice of tyres, a type referred to as "moto- cross, pulled from the Michelin range. These tyres were particularly well adapted to the muddy conditions but were a bit on the fragile side. Indeed the Mitsubishi driver had a minor off on the next stage as the tyres had worn prematurely. McRae made the most of it. Then the two drivers simply shared out the top honours on each stage between them. These guys simply got better as the conditions got worse. Nobody was capable of keeping up and one by one they dropped back. In the end, it took the second run at the Whaanga Coast stage towards the end of the day, to tip the balance of the New Zealand Rally.

While Makinen was going totally wild as he flew over "the mud, the mud, the mud" as he explained it, while Auriol was tackling the muck much more cautiously. Poor Sainz was stuck in first gear and McRae's arrival was awaited so eagerly that he never actually made the end of the stage! "Engine problem" said the depressed Scotsman. "We don't know what it is yet." The Focus had stopped in the middle of the stage and McRae never managed to get it going again. Strange, as when the mechanics finally got to the car, it fired up without too much bother. Some strange computer chip problem no doubt. As the crews splashed into Auckland, Makinen's fight with McRae had pushed the Finn into a 1m 15s lead over Auriol, a surprised inheritor of the second slot.

"It's really weird. It's not raining this morning," said the old lady manning the petrol pumps as Didier Auriol's note crew filled up for the fray ahead through the meadows. On the North Island, the winter can be mild but it is always very wet. The Frenchman turned out to be the big loser on this leg, which was totally dominated by Makinen. An excess of enthusiasm saw Didier compromise the chance of a good top three finish. Normally so surefooted, the Toyota driver got it wrong in the Batley stage. It was an expensive mistake, but it could have been worse and put him out of the rally. "I ran a bit wide in a quick right on this stage that I didn't know," he explained calmly afterwards. "I was off the line on ground that was not too muddy, but it was covered in gravel. There was a big rock. We were going quickly: 4th or 5th maybe. I hit it hard with the left rear, which pulled the wheel off and then the car started to spin and ended up on the edge of the road." On three wheels, the Frenchman managed to get out of the ditch and then made it all the way to the service area where his mechanics were waiting, armed to the teeth with spanners. That meant Auriol had left the way clear for Makinen. A solid lead at the end of the first leg, the world champion simply extended his lead in the next one. With Auriol out of the way, there was no stopping the Mitsubishi driver.

He did it again on the final leg. But counting the pennies was never his style and so he set about it with vim and vigour, taking the first three stages and putting success beyond doubt and out of reach of his opposition. "Of course I could have gone slower, but I love this! On top of that, these roads are not car breakers, so the risk was minimal." So Makinen did what he had to do, increasing his lead over Auriol in the championship and finishing ahead of his fellow countrymen, Kankkunen the old and Gardmeister the new. The Finnish finishing school had plenty of life in it yet.

MAKINEN BREAKS THE "KIWI" SIGN. He has won the world championship three times and no doubt he will win it again. In the meantime, Tommi Makinen has just one goal: to win everywhere. And up until today, New Zealand has proved a rally too far for him. Never had this insatiable winning machine, this fighter, managed to win in the land of the Maori. He had always shone here, putting a spark into the event in his four previous attempts. But usually they had ended badly, with three accidents and just one third place. But just as the island of the long cloud seemed to shake off its eternal and infernal rain and mist, it was only an illusion mind you, Tommi finally triumphed over his opponents and the Indian cloud sign, to take his eighteenth world championship win. Thus having also won in Monte Carlo this year, all that was missing to complete his master work was Corsica, the Acropolis, the RAC and China of course. As far as a fourth title was concerned, this win certainly could not have come at a better time. Firstly because his last victory dated back to an icy cold month of February, way up in Sweden and then because, after Sweden, the Mitsubishi team, almost invincible up to then, appeared to experience a run of technical misfortunes. From that point on, Andrew Cowan and his men had pushed as hard as the All Blacks front row in a scrum to fine tune the wider wheel tracks of the Lancer. "This give us a lot more options in terms of set-

up," explained Bernard Lindauer, the chief engineer. "The car is also more stable and has more grip. One evolution had already appeared in Greece. Now we are waiting for the next high speed flowing rally rather than a car breaking one to see if it all works properly." New Zealand was more than just a win. For starters, it allowed Mr. Tommi to fly off into the championship lead with just five rounds remaining and then it also proved to him that Mitsubishi was capable of providing a quick and reliable car after a long period of dodgy doubt. It would certainly help to ensure that the talented Finn kept his talents with Mitsubishi. It had been a long time since the Reds had won such an important victory.

GARDEMEISTER THE LITTLE WONDER. Tommi Makinen is an astute wine connoisseur, but when it comes to celebrating a matter of national pride, then nothing goes down better than a good glass of beer. So, on the night he won the rally, before heading off to sample a fine New Zealand wine in one of Auckland's smartest restaurants with a few close friends, the world champion knocked back a glass of the hop with his two fellow fighters, Juha Kankkunen and Toni Gardmeister. Everyone knows Kankkunen, the old lion with his four world championships and his twenty two wins to date, sharing the top spot for number of wins with Carlos Sainz. But Toni Gardmeister? You have to be a real rally fan to recognise the young lad with the moody expression and the unruly hair, who is still a driver in the making. Called up by Seat, to replace Piero Liatti, who was busy developing the Cordoba E2 on tarmac, the young man now had two rallies on his to-do list: New Zealand in order to get the hang of the car in preparation for Finland, a rally which was not a favourite with the Italian. With two fastest stage times to his name, Gardmeister had eclipsed his friend, team-mate and regular Seat jockey, Harri Rovanpera. This made his appearance on the all-Finnish podium alongside Makinen and Kankkunen, all the more remarkable. Not only did all three of them come from the same part of the world, they also all shared the same mentor, Timo Joukhi. The oldest among them, Mr. K, was quick to praise the youngest: "He's pushing me, but he is one of ours. Tommi and I can be proud of that." Kankkunen's co-driver Juha Repo went further: "here is the next Finnish World Champion!" "Little Toni" had just hoisted the Cordoba WRC onto the first podium of a young career. It was only the second in the company's history, after Zanini did it on the Monte in 1977 in a Seat 124. It goes without saying that the Spanish firm had nothing but praise for this talented, yet slightly arrogant young man. "I honestly never expected to do so well," he explained after the event. "I had only come here to get to grips with the car before Finland. In fact, I was never flat out." These words, spoken in front of his prestigious compatriots Makinen and Kankkunen had the effect of making these two gentlemen burst out laughing!

WHITHER TOYOTA? It was the top rumour doing the rounds in Auckland: what would become of Toyota? No decision had been made public, but the main players who knew better than the rest what was going on in the championship never stopped repeating the rumour that the Japanese company could pull out at the end of the 99 season. No matter that contracts were in place with drivers and sponsors until the end of 2000. And what of the drivers? Well, Auriol was struggling and having to fight like mad, to such an extent that he was making mistakes. Battling Didier was finding life tough on the Batley stage, hitting a rock and losing a wheel. He had been in a strong position but the Toyota Corolla WRC had never been up to putting either one of its virtuoso drivers in the lead. On the penultimate stage of the second leg, Sainz also went out. "The corner just started to slide, slide in a corner and I could do nothing about it. We ended up stuck with the left front wheel in the air. It took us nearly four minutes to get back on the track." Incredibly steady since the start of the year, the two Toyota drivers, whose ability cannot be called into question, were over-driving at the wheel of a car that was no longer on the pace and for which development appeared to have been exhausted. The Corolla's last win dated back exactly a year to this event, but now it was no longer able to fight for the win. It was from this lack of development that rumours of Toyota's imminent departure had grown. Because if the Japanese giant was really interested in rallying, it would do something about it, by investing heavily. The company is lucky to have Auriol and Sainz, because there is little doubt that it is their very considerable efforts which has put them in the lead of the Constructors' championship after an event where, despite all sorts of difficulties, the Frenchman finished fourth and the Spaniard was sixth. So what was the truth as regards its rallying future?

112.1

Handicapped by an off-song Corolla, Didier Auriol could not keep up with Makinen's pace.

112.2

On a downward spiral since the Safari, this third victory came in the nick of time to save Makinen's title hopes.

112.3-4

Thomas Radstrom began the destruction of his Ford Focus on stage 4.

113.1

Unaffected by a first off, Thomas Radstrom kept pushing before going off for good, despite being told to bring home some points.

NEW ZEALAND

"Shame about the clouds, damn the rain..."

114.1 - 115.1

Lacking motivation after losing a wheel, Didier Auriol saw his hopes of a second title slip away.

114.2

This first New Zealand win pushed Tommi Makinen closer to a fourth title.

114.3

Freddy Loix and Sven Smeets found the stages to be fast and slippery. It was a bit of pain which merited some comfort.

114.4

Toni Gardemeister was surprisingly on the pace at his first encounter with a WRC, offering Seat its first world championship podium.

115.2

A fourth blank for Malcolm Wilson's team.

114.1

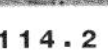

114.2

114.3

115.1

115.2

115.3

115.4

115.3

Juha Kankkunen chose to play a waiting game and it paid off, but the Subarus were not as well rewarded as in the previous events.

115.4

In the Seat camp, Rovanpera's problems met with incomprehension.

29TH NEW ZEALAND RALLY

TOP ENTRIES

1 Tommi Makinen - Risto Mannisenmaki
MITSUBISHI LANCER EV.6

2 Freddy Loix - Sven Smeets
MITSUBISHI CARISMA GT

3 Carlos Sainz - Luis Moya
TOYOTA COROLLA WRC

4 Didier Auriol - Denis Giraudet
TOYOTA COROLLA WRC

5 Richard Burns - Robert Reid
SUBARU IMPREZA WRC

6 Juha Kankkunen - Juha Repo
SUBARU IMPREZA WRC

7 Colin McRae - Nicky Grist
FORD FOCUS WRC

8 Thomas Radstrom - Fred Gallagher
FORD FOCUS WRC

9 Harri Rovanpera - Risto Pietilainen
SEAT CORDOBA WRC

10 Toni Gardemeister - Paavo Lukander
SEAT CORDOBA WRC

11 Possum Bourne - Craig Vincent
SUBARU IMPREZA WRC

12 Matthias Kahle - Dieter Schneppenheim
TOYOTA COROLLA WRC

14 Gustavo Trelles - Martin Christie
MITSUBISHI LANCER EV.5

15 Yoshihiro Kataoka - Satoshi Hayashi
MITSUBISHI LANCER EV.6

16 Frederic Dor - Kevin Gormley
SUBARU IMPREZA WRC

18 Hamed Al Wahaibi - Tony Sircombe
MITSUBUSHI LANCER EV.5

19 Michael Guest - David Green
SUBARU IMPREZA WRX

21 Toshihiro Araï - Roger Freeman
SUBARU IMPREZA WRX

22 Kenneth Eriksson - Staffan Parmander
HYUNDAI COUPE EV.2

23 Nobuhiro Tajima - Claire Parker
SUZUKI BALENO

24 Alister McRae - David Senior
HYUNDAI COUPE EV.2

9th leg of the 1999 world rally championships for constructors and drivers
9th leg of the constructors' «2 litre», production car drivers' and teams'world cups

Date: *15 - 18 July 1999*

Route: *1681,87 km divided into 3 legs, 27 stages on loose surface roads (401,56 km)*
1st leg : Thursday 15th et Friday 16th July, Auckland – Manukau – Auckland, 10 stages (141,89 km)
2nd leg : Saturday 17th July, Auckland – Maungaturoto – Auckland, 10 stages (174 km)
3rd leg : Sunday 18th July, Auckland – Manukau, 7 stages (85,67 km)

Starters/Finishers: *82/46*

In Group N, Hamed Al-Wahaibi watched Trelles triumph, but he picked up the Team's cup.

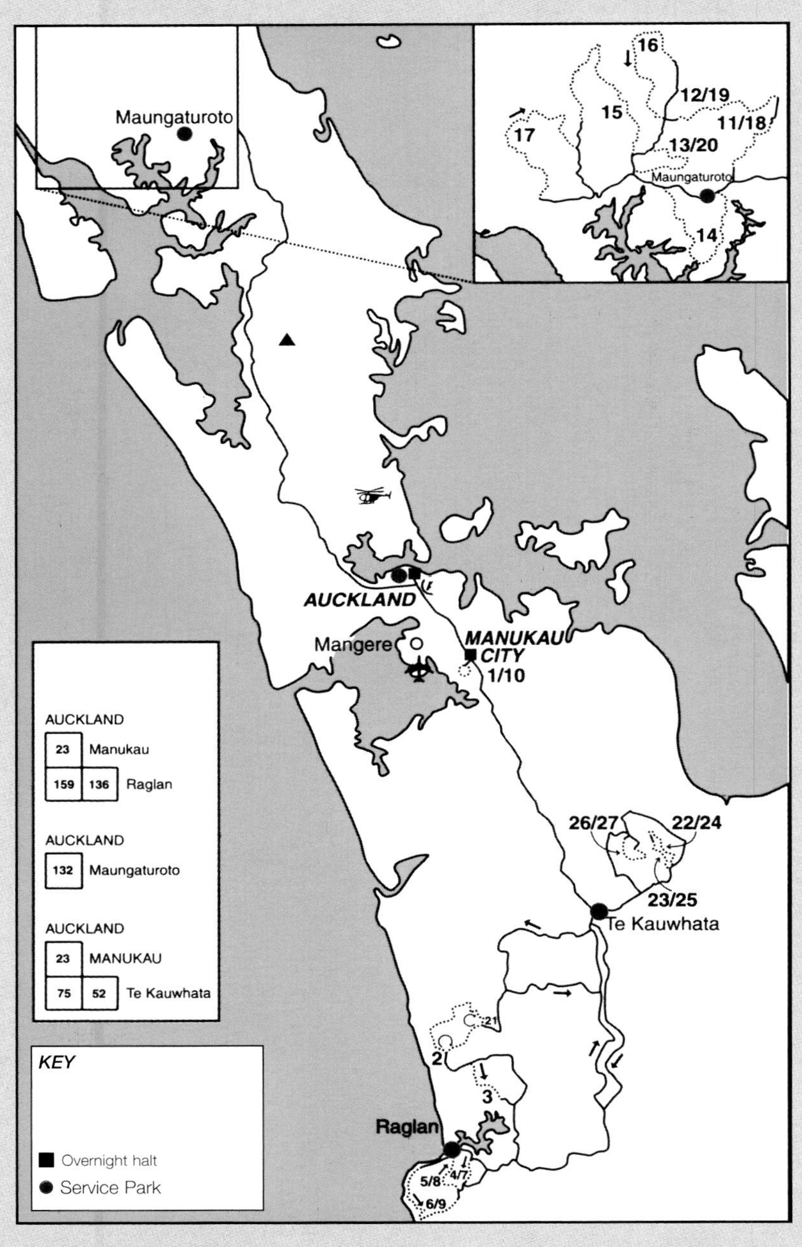

SPECIAL STAGE TIMES

SS.1 Super spéciale 1 (2,10 km)
1. Bourne 1'28"9 ; 2. Radstrom 1'29"2 ; 3. McRae 1'29"7 ; 4. Rovanpera 1'29"8 ; 5. Kankkunen 1'30"; Gr.N Nutahara 1'33" ; F2 Evans 1'36"4

SS.2 Te Akau North (31,83 km)
1. Makinen 18'30" ; 2. McRae 18'38" ; 3. Burns 18'54"4 ; 4. Auriol 18'55"8 ; 5. Sainz 18'58"1 ; Gr.N Trellss 20'07"2 ; F2 McRae 20'32"7

SS.3 Te Akau South (11,00 km)
1. McRae 6'58"4 ; 2. Sainz et Burns 7'03"4 ; 4. Makinen 7'03"5 ; 5. Auriol 7'04"1 ; Gr.N Trellss 7'29"6 ; F2 McRae 7'43"8

SS.4 Mangatawhiri 1 (6,52 km)
1. Makinen 3'42"5 ; 2. Sainz 3'43"2 ; 3. McRae 3'44"5 ; 4. Burns 3'45"1 ; 5. Kankkunen 3'46"8 ; Gr.N Trellss 3'58"9 ; F2 Eriksson 4'11"8

SS.5 Te Hutewai 1 (11,39 km)
1. Makinen 8'05"2 ; 2. McRae 8'05"4 ; 3. Auriol 8'09"5 ; 4. Sainz 8'11"2 ; 5. Kankkunen 8'14"5 ; Gr.N Trellss 8'37"9 ; F2 McRae 8'55"

SS.6 Whaanga Coast 1 (29,52 km)
1. McRae 21'39"7 ; 2. Makinen 21'41"8 ; 3. Auriol 21'49"4 ; 4. Sainz 21'50"5 ; 5. Burns 21'51" ; Gr.N Trellss 23'14"9 ; F2 McRae 24'16"5

SS.7 Mangatawhiri 2 (6,52 km)
1. Sainz 3'47"4 ; 2. Auriol 3'48"4 ; 3. Kankkunen 3'49" ; 4. Makinen 3'50" ; 5. Gardemeister 3'50"2; Gr.N Trellss 4'01" ; F2 McRae 4'11"8

SS.8 Te Hutewai 2 (11,39 km)
1. McRae 8'18"5 ; 2. Sainz 8'20"2 ; 3. Makinen 8'23"9 ; 4. Kankkunen 8'24"8 ; 5. Auriol 8'26"8 ; Gr.N Trellss 8'43"3 ; F2 McRae 9'02"8

SS.9 Whaanga Coast 2 (29,52 km)
1. Makinen 23'12"1 ; 2. Kankkunen 23'16"8 ; 3. Gardemeister 23'24" ; 4. Radstrom 23'33"6 ; 5. Auriol 23'38"8 ; Gr.N Al Wahaibi 24'41" ; F2 Eriksson 25'27"3

SS.10 Super Spéciale 2 (2,10 km)
1. Radstrom 1'36"7 ; 2. Kankkunen 1'37"9 ; 3. Sainz et Rovanpera 1'38"1 ; 5. Kataoka 1'39"3 ; Gr.N Arai 1'41"3 ; F2 McRae 1'43"3

SS.11 Waipu Gorge 1 (11,24 km)
1. Auriol 6'40"7 ; 2. Makinen 6'41"6 ; 3. Sainz 6'42"5 ; 4. Kankkunen 6'43"3 ; 5. Rovanpera 6'44"4 ; Gr.N Trellss 7'08"2 ; F2 McRae 7'19"1

SS.12 Brooks 1 (16,15 km)
1. Sainz 10'08"6 ; 2. Makinen 10'10"7 ; 3. Auriol 10'11"1 ; 4. Kankkunen 10'12"8 ; 5. Gardemeister 10'15"9 ; Gr.N Trellss 10'55"3 ; F2 McRae 11'11"5

SS.13 Paparoa Station 1 (11,66 km)
1. Makinen 6'31"7 ; 2. Auriol 6'32"4 ; 3. Sainz 6'33"4 ; 4. Kankkunen 6'33"7 ; 5. Radstrom 6'35"7; Gr.N Al Wahaibi 7'04"9 ; F2 McRae 7'08"5

SS.14 Batley (19,89 km)
1. Radstrom 11'22" ; 2. Sainz 11'22"3 ; 3. Gardemeister 11'24"7 ; 4. Makinen 11'25"4 ; 5. Kankkunen 11'31"1 ; Gr.N Trellss 12'08"8 ; F2 Eriksson 12'37"2

SS.15 Ararua (31,95 km)
1. Makinen 20'22"3 ; 2. Sainz 20'25"4 ; 3. Kankkunen 20'31"3 ; 4. Radstrom 20'32"6 ; 5. Gardemeister 20'33"2 ; Gr.N Trellss 21'48"9 ; F2 Eriksson 22'27"4

SS.16 Cassidy (20,06 km)
1. Makinen 11'36"9 ; 2. Kankkunen 11'39"7 ; 3. Sainz 11'40"5 ; 4. Radstrom 11'40"5 ; 5. Gardemeister 11'42"4 ; Gr.N Trellss 12'28"5 ; F2 McRae 13'21"4

SS.17 Parahi (24,00 km)
1. Kankkunen 12'59"8 ; 2. Makinen 13'03"7 ; 3. Sainz 13'05"4 ; 4. Gardemeister 13'09" ; 5. Auriol 13'10"4; Gr.N Trellss 14'06"3 ; F2 Eriksson 14'32"

SS.18 Waipu Gorge 2 (11,24 km)
1. Radstrom 6'44"7 ; 2. Gardemeister 6'45"1 ; 3. Kankkunen 6'47"2 ; 4. Sainz 6'47"7 ; 5. Makinen 6'49"4 ; Gr.N Trellss 7'07"5 ; F2 McRae 7'23"2

SS.19 Brooks 2 (16,15 km)
1. Kankkunen 10'18"4 ; 2. Radstrom 10'20"6 ; 3. Makinen 10'21" ; 4. Gardemeister 10'21"9 ; 5. Bourne 10'36"5 ; Gr.N Trellss 10'58"9 ; F2 McRae 11'22"5

SS.20 Paparoa Station 2 (11,66 km)
1. Kankkunen 6'43"2 ; 2. Gardemeister 5'43"3 ; 3. Sainz 6'46" ; 4. Makinen 6'46"1 ; 5. Radstrom 6'48"1; Gr.N Al Wahaibi 7'07"2 ; F2 McRae 7'19"

SS.21 Te Akau North 2 (32,23 km)
1. Makinen 19'25"5 ; 2. Kankkunen 19'30"7 ; 3. Sainz 19'39"9 ; 4. Gardemeister 19'40"2 ; 5. Auriol 19'40"7; Gr.N Trellss 20'46"3 ; F2 Eriksson 21'33"8

SS.22 Ridge 1 (8,60 km)
1. Makinen 4'55"2 ; 2. Kankkunen 4'58"7 ; 3. Sainz 4'59"8 ; 4. Auriol 5'00"7 ; 5. Bourne 5'01"3 ; Gr.N Arai 5'21"7 ; F2 Eriksson 5'31"7

SS.23 Campbell 1 (7,49 km)
1. Makinen 4'01"8 ; 2. Sainz 4'03"9 ; 3. Kankkunen 4'04"7 ; 4. Gardemeister 4'06"2 ; 5. Bourne 4'06"8 ; Gr.N Holmss 4'23"5 ; F2 McRae 4'31"7

SS.24 Ridge 2 (8,60 km)
1. Auriol 4'58"3 ; 2. Sainz 4'58"6 ; 3. Makinen 4'58"8 ; 4. Kankkunen 4'59"2 ; 5. Gardemeister 4'59"3 ; Gr.N Mendez 5'13"6 ; F2 McRae 5'29"8

SS.25 Campbell 2 (7,49 km)
1. Sainz 4'02"5 ; 2. Gardemeister 4'03"7 ; 3. Bourne 4'04"2 ; 4. Makinen 4'04"6 ; 5. Auriol 4'04"8 ; Gr.N Al Wahaibi et Taguchi 4'22" ; F2 McRae 4'30"1

SS.26 Fyfe 1 (10,63 km)
1. Auriol 5'58"9 ; 2. Sainz et Kankkunen 5'59"3 ; 4. Gardemeister 6'02"2 ; 5. Bourne 6'03"6 ; Gr.N Al Wahaibi 6'25"2 ; F2 Eriksson 6'37"8

SS.27 Fyfe 2 (10,63 km)
1. Sainz 5'56"9 ; 2. Auriol 5'58"7 ; 3. Bourne 5'59"5 ; 4. Kankkunen 6'00"4 ; 5. Gardemeister 6'01"8 ; Gr.N Mendez et Argyle 6'22"4 ; F2 Eriksson 6'32"9

RESULTS AND RETIREMENTS

	Driver/Co-Driver	Car	Gr	Total Time
1	**Tommi Makinen – Risto Mannisenmaki**	**Mitsubishi Lancer Ev.6**	**A**	**4h11m07,1s**
2	Juha Kankkunen – Juha Repo	Subaru Impreza WRC	A	4h12m44,1s
3	Toni Gardemeister – Paavo Lukander	Seat Cordoba WRC	A	4h13m56,1s
4	Didier Auriol – Denis Giraudet	Toyota Corolla WRC	A	4h17m22,9s
5	Possum Bourne – Craig Vincent	Subaru Impreza WRC	A	4h17m55,4s
6	Carlos Sainz – Luis Moya	Toyota Corolla WRC	A	4h19m23s
7	Matthias Kahle – Dieter Schneppenheim	Toyota Corolla WRC	A	4h25m44,2s
8	Freddy Loix – Sven Smeets	Mitsubishi Carisma GT	A	4h26m34,4s
9	**Gustavo Trelles – Martin Christie**	**Mitsubishi Lancer Ev.5**	**N**	**4h28m32,8s**
10	**Hamed Al Wahaibi – Tony Sircombe**	**Mitsubishi Lancer Ev.5**	**N**	**4h30m21,2s**
17	**Kenneth Eriksson – Staffan Parmander**	**Hyundai Coupe Ev.2**	**A**	**4h38m37,5s**
SS.6	Richard Burns – Robert Reid	Subaru Impreza WRC	A	Gearbox
SS.9	Colin McRae – Nicky Grist	Ford Focus WRC	A	Electrics
SS.9	Michael Guest – David Green	Subaru Impreza WRX	A	Accident
SS.15	Yoshihiro Kataoka – Satoshi Hayashi	Mitsubishi Lancer Ev.6	A	Suspension
SS.17	Harri Rovanpera – Risto Pietilainen	Seat Cordoba WRC	A	Engine
SS.21	Thomas Radstrom – Fred Gallagher	Ford Focus WRC	A	Accident

EVENT LEADERS

SS.1	Bourne
SS.2 – SS.7	Makinen
SS.8	McRae
SS.9 – SS.27	Makinen

BEST PERFORMANCES

	1	2	3	4	5	6
Makinen	10	4	3	5	1	2
Sainz	4	8	8	3	1	-
Kankkunen	3	6	5	5	4	2
Auriol	3	3	4	2	6	4
McRae	3	2	2	-	-	1
Radstrom	3	2	-	3	2	5
Bourne	1	-	2	-	4	5
Gardemeister	-	3	2	5	6	5
Burns	-	1	1	1	1	1
Rovanpera	-	-	1	1	1	1
Kataoka	-	-	-	-	1	-
Loix	-	-	-	-	-	3

CHAMPIONSHIP CLASSIFICATIONS

Drivers

1. Tommi Makinen	46
2. Didier Auriol	35
3. Carlos Sainz	30
4. Juha Kankkunen	24
5. Colin McRae	23
5. Richard Burns	23

Constructors

1. Toyota	78
2. Mitsubishi	59
3. Subaru	52
4. Ford	35
5. Seat	12

Group N

1. Gustavo Trelles	61
2. Hamed Al Wahaibi	52
3. Manfred Stohl	14

Two Litres

1. Renault	77
2. Hyundai	55
3. Volkswagen	16

Team's Cup

1. Valencia Terra Mar Team Luis Climent	40
2. F.Dor Rally Team Frederic Dor	34
3. Team Mitsubishi Oman Hamed Al Wahaibi	19

PREVIOUS WINNERS

1977	Bacchelli - Rosetti Fiat 131 Abarth
1978	Brookes - Porter Ford Escort RS
1979	Mikkola - Hertz Ford Escort RS
1980	Salonen - Harjanne Datsun 160J
1982	Waldegaard - Thorzelius Toyota Celica GT
1983	Rohrl - Geistdorfer Opel Ascona 400
1984	Blomqvist - Cederberg Audi Quattro A2
1985	Salonen - Harjanne Peugeot 205 T16
1986	Kankkunen - Piironen Peugeot 205 T16
1987	Wittmann - Patermann Lancia Delta HF 4WD
1988	Haider - Hinterleitner Opel Kadett GSI
1989	Carlsson - Carlsson Mazda 323 Turbo
1990	Sainz - Moya Toyota Celica GT-Four
1991	Sainz - Moya Toyota Celica GT-Four
1992	Sainz - Moya Toyota Celica Turbo 4WD
1993	McRae - Ringer Subaru Legacy RS
1994	McRae - Ringer Subaru Impreza
1995	McRae - Ringer Subaru Impreza
1996	Burns - Reid Mitsubishi Lancer Ev.3
1997	Eriksson - Parmander Subaru Impreza WRC
1998	Sainz - Moya Toyota Corolla WRC

GOSSIP

• ERIKSSON'S CENTURY

In New Zealand, Kenneth Eriksson started his one hundredth world championship rally, taking the win in the two litre class at the wheel of his Hyundai Coupe. The Swede took part in his first world championship rally in Sweden back in 1980 and finished 51st. At the age of 43, he intends to continue for a good while yet. Certainly the Korean constructor is counting on his presence behind the wheel of the WRC that they will enter starting in 2000.

• BURNS DOES NOT CONFIRM

Everyone was waiting to see what Richard Burns could do after his win in Greece, but he was unable to confirm his form, despite being on the kind of terrain which suits him perfectly. In the middle of the second leg, when his team had just changed his faulty gearbox, the Englishman had to retire just after he had got going again from the service area where the repair was carried out. He retired a few kilometres down the road when a joint in the hydraulic system let go.

• THE CUNNING OF AL-WAHAIBI

Although beaten by Gustavo Trelles in Group N, Hamed Al-Wahaibi drove a very intelligent race. Not at all at ease in the New Zealand mud, as this was only his third event on this type of surface, the man from Oman chose to make sure of the second place in the category, rather than risk going off the road. However, this meant giving away a fair few points to the Uruguayan, who thus took the lead in the championship.

• THE LION'S SHARE FOR MICHELIN

Tommi Makinen's and Mitsubishi's win was the seventh out of nine starts for Michelin this season. It was a healthy score for the French manufacturer, much appreciated by the Finnish driver. He was particularly keen on the mud tyres, which he chose on several occasions to stop the watch in some impressive times.

• YOU HAVE TO BE MAD TO TRUST IN THE RAIN

A heavy shower hit the small town of Maungaturoto, the site of the service area for the second leg. All the front runners opted for a tyre change therefore, opting for the softest tyre as being the best option. All this happened within seconds of heading off for the final few stages. However, the very next stage had escaped the rain and so all the front runners were on equal terms yet again and on the wrong tyres as well.

"More foolhardy than brave..."

FINLAND

The brio of the Peugeot 206 driven by Marcus Gronholm was extinguished by the lack of reliability of the baby WRC with the promising performance level. Tommi Makinen went out with mechanical failure and Richard Burns was beaten. This left Juha Kankkunen to rule over his national rally. The old master had handed out a lesson and on the way he racked up his record twenty third world rally championship win and relaunched his bid for the title at

the perfect moment. Especially as, apart from Makinen's retirement, Didier Auriol had been seriously slowed by a Corolla which was so badly set up that it was almost dangerous.

A RECORD WIN FOR KANKKUNEN. Here we were back in the land of the brave. The world championship was making its annual pilgrimage to the land of yumps, fast curves and speeds that were best not thought about. You needed guts to jump into the first stage which was run at an average speed of over 135 km/h. Juha Kankkunen has never been short of guts. Mr. K was inspired, mounting a prodigious attack made up of slides, avoidances and jumps, all at the wheel of a Subaru he drove with true brio and pace. He was the first to lead, but after just two stages, he was forced to concede it to team-mate Richard Burns. This was only the lanky Englishman's second visit to these shores, but already he had the hang of it. He led for most of the first leg, using all his skill and helped by the fact he was taking to the stages in the best possible place in the running order.

On the dry tracks, covered with a light coating of gravel, the wheels of the first few competitors do a marvellous job of sweeping the moving carpet, the classic loose surface conundrum. "Especially over the last stages, its a big disadvantage," explained championship leader Makinen who was first on the road. However, Kankkunen and Burns were starting the day's seven stages from fourth and sixth places respectively, which meant they were running on a surface which provided plenty of bite for the tyres. The same applied to the other dominant player in this section, the Finn Gronholm, who was twelfth on the road. Because once the blue cars had gone flying, it was time for the little white rocket to do the same. Once warmed up, the 206 WRC overcame a few trivial problems like a harmless oil leak from the central differential and it was time for Gronholm, nicknamed "Marcus Full Pedal" to set two fastest times in what was a thrilling battle. The brilliant young driver moved up from fifth to second before being promoted to the lead. Because the lead changed yet again towards the end of the day in the very last stage. Mainly to avoid being first on the road the following day, Burns ran at a pace which might have disgraced the Queen's carriage as she rode down the Mall, losing a handful of seconds and the lead at the same time. It was a clever move as no such finesse was permissible for Gronholm and Peugeot, who had just set the first leg of a rally of its short career. For them, that was important.

Right from the opening kilometres of the second leg, the previous day's form started to repeat itself. Makinen was out to play the role of the cat, made easier by the fact he was starting fifth on the road, allowing him to stretch out a lazy paw to worry those in front of him with his claws. The first stage went to Gronholm, never mind, and the next three to a flamboyant Sainz, doesn't matter, and Kankkunen still led overall but Makinen was not far behind. He took a little while to fine tune his settings, stiffening his dampers and confirming all was well by finally taking his first stage win. The beast was ready and all its claws had been sharpened. Until now, it had simply played with the mice, letting the pack close up. Kankkunen, who led from the second stage of the day was unable to build a substantial lead of Burns, Gronholm, Sainz and of course Makinen. This fantastic rally was heading for a tantalising climax. With 311 out of 377 competitive kilometres completed, nothing was certain as five escapees were locked in the same eight seconds.

Still to come was Ouninpohja, hard to say without sneezing, a 34.21 kilometre stage. The official programme described it as the height of the rally. "A hard surface with sudden jumps and tight corners which go on without pause." You had to be more foolhardy than brave. Its first victim was named Radstrom, who split open the front of his Focus when he fell off the edge. The second unfortunate was ......Makinen! His Mitsubishi had packed up with a sudden transmission failure, 16 kilometres into the stage. And just to make the Japanese team's misery complete, its second driver Loix, who had been off the pace up until that point, decided to roll his car into a ball. Ouninpohja would claim one more victim and that was Gronholm. An impromptu loss of hydraulic fluid took an eternity to fix and cost him a 50 second penalty. This stage had completely changed the tenor of the event, with three drivers flying off into the distance; Kankkunen, Sainz and Burns. But Mr. K had this rally so well under control that he managed to keep everything in hand and his two chasers at bay, even when faced with the difficulty of being first car on the road for the final leg. No one could denigrate this win, his 23rd and a new record to boot, on his home turf. Adding to the joy, it was a one-two finish for Subaru and he was now chasing Makinen hard for the drivers' championship. How could he have dreamed of anything better?

PEUGEOT COMES CLOSE. In the lead after just two stages on the Tour of Corsica, taking its very first stage win on the Acropolis and winning its first rally leg in Finland and scoring its first world championship points thanks to Gronholm's fourth place, the 206 WRC had not stopped making progress since its first appearance. On top of that, it had won the Mantta Rally, two weeks before the 1000 Lakes. The most surprising aspect of its performance is that the pocket rocket has proved equally adept on the tarmac of the

"And Juha Kankkunen could now dream openly of a fifth and final world crown."

120.1 - 121.3-4
Twenty third world championship win for Juha Kankkunen and the Finn's delight was plain to see on the podium.

121.1
With five fastest times, Marcus Gronholm was the best performer, equal with Kankkunen.

121.2
Once again the Mitsubishi's reliability was suspect, which prevented Tommi Makinen from racking up a sixth consecutive win on his home rally.

121.5
Carlos Sainz tried all he knew, but he could not match Kankkunen's pace.

120.1

121.1

121.2

121.3

121.4

121.5

Island of Beauty and the unforgiving rough roads of Greece and the ultra-fast Nordic roads. All that it needs now is for its reliability to come up to scratch. In Finland, the first alert came at the end of the first leg. While fitting a new gearbox in preparation for the second leg, a hydraulic union was badly fitted, causing a drop in oil pressure. Despite having to drop the engine subframe and the power steering, Gronholm still checked in on time. Well done the lads. The next day, it was all over because of a hydraulic leak. Five minutes too long taken to fix the problem meant a 50 second penalty, which effectively put him out of the running for a win. At the same time, Delecour was not really feeling comfortable on a rally he had not tackled since 1994 and his car's handling was erratic. Sometimes the 206 lost its brakes or would suddenly switch to two wheel drive before kicking in again on all four without warning. It was due no doubt to a fault in the electronic control of the differentials; a problem which had already occurred in Corsica. Despite it all, he finished ninth. As for Gilles Panizzi (33rd) an electronics glitch stopped him for fifteen minutes during the second leg, but the two time French champion never got into the swing of the Finnish event. All these little irritations prevented Peugeot from pulling off something special. They would have to wait for another chance at the ultimate prize.

AURIOL, BETWEEN TERROR AND ACHIEVEMENT. Looking at his rally, the first day had not been catastrophic for Didier Auriol. Seventh, 24.3 seconds down on Gronholm the leader, he could still hope for a good event. "The car has a few problems," he explained at the end of the day. "Sometimes, when I brake, it pulls hard to the right. It's alright when you are in second gear, but in sixth it's a bit more exciting. Really, it all came down to the running order on the road. I really pushed very hard. It was all under control though. And then, Makinen (6th) and me are quite close in the classification." It was an analysis full of hope for the forthcoming stages. Sadly, what followed did not live up to those hopes. Getting behind the wheel of a Corolla which was handling so unpredictably was becoming positively dangerous, but he managed a major achievement all the same. What was it? He stayed on the road! His WRC was full of surprises and even when travelling in a straight line, spectators would throw themselves in the ditches, scared they were about to be hit. It took a lot of driving talent and infinite patience and Didier was constantly on at his crew to make various changes. It was all in vain. Having put up with this for two days, Toyota decided to stop Auriol-Giraudet in the middle of the final leg, to change the two elements they had not so far replaced; the central differential and the steering rack. This was done with the aim of tackling the final televised stage, which is open to the leading drivers, even if they are out of the rally proper. And lo, there was a miracle. The Corolla was reborn and he set the quickest time! Despite constant demands from the driver, the team had not changed these parts earlier without really explaining why not. It might have been because this same component had caused Hagstrom's Toyota Number 3 to retire. But given the parlous state they were in, the French crew were up for anything. Winner of the final stage and collector of the three points which go with that victory, Auriol at least had some consolation to take home with him. But given how well he was driving and seeing what Sainz achieved with a properly sorted Toyota, who knows what Auriol would have achieved with a decent car.

KANKKUNEN DREAMS OF FANGIO! Juha Kankkunen is not an easy man to deal with. An English television reporter asked him at the end of the final stage, the rather mundane question as to his tyre choice and although there was no great mystery to this matter, the Finn replied, "round and black Pirellis!" The Finn certainly lived up to his reputation as a laconic smoker of cigarillos. But as the event winner, he should have been a bit more forthcoming. That's the way he is, Mr. K, the man from the woods and the blue lakes. Nevertheless, he can shows signs of humanity. Knocked out by Richard Burns' performance at only his second attempt at this very specialised event, Kankkunen was full of praise for the Englishman, although this was all done through third parties, as the two men had virtually stopped talking to one another after the prickly situation regarding team orders at the end of the rally in Argentina. "To be able to be in with a chance of winning is all the more fantastic as this is only his second Thousand Lakes," said the mustachioed one. "In fact I reckon that a foreign driver has never done so well!" Burns had definitely produced the best ever performance from a British driver on these stages.

Subaru's Finnish jaunt had ended in total success. Another one-two finish, the second of the season after the one acquired in South America and a new record number of wins - 23 - for Kankkunen, who was now one victory ahead of Sainz and finally two drivers in with a crack at the title. While Burns was 19 points down on Makinen and therefore had a very slim chance of victory, Mr. K had improved his cause with this win and his deficit stood at just 15 points. This meant he could now dream openly of a fifth and final world crown to round off a glorious career. That would have put him right up there with a certain Juan-Manuel Fangio.

122.1

122.2

122.3

FINLAND

"The speed of a leopard at full stretch..."

122.1

Marcus Gronholm gave Peugeot its constructors' championship points.

122.2

Didier Auriol's rally was a nightmare at the wheel of a virtually undriveable Corolla.

122.3

Before the start of the final stage, McRae spotted traces of oil on his engine and a few metres down the road it was all over, when he had been a comfortable fourth.

123.1

Delayed by yet another off, Freddy Loix was a disappointing tenth.

123.2-4

Toni Gardemeister took the Seat Cordoba Ev. 2 to its first stage win and Rovanpera was no slouch either.

123.3

Richard Burns put on a remarkable performance for his second attempt at the Nordic event.

123.1

123.2

123.3

123.4

10
NESTE Rally 1999

49TH RALLY OF FINLAND

TOP ENTRIES

1 Tommi Makinen - Risto Mannisenmaki
MITSUBISHI LANCER EV.6
2 Freddy Loix - Sven Smeets
MITSUBISHI CARISMA GT
3 Carlos Sainz - Luis Moya
TOYOTA COROLLA WRC
4 Didier Auriol - Denis Giraudet
TOYOTA COROLLA WRC
5 Richard Burns - Robert Reid
SUBARU IMPREZA WRC
6 Juha Kankkunen - Juha Repo
SUBARU IMPREZA WRC
7 Colin McRae - Nicky Grist
FORD FOCUS WRC
8 Thomas Radstrom - Fred Gallagher
FORD FOCUS WRC
9 Harri Rovanpera - Risto Pietilainen
SEAT CORDOBA WRC EV.2
10 Toni Gardemeister – Paavo Lukander
SEAT CORDOBA WRC EV.2
11 Armin Schwarz – Manfred Hiemer
SKODA OCTAVIA WRC
12 Emil Triner – Milos Hulka
SKODA OCTAVIA WRC
14 François Delecour – Daniel Grataloup
PEUGEOT 206 WRC
15 Marcus Gronholm – Timo Rautiainen
PEUGEOT 206 WRC
16 Gilles Panizzi – Herve Panizzi
PEUGEOT 206 WEC
17 Petter Solberg - Philip Mills
FORD FOCUS WRC
18 Markko Martin - Toomas Kitsing
TOYOTA COROLLA WRC
19 Pasi Hagstrom - Tero Gardemeister
TOYOTA COROLLA WRC
20 Sebastian Lindholm - Jukka Aho
FORD ESCORT WRC
21 Volkan Isik - Erkan Bodur
TOYOTA COROLLA WRC
22 Luis Climent - Alex Romani
SUBARU IMPREZA WRC
23 Jouko Puhakka - Jakke Honkanen
MITSUBISHI LANCER EV.5
24 Gustavo Trelles - Martin Christie
MITSUBISHI LANCER EV.6
25 Janne Tuohino - Miikka Anttila
FORD ESCORT WRC
26 Alister McRae - David Senior
HYUNDAI COUPE EV.2
27 Tapio Laukkanen - Kaj Lindstrom
RENAULT MEGANE MAXI
28 Kenneth Eriksson - Staffan Parmander
HYUNDAI COUPE EV.2
29 Jarmo Kytoletho - Arto Kapanen
VAUXHALL ASTRA KIT CAR
30 Mark Higgins - Bryan Thomas
VOLKSWAGEN GOLF GTI 16V
31 Martin Rowe - Derek Ringer
RENAULT MEGANE MAXI
32 Per Svan - Johan Olsson
OPEL ASTRA KIT CAR
34 Juuso Pykalisto - Esko Mertsalmi
MITSUBISHI CARISMA GT
36 Juha Kangas - Mika Ovaskainen
SUBARU IMPREZA
38 Hamed Al Wahaibi - Tony Sircombe
MITSUBUSHI LANCER EV.5
39 Manfred Stohl - Peter Muller
MITSUBISHI LANCER EV.5
40 Jesus Puras - Marc Marti
SUBARU IMPREZA
41 Frederic Dor - Didier Breton
SUBARU IMPREZA WRC
43 Pernilla Walfridsson-Ulrika Mattsson
MITSUBISHI LANCER EV.5
58 Adruzilo Lopes - Luis Lisboa
MITSUBISHI LANCER EV.5
68 Simon Jean-Joseph - Patrick Pivato
FORD PUMA KIT CAR

10th leg of the 1999 world rally championships for constructors and drivers
10th leg of the constructors' "2 litre", production car drivers' and teams'world cups

Date: *20 - 22 August 1999*

Route: *1156,59 km divided into 3 legs, 23 stages on loose surface roads (377,26 km)*
1st leg : Friday 20th August, Jyvaskyla – Laajavuori, 7 stages (82,29 km)
2nd leg : Saturday 21st August, Laajavuori – Orivesi – Laajavuori, 10 stages (201,21 km)
3rd leg : Sunday 22nd August, Laajavuori – Josemora – Lievestuore, 6 stages (93,76 km)

Starters/Finishers: *129/64*

First world championship win for Tappio Laukkanen in the 2 litre category.

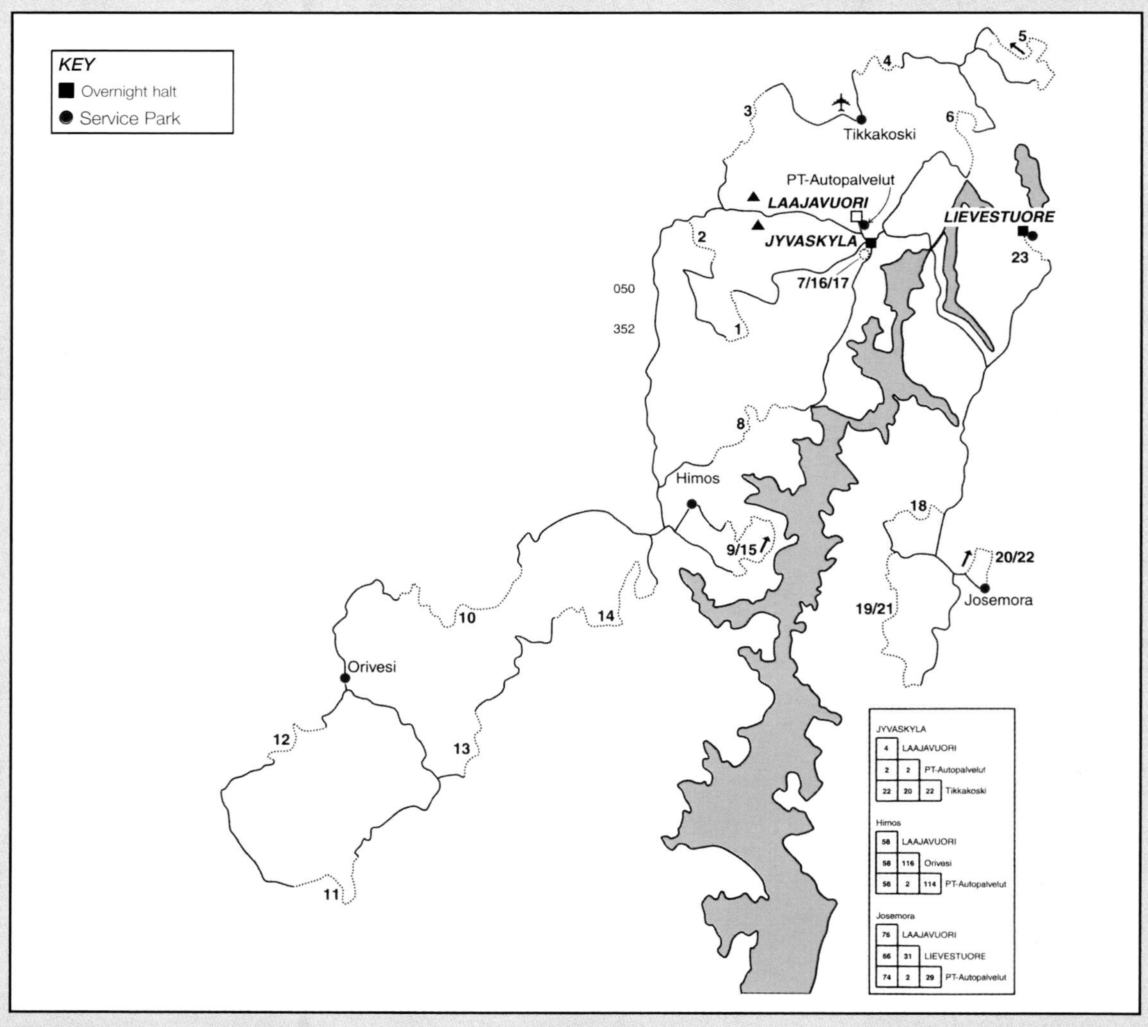

SPECIAL STAGE TIMES

SS.1 Parkkola (11,07 km)
1. Kankkunen 4'54"9 ; 2. Makinen 4'54"2 ; 3. Hagstrom 4'55"3 ; 4. Sainz 4'55"7 ; 5. Rovanpera 4'55"9 ; Gr.N Puhakka 5'08"8 ; F2 Kytholetho 5'12"5

SS.2 Tiilimaa (10,26 km)
1. Radstrom 5'03"4 ; 2. Makinen 5'03"6 ; 3. Kankkunen 5'03"7 ; 4. Burns 5'04"1 ; 5. Gardemeister 5'05"6 ; Gr.N Puhakka 5'22"6, F2 Kytholetho 5'29"5

SS.3 Mokkipera (13,39 km)
1. Burns 6'36"3 ; 2. Gronholm 6'40"1 ; 3. Kankkunen 6'40"3 ; 4. Auriol et Radstrom 6'40"7 ; Gr.N Puhakka 7'01"6 ; F2 Kytholetho 7'08"1

SS.4 Valkola (8,40 km)
1. Kankkunen 4 '35"7 ; 2. Makinen 4'35"8 ; 3. Gronholm 4'36" ; 4. Burns 4'36"5 ; 5. McRae 4'37"7 ; Gr.N Puhakka 4'54"6 ; F2 Laukkanen 4'58"1

SS.5 Lankamaa (25,12 km)
1. Gronholm 12'44"6 ; 2. Burns 12'49"6 ; 3. Kankkunen 12'49"9 ; 4. Sainz 12'52"6 ; 5. Radstrom 12'52"7 ; Gr.N Puhakka 13'29"8 ; F2 Laukkanen 13'24"6

SS.6 Laukaa (12,36 km)
1. Gronholm 6'19"7 ; 2. Kankkunen et Burns 6'21"6 ; 4. Rovanpera et Sainz 6'22"9 ; Gr.N Puhakka 6'38"5 ; F2 Laukkanen 6'41"4

SS.7 Hippos 1 (1,69 km)
1. Radstrom 1'34"8 ; 2. McRae 1'35"3 ; 3. Martin 1'35"4 ; 4. Sainz 1'35"5 ; 5. Makinen et Gronholm 1'36" ; Gr.N Backlund 1'39"9 ; F2 Kytoletho 1'42"2

SS.8 Leustu (23,57 km)
1. Gronholm 11'49" ; 2. Kankkunen 11'49"9 ; 3. Makinen 11'51"9 ; 4. Sainz 11'53"6 ; 5. Burns 11'53"9 ; Gr.N Puhakka 12'47"3 ; F2 Laukkanen 12'42"6

SS. 9 Vahari 1 (31,03 km)
1. Sainz 15'29"9 ; 2. Makinen 15'31"8 ; 3. Kankkunen 15'32" ; 4. Burns 15'34"5 ; 5. Gardemeister 15'34"9 ; Gr.N Puhakka 16'36" ; F2 Laukkanen 16'30"6

SS.10 Juupajoki (30,39 km)
1. Sainz 15'19"5 ; 2. McRae 15'22 ; 3. Burns 15'22"3 ; 4. Makinen 15'27"7 ; 5. Kankkunen 15'27"9 ; Gr.N Puhakka 16'20"4 ; F2 Laukkanen 16'18"9

SS.11 Sahalahti (20,48 km)
1. Sainz 9'45"9 ; 2. Makinen 9'48"6 ; 3. Kankkunen 9'50" ; 4. Gronholm 9'52"5 ; 5. Burns 9'53" ; Gr.N Puhakka 10'19"8 ; F2 Kytoletho 10'19"5

SS.12 Siitama (14,70 km)
1. Makinen 7'23"3 ; 2. Sainz 7'24"2 ; 3. Gardemeister 7'24"9 ; 4. Burns 7'27"5 ; 5. Kankkunen 7'27"8 ; Gr.N Puhakka 7'47"7 ; F2 Laukkanen 7'50"5

SS.13 Vastila (12,42 km)
1. Sainz 5'53"1 ; 2. Gardemeister 5'54"1 ; 3. Makinen 5'54"4 ; 4. Burns 5'56"3 ; 5. McRae 5'56"3 ; Gr.N Puhakka 6'12" ; F2 Kytoletho 6'09"9

SS.14 Ouninpohja (34,21 km)
1. Kankkunen 16'26"2 ; 2. Burns 16'31"1 ; 3. Gronholm 16'33"5 ; 4. Sainz 16'34"3 ; 5. McRae 16'41"8 ; Gr.N Puhakka 16'35" ; F2 Laukkanen 16'31"5

SS.15 Vaheri 2 (31,03 km)
1. McRae 15'26"2 ; 2. Kankkunen 15'26"4 ; 3. Sainz 16'26"8 ; 4. Burns 15'32"9 ; 5. Gronholm 15'32"9 ; Gr.N Puhakka 16'44"6 ; F2 Laukkanen 16'29"6

SS.16 Hippos 2 (1,69 km)
1. McRae 1'35" ; 2. Radstrom 1'36"2 ; 3. Sainz et Kankkunen 1'36"3 ; 5. Burns 1'36"4 ; Gr.N Puhakka 1'39" ; F2 McRae 1'41"4

SS.17 Hippos 3 (1,69 km)
1. McRae et Gronholm 1'33"3 ; 3. Burns et Radstrom 1'34"3 ; 5. Sainz 1'35" ; Gr.N Puhakka 1'39"7 ; F2 Laukkanen 1'42"8

SS.18 Hauhanpohja (11,27 km)
1. Gardemeister 5'39"6 ; 2. Burns 5'41"8 ; 3. Rovanpera 5'42"1 ; 4. Kankkunen 5'43"6 ; 5. Sainz 5'43"7 ; Gr.N Puhakka 6'04"8 ; F2 Kytoletho 6'10"1

SS.19 Lempaa 1 (28,47 km)
1. Burns 13'48" ; 2. Kankkunen 13'49"4 ; 3. McRae 13'52"3 ; 4. Sainz 13'54"1 ; 5. Rovanpera 13'54"5 ; Gr.N Puhakka 14'44"2 ; F2 Rowe 14'49"3

SS.20 Tammimaki 1 (9,27 km)
1. Gronholm 4'29"8 ; 2. McRae 4'30"7 ; 3. Burns 4'31"5 ; 4. Rovanpera 4'33"8 ; 5. Gardemeister 4'33"8 ; Gr.N Puhakka 4'50"2 ; F2 Rowe 4'53"5

SS.21 Lempaa 2 (28,47 km)
1. Kankkunen 13'32"9 ; 2. McRae 13'33"9 ; 3. Burns 13'34" ; 4. Sainz 13'37"2 ; 5. Gardemeister 13'40"4 ; Gr.N Puhakka 14'27"9 ; F2 Laukkanen 14'29"6

SS.22 Tammimaki 2 (9,27 km)
1. Kankkunen 4'30"7 ; 2. Burns 4'30"8 ; 3. Gronholm 4'31"4 ; 4. Sainz 4'32"1 ; 5. Gardemeister 4'32"5 ; Gr.N Puhakka 4'49"3 ; F2 Svan 4'51"8

SS.23 Ruuhimaki (7,01 km)
1. Auriol 3'20"4 ; 2. Makinen 3'21"2 ; 3. Gardemeister 3'23"8 ; 4. Radstrom 3'24" ; 5. Sainz 3'26"6 ; Gr.N Puhakka 3'41"8 ; F2 Svan 3'45"

RESULTS AND RETIREMENTS

	Driver/Co-Driver	Car	Gr	Total Time
1	**Juha Kankkunen – Juha Repo**	**Subaru Impreza WRC**	**A**	**3h08m54,5s**
2	Richard Burns – Robert Reid	Subaru Impreza WRC	A	3h09m04,2s
3	Carlos Sainz – Luis Moya	Toyota Corolla WRC	A	3h09m12,5s
4	Marcus Gronholm – Timo Rautiainen	Peugeot 206 WRC	A	3h10m26,7s
5	Harri Rovanpera – Risto Pietilainen	Seat Cordoba WRC Ev.2	A	3h11m04,6s
6	Toni Gardemeister – Paavo Lukander	Seat Cordoba WRC Ev.2	A	3h12m04s
7	Sebastian Lindholm – Jukka Aho	Ford Escort WRC	A	3h12m59,2s
8	Jannne Tuohino – Miikka Anttila	Ford Escort WRC	A	3h17m59,5s
9	François Delecour – Daniel Grataloup	Peugeot 206 WRC	A	3h18m48,9s
10	Freddy Loix – Sven Smeets	Mitsubishi Carisma GT	A	3h19m43,5s
11	**Jouko Puhakka – Jakke Honkanen**	**Mitsubishi Lancer Ev.5**	**N**	**3h20m46s**
13	**Tapio Laukkanen – Kaj Lindstrom**	**Renault Megane Maxi**	**A**	**3h21m31,7s**
15	**Volkan Isik – Erkan Bodur**	**Toyota Corolla WRC**	**A**	**3h22m48s**
SS.1	Armin Schwarz – Manfred Hiemer	Skoda Octavia WRC	A	Accident
SS.5	Luis Climent – Alex Romani	Subaru Impreza WRC	A	Accident
SS.8	Hamed Al Wahaibi – Tony Sircombe	Mitsubishi Lancer Ev.5	N	Engine
SS.9	Kenneth Eriksson – Staffan Parmander	Hyundai Coupe Ev.2	A	Brakes
SS.9	Mark Higgins – Bryan Thomas	Volkswagen Golf GTI 16V	A	Accident
SS.10	Markko Martin – Toomas Kitsing	Toyota Corolla WRC	A	Turbo
SS.14	Tommi Makinen – Risto Mannisenmaki	Mitsubishi Lancer Ev.6	A	Transmission
SS.19	Gustavo Trelles – Martin Christie	Mitsubishi Lancer Ev.6	N	Suspension
SS.20	Thomas Radstrom – Fred Gallagher	Ford Focus WRC	A	Retired
SS.21	Didier Auriol – Denis Giraudet	Toyota Corolla WRC	A	Retired
SS.23	Colin McRae – Nicky Grist	Ford Focus WRC	A	Engine

EVENT LEADERS

SS.1 – SS.2	Kankkunen
SS.3 – SS.6	Burns
SS.7 – SS.8	Gronholm
SS.9 – SS.23	Kankkunen

BEST PERFORMANCES

	1	2	3	4	5	6
Kankkunen	5	4	6	1	2	2
Gronholm	5	1	4	1	1	4
Sainz	4	1	2	8	3	1
McRae	3	3	1	-	3	1
Burns	2	4	5	6	3	1
Radstrom	2	1	1	1	2	-
Makinen	1	6	3	1	-	1
Gardemeister	1	1	2	-	5	4
Auriol	1	-	-	1	-	2
Rovanpera	-	-	1	2	2	6
Hagstrom	-	-	1	-	-	-
Delecour	-	-	-	-	1	-
Solberg	-	-	-	-	-	1
Loix	-	-	-	-	-	1

CHAMPIONSHIP CLASSIFICATIONS

Drivers	
1. Tommi Makinen	48
2. Didier Auriol	38
3. Juha Kankkunen	34
3. Carlos Sainz	34
5. Richard Burns	29
Constructors	
1. Toyota	85
2. Subaru	68
3. Mitsubishi	61
4. Ford	35
5. Seat	16
Group N	
1. Gustavo Trelles	61
2. Hamed Al Wahaibi	52
3. Jouko Puhakka	26
Two Litres	
1. Renault	89
2. Hyundai	59
3. Volkswagen	21
Team's Cup	
1. Valencia Terra Mar Team Luis Climent	40
1. F.Dor Rally Team Frederic Dor	40
3. Toyota Mobil Team Turkey Volkan Isik	26

PREVIOUS WINNERS

1973	Makinen - Liddon Ford Escort RS 1600
1974	Mikkola - Davenport Ford Escort RS 1600
1975	Mikkola - Aho Toyota Corolla
1976	Alen - Kivimaki Fiat 131 Abarth
1977	Hamalaiinen - Tiukkanen Ford Escort RS
1978	Alen - Kivimaki Fiat 131 Abarth
1979	Alen - Kivimaki Fiat 131 Abarth
1980	Alen - Kivimaki Fiat 131 Abarth
1981	Vatanen - Richards Ford Escort RS
1982	Mikkola - Hertz Audi Quattro
1983	Mikkola - Hertz Audi Quattro
1984	Vatanen - Harryman Peugeot 205 T16
1985	Salonen - Harjanne Peugeot 205 T16
1986	Salonen - Harjanne Peugeot 205 T16
1987	Alen - Kivimaki Lancia Delta HF Turbo
1988	Alen - Kivimaki Lancia Delta Integrale
1989	Ericsson - Billstam Mitsubishi Galant VR4
1990	Sainz - Moya Toyota Celica GT-Four
1991	Kankkunen - Piironen Lancia Delta Integrale 16v
1992	Auriol - Occelli Lancia Delta Integrale
1993	Kankkunen - Giraudet Toyota Celica Turbo 4WD
1994	Makinen - Harjanne Ford Escort RS Cosworth
1995	Makinen - Harjanne Mitsubishi Lancer Ev.3
1996	Makinen - Harjanne Mitsubishi Lancer Ev.3
1997	Makinen - Harjanne Mitsubishi Lancer Ev.4
1998	Makinen - Mannisenmaki Mitsubishi Lancer Ev.5

GOSSIP

• SEAT CONFIRMS

Running consistently near the front, the two Seats of Rovanpera and Gardemeister finished fifth and sixth respectively. On top of that, the evolution of the Cordoba WRC, called E2, made its rally debut and scored the first stage win of its career on the opening stage of the final day, thanks to Gardemeister. It augured well for this car which was reliable and getting quicker by the day, confirming the potential of its third place in New Zealand. The first version had actually made its debut, here in Finland, one year earlier.

• A DRAW IN GROUP N

Finland's Juha Puhakka dominated Group N, while the worthy Hamed Al- Wahaibi, second in the championship, shone briefly in Finland before crashing out of the event. Luckily for the Omani, Gustavo Trelles, the class leader, also retired with an engine failure on the final day.

• THE FAILURE OF THE FINAL FLING

Just as in Corsica, the Rally of Finland culminated with a televised special stage, shown live by Finnish television. The point of it all was the distribution of additional points for the world championship: 3 for the first, 2 for second and 1 for third. Auriol and Makinen were the first away and therefore avoided the shower which hit the stage shortly after they had performed and meant they easily set the best times ahead of Gardemeister. A shame for the Kankkunens, Burns, Sainzs and all, who would have like the chance to fight it out on equal terms, rather than having to splash through the puddles. Not a very fair system.

• JEAN-JOSEPH UNLUCKY AGAIN

He came to tackle this rally in a Puma Kit-Car 1600 cc in order to get to know the event. But the official Focus WRC tarmac driver, did not even make it to the end of the first leg as his engine broke. In fact, it had never run right all day. Having already driven the car on the Acropolis, with no better luck as his suspension broke, the man from Martinique was not exactly thrilled at getting back behind the wheel of the Puma on the RAC.

• ROYAL VISIT

The Formula 1 World Champion had never attended his home rally, which is the number one sporting event in Finland. It was finally sorted on the final stage, where, invited by the organisers, he came to watch and support his rallying friends. In fact, Makinen had made the journey in the other direction, attending the German Grand Prix to support Mika Hakkinen. It was a protocol of sorts by royal arrangement - the politeness of kings. It is worth noting that in both cases the two world champions were forced to retire!

"In the land of Confucius, Aurio

was the wise one..."

CHINA

The first Chinese Rally to feature as part of the world championship brought its fair share of surprises. The event was run in very muddy conditions after thirty six uninterrupted hours of torrential rain. Two stages were impassable and had to be cancelled. Emerging from the quagmire ahead of the rest was Didier Auriol, who was on absolute top form. It was a particularly convincing win from the Frenchman, because no one, apart from McRae, Liatti and Eriksson had ever seen this very treacherous terrain before the start. It was the perfect test to see who was the most talented driver of them all. This win, from Burns and Sainz, meant the Toyota driver was now back in the lead of the championship, on equal terms with Tommi Makinen. The Finn had driven brilliantly here until he crashed out.

Didier Auriol is congratulated by his engineer Guert Pfeiffer after he took the Corolla WRC to its first 1999 win. Toyota had not won since the 1998 New Zealand rally.

"Didier Auriol's success on unknown territory constituted the clearest indicatio

"Idiots." Malcolm Wilson is not hiding his feelings. Mr. Wilson is very angry. Mr. Wilson has just come from the other side of the world to run his team in a rally; a rally which would last all of 2000 metres! So, yes, Mr. Wilson had every right to be angry, while Mrs. Wilson wiped away the odd tear. First leg, first stage, second kilometre, a right hand corner and a Ford which takes too much of a shortcut, hits a rock and breaks its suspension. The authors of this incident were McRae/Grist; two men who are capable of taking charge of an event, but also of crashing out of one. Then Loix went by and along came the second Ford, crewed by Radstrom-Gallagher. The yin had obviously not informed the yang and bang! Same corner, same mistake, same punishment. Recognising they were at fault, the two drivers attempted to clear their names. "It's the same suspension part which has broken on both cars," explained the Scot. "We will have to find out why." And so we said farewell to Ford and its daft drivers. They would not win in China, or at least not this year. So no McRae in a land where McDonalds had even reached this far and its bright colours could be seen shining, even in the streets of Huai Rou.

As McRae and Radstrom crept off stage in the Chinese theatre, Didier Auriol and his trusty Corolla emerged from the wings to drive off in search of stage wins. "It wasn't easy," he puffed as he got out of the car. "The stages are very, very narrow and rough and with the mud the roads are extremely slippery. I just concentrated on staying on the road. You are driving on a wire. One mistake, just one and you slide and break something." This did not hold him back much and he also profited from Subaru's very bad tyre choice and King Makinen showing clemency. In the land of the panda, the cat, so beloved of painters and sculptors int this country, was feeling pretty much at home. The Finn was in fine form. He watched the mice dance in the mud and got his claws out. In the second special stage of the day, which was long and hard, he set an incredible time. Da Xi Chan will be forever on his record book. After 26.46 kilometres, second placed Burns was 12.4 seconds down while Auriol next was at 28.7 seconds from the leader. The others, all of them no longer existed; skin fur, claws and tyres, he had destroyed them all. He was one second a kilometre quicker than the Frenchman. The world champion could have draped himself in the imperial robes. He did not, which was a shame for him, but it spiced up the event. He had decided to demolish the opposition and he was quickest again on the next stage. But then he got his paint brushes caught up in his royal robes. A long tightening right hander and an attempt at a racing line at excessive racing speeds and the next thing we knew, there was a Lancer parked with its left rear door in a tree, damaging the transmission. Makinen's championship chances took a knock, but hardly a knock out. "I am disappointed that I made such a stupid mistake because I was leading by around 30 seconds." Burns, who had been much more aggressive, once the morning's tyre selection problems were out of the way, could not have asked for more. He took the lead, thanks to two consecutive stage wins in the final part of the day ahead of Auriol, who was being cautious, having clobbered a rock. A long way ahead of Kankkunen and with Sainz out of it, the Englishman could start to dream, but it would not be for long.

It certainly seemed that, in the land of Confucius, Didier Auriol was the wise one. Maybe after his visit to the Forbidden City between the Gate of Supreme Harmony and the Palace of Tranquillity, Auriol had adopted the Chinese philosophy. Because on two occasions in the second leg, Didier did not so much dominate the opposition, as annihilate them. At the end of both runs through Di Shui Hui, a technical and treacherous stage under 12 kilometres long, those who set the second best time were beaten by ten seconds courtesy of a very on-form Auriol. "It is very risky at every corner," explained the Toyota driver. Taking it steady on the car breaking stages and attacking hard in the technical ones, he was in control of a rally where Makinen kept going off the road, before staying off for good, at dusk and under driving rain, with Burns the only one to hang on to the Toyota's coat tails. The world champion was the big loser, because the Frenchman was determined to win now and did not budge an inch under attack from the Englishman in the final leg. Burns was only allowed one stage win to Auriol's five. This was his first win for eighteen months, since the Catalunya event in 1998 and it put him back in joint equal lead of the championship with Makinen. And, thanks to third place from Sainz, who ran a discrete rally, Toyota confirmed its position as leader of the constructors' championship.

ROAD BOOK. Although they were heavily criticised, the roads in China were an excellent judge of competence in the final analysis. This time, the stopwatches, slightly more accurate than the mini wooden sun dials sold by Miss Lui, of Dashalan Street in Peking, in between bottles of strange perfume and mass produced etchings, had a more significant importance than usual. Because, apart from McRae and Liatti, the only two WRC drivers to have competed in this event before, all the rest of the bunch were discovering the joys of China for the very first time. As both the two with previous experience retired on the first day, they were unable to bring that experience into play. So, the rest of the pack had to learn its way around in just three runs carried out through each leg, during the reconnaissance. It was essential to

A few minutes before the finish, the sun came up on Didier Auriol and Denis Giraudet's win against the impressive backdrop of the wall.

f the extent of his talent." Denis Giraudet

dictate the best notes possible to the co-driver, so that they would do the job when it came to driving the stages for real. Between Makinen, Sainz, Auriol and their side men, no one knew the route by heart. At home in Finland, the world champion had started the event on no less than thirteen times and for Kankkunen, the number was eighteen. The same applied to Auriol in Corsica, Sainz in Catalunya, Radstrom in Sweden and so forth. This time however, the purest driving science, improvised in part was going to split them. Denis Giraudet is currently Auriol's navigator, but he has co-driven for many of the greats and he came up with an interesting analysis before the start. Of course the British like Burns and McRae will be more at ease. Their system of notes consists mainly of an objective description of the road and not instructions as to how it should be driven. For the others, improvisation will be more important and difficult. And in these situations, Didier is very good." He was not wrong. The success of Didier Auriol, often accused of recceing himself to bits, was a very convincing demonstration of his talent. And also that of the others!

HAS CHINA WOKEN UP TOO EARLY? Once the event was over, the question on everyone's lips was, had the world rally championship come to China too early? Should there be an event at all in country which was a forbidden place for so long? Proud of their country and with good reason, the Chinese people were constantly quizzing every visitor as to the impression he would retain of their country. There were so many strange incidents in a land so splendid and yet so confusing to the westerner. It has to be said the rally was perfectly organised. There was absolutely no sign of spectator problems, mainly because there were hardly any. That was pretty much it for the rally of China, but there were some questions to be asked. Was it necessary on a sports event to evacuate whole villages just because they were near the special stages? Was it necessary to stop all traffic from using the roads linking the stages so that the rally circus could travel unhindered. Should one tolerate the terrible accidents which took place during the recce and then when the service vehicles, organisers and press were dashing about? Then there were all the oriental haggles on the administrative front. There was very little media interest, which must have upset the manufacturers who had done nothing but talk about the exciting possibilities of this new market. Racketeering was everywhere, with a coffee in the hotels used as a base by the crews in Huai Rou costing over two pounds. So, at the end of it all there were many who felt they had not really visited China at all, but had simply sailed close by and helped to pour sack loads of dollars into the pockets of those who did not really need them.

MAKINEN LOSES BUT then has a big win "As for him, he's only happy when he can crush a rally in just one stage time; when he manages to stuff you by thirty seconds at one go." Denis Giraudet is not wrong in his analysis of Makinen's times like saw teeth, as he pours over the notebook, where he records everyone's times. From the start, the world champion brought out his big guns. A section called Da Xi Chan will long be remembered for his exploits there. After its 26.4 kilometres, second placed Burns was 12.4 seconds down while Auriol, in third place was 28.7 seconds behind as Makinen reclaimed the lead. Trying to hammer his advantage home, he only missed falling off the road, when he hit a tree head on, which did the sort of damage to his Mitsubishi, which makes engineers weep. He also twisted the rear drive line. The next day, Tommi started all over again. He attacked and attacked and attacked, setting fastest times one after the other, until he went off, once on the second stage and then for good on the last stage of this leg, run under the rain. All rally long, he had been trying too hard and each time, he explained his brushes with the undergrowth as " a problem with the notes. His hot headed approach allowed Auriol's brilliant driver to hoist the Frenchman back onto level pegging with the Finn in the world championship. In the race for the title, Makinen was the big loser.

But a little earlier he had been the big winner. One week before the Chinese event and after some hesitation, Makinen confirmed that he would stay with Mitsubishi in 2000. The routes leading to Peugeot, Seat or maybe Ford had finally been brushed aside one at a time. Sitting at the centre of the driver market, Makinen had finally been convinced. By Marlboro who answered his financial needs with talk of 6.4 million dollars a year. He was also convinced by his team. "My choice was guided by the fact it is a team I know well, where I know exactly what they can do and I also appreciate just how much work the test team carries out," explained the world champion. "As for the car itself, although it is at the end of its career, some new improvements should see it being competitive in 2000." Of course, Makinen has been working for a while now on the future Mitsu WCR which should make its competition debut in 2001. Chances are that, just like the current Lancer, the new car will be built around his own driving needs, to the detriment of current team-mate Freddy Loix and all the other drivers actually, who will find it difficult to dislodge him. In the past, Makinen had only ever agreed to sign on for one year at a time, but on this occasion he felt confident enough to put pen to paper for the following two seasons.

CHINA

"In the land of Confucius, the bigwig was the wise one..."

130.1

Out of the running, a de-motivated Juha Kankkunen settled for getting to the finish.

130.2

Three offs and you're out for Tommi Makinen.

130.4

After hitting a rock on the first stage, Colin McRae was unable to exploit his knowledge of the terrain.

130.1

130.2

130.4

131.1-4
On roads that were new to everyone, Didier Auriol demonstrated once again his talent for improvisation.

131.2
Didier Auriol's attempts to take the title seemed to have little affect on Tommi Makinen.

131.3
For many of the locals, this was their first encounter with Westerners.

131.5
With no opposition, Kenneth Eriksson's mission was to make sure he brought home the points for the Korean manufacturer.

131.1

131.2

31.3

131.5

11

3RD RALLY OF CHINA

TOP ENTRIES

1 Tommi Makinen - Risto Mannisenmaki
MITSUBISHI LANCER EV.6

2 Freddy Loix - Sven Smeets
MITSUBISHI CARISMA GT

3 Carlos Sainz - Luis Moya
TOYOTA COROLLA WRC

4 Didier Auriol - Denis Giraudet
TOYOTA COROLLA WRC

5 Richard Burns - Robert Reid
SUBARU IMPREZA WRC

6 Juha Kankkunen - Juha Repo
SUBARU IMPREZA WRC

7 Colin McRae - Nicky Grist
FORD FOCUS WRC

8 Thomas Radstrom - Fred Gallagher
FORD FOCUS WRC

9 Harri Rovanpera - Risto Pietilainen
SEAT CORDOBA WRC EV.2

10 Piero Liatti - Carlo Cassina
SEAT CORDOBA WRC EV.2

11 Volkan Isik - Erkan Bodur
TOYOTA COROLLA WRC

13 Jesus Puras - Marc Marti
TOYOTA COROLLA WRC

14 Possum Bourne - Craig Vincent
SUBARU IMPREZA WRC

15 Gustavo Trelles - Martin Christie
MITSUBISHI LANCER EV.5

16 Hamed Al Wahaibi - Tony Sircombe
MITSUBUSHI LANCER EV.5

17 Yoshihiro Kataoka - Satoshi Hayashi
MITSUBISHI LANCER EV.5

21 Toshihiro Arai - Roger Freeman
SUBARU IMPREZA

24 Kenneth Eriksson - Staffan Parmander
HYUNDAI COUPE EV.2

25 Nobuhiro Tajima - Visut Sukosi
SUZUKI BALENO

26 Alister McRae - David Senior
HYUNDAI COUPE EV.2

11th leg of the 1999 world rally championships for constructors and drivers
11th leg of the constructors' «2 litre», production car drivers' and teams'world cups

Date: *16 - 19 September 1999*

Route: *1394,12 km divided into 3 legs, 22 stages on loose surface roads (370,56 km)*
1st leg : Friday 17th September, Huairou – Ba dao He – Hongda, 8 stages (136,02 km)
2nd leg : Saturday 18th September, Hongda – Nian Zi – Hongda, 8 stages (148,14 km)
3rd leg : Sunday 19th September, Hongda – Jin Shan Ling, 6 stages (86,40 km)

Starters/Finishers: *67/25*

The Seat team was not impressed with Piero Liatti's retirement. He was unable to capitalise on his knowledge of the terrain.

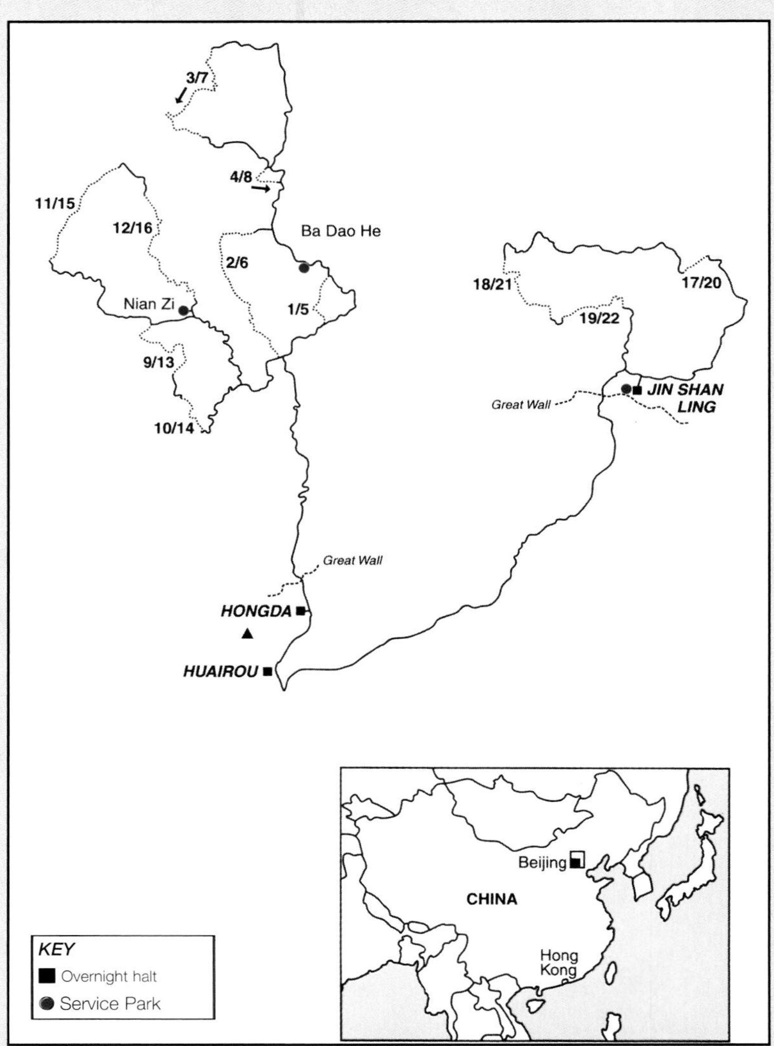

SPECIAL STAGE TIMES

SS.1 Qi Dao He 1 (9,03 km)
1. Auriol 7'01"7 ; 2. Makinen 7'04"1 ; 3. Sainz 7'05"5; 4. Kankkunen 7'13"4 ; 5. Burns 7'14" ; Gr.N Arai 7'36" ; F2 McRae 8'06"6

SS.2 Zhuang Hu 1 (33,07 km)
Cancelled

SS.3 Da Xi Shan 1 (26,46 km)
1. Makinen 19'59"3 ; 2. Burns 20'11"7 ; 3. Auriol 20'28" ; 4. Kankkunen 20'33"2 ; 5. Liatti 20'39"9 ; Gr.N Arai 21'27"8 ; F2 McRae 22'57"6

SS.4 Sun Zha Zi (7,00 km)
1. Makinen 6'38"7 ; 2. Burns 6'45"2 ; 3. Auriol 6'46"2; 4. Kankkunen 6'46"9 ; 5. Sainz 6'47"3 ; Gr.N Arai 7'11"6 ; F2 McRae 7'49"4

SS.5 Qi Dao He 2 (9,03 km)
1. Auriol 6'48"1 ; 2. Burns 6'52"2 ; 3. Sainz 6'54"5 ; 4. Kankkunen 6'59"6 ; 5. Loix 7'07"8 ; Gr.N Al Wahaibi 7'25"8 ; F2 Eriksson 8'16"1

SS.6 Zhuang Hu 2 (33,07 km)
Cancelled

SS.7 Da Xi Shan 2 (24,46 km)
1. Burns 19'35"8 ; 2. Kankkunen 19'39"9 ; 3. Sainz 19'45"5 ; 4. Auriol 19'50"5 ; 5. Makinen 20'00"6 ; Gr.N Arai 21'18"2 ; F2 McRae 23'02"8

SS.8 Sun Zha Zi 2 (7, 00 km)
1. Burns 6'23"6 ; 2. Makinen et Auriol 6'27"8 ; 4. Kankkunen 6'28"7 ; 5. Sainz 6'29"1 ; Gr.N Al Wahaibi 6'52" ; F2 McRae 7'33"3

SS.9 Si Dao Dian 1 (15,94 km)
1. Burns 7'55"7 ; 2. Auriol 7'57"4 ; 3. Makinen 8'03"7 ; 4. Sainz 8'06"8 ; 5. Kankkunen 8'10"2 ; Gr.N Al Wahaibi 8'46"4 ; F2 McRae 8'55"4

SS.10 Di Shui Hu 1 (12,47 km)
1. Auriol 10'34"7 ; 2. Rovanpera 10'44"8 ; 3. Sainz 10'45"1 ; 4. Kankkunen 10'45"3 ; 5. Burns 10'47"8 ; Gr.N Al Wahaibi 11'25"3 ; F2 McRae 11'49"3

SS.11 Dao De Gou 1 (19,78 km)
1. Makinen 13'54"2 ; 2. Burns 14'00"7 ; 3. Auriol 14'03"8 ; 4. Sainz 14'04"1 ; 5. Kankkunen 14'09"1 ; Gr.N Nutahara 15'24"5 ; F2 McRae 16'08"4

SS.12 Hei Niu Shan 1 (25,88 km)
1. Makinen 14'05"9 ; 2. Sainz 14'11"9 ; 3. Burns 14'16"1 ; 4. Auriol 14'17"1 ; 5. Kankkunen 14'22"1 ; Gr.N Arai 15'31"1 ; F2 McRae 16'12"

SS.13 Si Dao Dian 2 (15,94 km)
1. Makinen 7'42"3 ; 2. Auriol 7'42"6 ; 3. Kankkunen 7'47" ; 4. Burns 7'50"1 ; 5. Sainz 7'52" ; Gr.N Al Wahaibi 8'34" ; F2 Eriksson 8'46"4

SS.14 Di Shui Hu 2 (12,47 km)
1. Auriol 10'16"4 ; 2. Makinen 10'24"7 ; 3. Kankkunen 10'25"6 ; 4. Sainz 10'26"9 ; 5. Burns 10'28"7 ; Gr.N Arai 10'58"5 ; F2 Eriksson 11'23"4

SS.15 Dao De Gou 2 (19,78 km)
1. Makinen 13'35"2 ; 2. Auriol 13'46"4 ; 3. Burns 13'51"9 ; 4. Sainz 13'53"3 ; 5. Rovanpera 14'21"7 ; Gr.N Arai 15'10"9 ; F2 Eriksson 16'21"6

SS.16 Hei Niu Shan 2 (25,88 km)
1. Sainz 14'26"1 ; 2. Burns 14'26"3 ; 3. Auriol 14'28"4 ; 4. Kankkunen 14'40"2 ; 5. Rovanpera 15'21"1 ; Gr.N Al Wahaibi ; F2 McRae 17'42"6

SS.17 Cha Dao Kou 1(7,38 km)
1. Auriol 5'37"3 ; 2. Burns 5'39"5 ; 3. Sainz 5'40"9 ; 4. Kankkunen 5'46"9 ; 5. Isik 5'59"7 ; Gr.N Arai 6'04"8 ; F2 Eriksson 6'27"1

SS.18 Bei Gou 1 (19,15 km)
1. Auriol 13'15"7 ; 2. Burns 13'21"3 ; 3. Sainz 13'37"8 ; 4. Kankkunen 13'39"3 ; 5. Rovanpera 14'31"4 ; Gr.N Arai 14'41"4 ; F2 McRae 15'18"2

SS.19 Wu Ying Zi 1 (16,67 km)
1. Auriol 10'15"8 ; 2. Kankkunen 10'26"9 ; 3. Sainz 10'28"6 ; 4. Burns 10'29" ; 5. Rovanpera 11'02"8 ; Gr.N Arai 11'12"4 ; F2 McRae 11'52"6

SS.20 Cha Dao Kou 2 (7,38 km)
1. Burns 5'49"4 ; 2. Auriol 5'54"3 ; 3. Sainz 5'56"4 ; 4. Kankkunen 5'58"3 ; 5. Arai 6'03" ; F2 McRae 6'32"1

SS.21 Bei Gou 2 (19,15 km)
1. Auriol 13'06"3 ; 2. Burns 13'15" ; 3. Kankkunen 13'24" ; 4. Sainz 13'29"4 ; 5. Rovanpera 13'50"7 ; Gr.N Arai 14'26"7 ; F2 McRae 14'41"6

SS.22 Wu Ying Zi 2 (16,67 km)
1. Auriol 9'58"1 ; 2. Sainz 10'14"5 ; 3. Burns 10'18"4; 4. Kankkunen 10'20" ; 5. Rovanpera 10'23"2 ; Gr.N Arai 10'52"1 ; F2 Eriksson 10'58"7

RESULTS AND RETIREMENTS

	Driver/Co-Driver	Car	Gr	Total Time
1	Didier Auriol - Denis Giraudet	Toyota Corolla WRC	A	3h38m36,6s
2	Richard Burns - Robert Reid	Subaru Impreza WRC	A	3h39m32,4s
3	Carlos Sainz - Luis Moya	Toyota Corolla WRC	A	3h40m56s
4	Juha Kankkunen - Juha Repo	Subaru Impreza WRC	A	3h43m54,7s
5	Harri Rovanpera - Risto Pietilainen	Seat Cordoba WRC Ev.2	A	3h47m52s
6	Volkan Isik - Erkan Bodur	Toyota Corolla WRC	A	3h54m42,3s
7	Toshihiro Arai - Roger Freeman	Subaru Impreza	N	3h58m32,5s
8	Gustavo Trelles - Martin Christie	Mitsubishi Lancer Ev.5	N	4h06m33,6s
9	Katsuhiko Taguchi - Ron Teoh	Mitsubishi Lancer Ev.6	N	4h09m46,8s
10	Alister McRae - David Senior	Hyundai Coupe Ev.2	A	4h11m51,7s
SS.1	Colin McRae - Nicky Grist	Ford Focus WRC	A	Suspension
SS.1	Thomas Radstrom - Fred Gallagher	Ford Focus WRC	A	Suspension
SS.5	Jesus Puras - Marc Marti	Toyota Corolla WRC	A	Electrics
SS.5	Nobuhiro Tajima - Visut Sikosi	Suzuki Baleno	A	Accident
SS.7	Freddy Loix - Sven Smeets	Mitsubishi Carisma GT	A	Accident
SS.7	Yoshihiro Kataoka - Satoshi Hayashi	Mitsubishi Lancer Ev.5	A	Engine
SS.8	Piero Liatti - Carlo Cassina	Seat Cordoba WRC	A	Engine
SS.12	Abdullah Bakhashab - Michael Park	Toyota Corolla WRC	A	Suspension
SS.16	Tommi Makinen - Risto Mannisenmaki	Mitsubishi Lancer Ev.6	A	Suspension
SS.21	Hamed Al Wahaibi - Tony Sircombe	Mitsubishi Lancer Ev.5	N	Engine

Volkan Isik became the first Turkish driver to score a point in the drivers' championship.

GOSSIP

• HYUNDAI AT WORK

Forty eight hours before the start, at the Frankfurt Motor Show, Hyundai unveiled its new WRC. Built around the new Accent, this impressive looking car had run just before back in England for the very first time. The test was virtually trouble free and ran for two days. In 2000 it will be driven by the same guys currently piloting the Coupe Kit-Car; Sweden's Kenneth Eriksson and Scotsman Alister McRae, Colin's little brother.

• A QUESTION OF NAMES

For once and contrary to tradition, the Toyota mechanics had not given a pet name to Auriol's Corolla on the Rally of China. "It is a bit impersonal," underlined Giraudet, as it does not even have the traditional French flag in the middle of the steering wheel. However, Sainz's car had been given the lovely name of Sofia. What a shame that it now seemed as though anonymity produced better results.

• TRELLES IN MOURNING

Gustavo Trelles was very upset at the death shortly before the event, if his fellow countryman Gonzalo Rodriguez. The two men had been close friends and Rodriguez's death in a CART race in the USA had left Trelles unable to give his best on the rally, something he readily admitted to. The championship leader simply looked on as a great battle was waged between Japan's Arai and Al-Wahaibi. Sadly for the Omani driver, who was on fine form, his engine let go in the penultimate stage.

• MICHELIN CELEBRATES

"Thank you Michelin," Carlos Sainz was shouting through his intercom to the Bibendum men. On the last two stages, the Spaniard suffered punctures to all four wheels, but the anti-puncture foam allowed him to keep going, setting a fastest time on the way. All rally long, the French tyres were clearly better than the Pirellis and Subaru made their situation worse by choosing the wrong ones.

• SEAT SULKS

Although Rovanpera scored two points in China, having come home fifth, the Spanish team was not happy as it headed for home. It had never been capable of operating as one of the front runners. Too aggressive, Liatti had drowned out his Cordoba WRC in a ford on the very first day. As for Rovanpera, he was pretty inconsistent. He set the second fastest time on one stage but after that he never seemed capable of repeating that form. He simply was not able to fight hard enough.

EVENT LEADERS

SS.1	Auriol
SS.3 – SS.5	Makinen
SS.7 – SS.13	Burns
SS.14 – SS.22	Auriol

CHAMPIONSHIP CLASSIFICATIONS

Drivers

1. Tommi Makinen	48
1. Didier Auriol	48
3. Carlos Sainz	38
4. Juha Kankkunen	37
5. Richard Burns	35

Constructors

1. Toyota	99
2. Subaru	77
3. Mitsubishi	61
4. Ford	35
5. Seat	18

Group N

1. Gustavo Trelles	69
2. Hamed Al Wahaibi	52
3. Jouko Puhakka	26

Two Litres

1. Renault	89
2. Hyundai	75
3. Volkswagen	21

Team's Cup

1. Valencia Terra Mar Team Luis Climent	40
1. F.Dor Rally Team Frederic Dor	40
3. Toyota Mobil Team Turkey Volkan Isik	36

BEST PERFORMANCES

	1	2	3	4	5	6
Auriol	9	5	4	2	-	-
Makinen	6	3	1	-	1	-
Burns	4	8	3	2	3	-
Sainz	1	2	8	5	3	1
Kankkunen	-	2	3	11	3	-
Rovanpera	-	1	-	-	6	9
Isik	-	-	-	-	1	7
Arai	-	-	-	-	1	1
Liatti	-	-	-	-	1	1
Loix	-	-	-	-	1	-

PREVIOUS WINNERS

1997	McRae - Grist SUBARU IMPREZA WRC
1998	Fujimoto - Sircombe TOYOTA CELICA GT - FOUR

“The lions have their claws

clipped...”

SANREMO

Its rivals thought as much and now they had been warned: Peugeot was back in the world championship in a big way. The 206 was back and running in the wheel tracks left by the legendary 205. Francois Delecour, Gilles Panizzi and Marcus Gronholm had even been able to contemplate victory , or better still a one-two finish, or almost unthinkable a winning trio, after an awesome start to the rally. But maybe because of a lack of experience and certainly because of a bit of bad luck, the assault of the

Lions was set to fade. That meant that Tommi Makinen, who had sat back and watched and bided his time, chose the right moment to attack and strengthen his hold over the world championship. But the Peugeots would be back.

"For Tommi, driving is like breathing. He is not in the habit of braking until the final corner."

Gilles Panizzi

136.1 - 137.1

Disappointment for Peugeot who came within a whisker of a first win, but at least Jean-Pierre Nicolas and Corrado Provera could celebrate a first podium for the 206 WRC.

136.3

Marcus Gronholm was denied an excellent result by an off on the second leg.

136.2

DIDIER AURIOL IS A FREE THINKING MAN. He talks, he talks a lot and with enthusiasm. He can be forceful when he needs to and more often than not, he is right. This season, he adopted the mantle of the dominant figure in the rally circus. Didier the Boss. So, his comments were worthy of attention when he spoke in L'Equipe, the French newspaper. "They should not have lost. It is up to them now to analyse what happened and sort it out." Of course, he was talking about the Peugeot team. Reading between the lines, one could see signs of a rivalry worthy of the Jets and the Sharks between Didier Auriol and Francois Delecour. There was that misunderstanding which, for some strange reason, ended up with Didier walking out of an office in Velizy without putting his signature to the contract which was on offer. But, at his age, Auriol was above all that and so his opinion is worth considering. Peugeot should not have lost, he claimed. For sure, Peugeot could have won. For a long time, the Lions ran in the podium places. But in the end it was the Mitsubishi triple diamond and its pearl of a driver, Tommi Makinen who shone brightest. However, after eight of the eighteen stages, Peugeot was still in a position to dream of capturing all the top three placings. It had led for 294 of the 385 kilometres and set ten fastest times. "You wanted a win," said Jean-Pierre Nicolas, "while we would have settled for a podium."

The first Peugeot driver to go out was Marcus Gronholm. Up until that point, the Finn had seriously dented the perceived wisdom that, while naturally rapid on any loose surface road, the Scandinavians were not quite up to the mark whenever tarmac came into view. Certainly, Marcus was not quite up to the speed of his two specialist neighbours, Francois Delecour and Gilles Panizzi. However, this being only his third tarmac event (after the Bianchi and the Catalunya) perhaps his was the greatest achievement. "To be honest, I thought I would struggle to get into the top five," he commented. Surprising, fantastic, super. Or at least it was up until stage nine. Big Marcus ran a bit wide in a right hander and only got it back on its wheels after a double roll. It probably affected his concentration, because on the next stage, he lost over four minutes after he put it in a ditch. But Marcus, already great in the physical sense will be greater still one day. "He is a future world champion," reckoned an admiring Delecour. As for Francois Delecour himself, well he was keen to conquer again and he almost got there, or at least he made it to stage sixteen, having led for most of the event. Hit by gearbox problems, he finally gave up because of electrical problems. Gronholm had been thrown off the podium, Delecour joined him in the hard luck camp, but Gilles Panizzi was still going strong. At the start of the final stage, 40.34 kilometres called Colle Langlan 2, the Frenchman had a tiny advantage of 1.8 seconds over Tommi Makinen. Brake problems were nibbling away at that lead, which did not inspire confidence before a long stage where the terrain and weather are reckoned to be changeable. "Tommi is in his car every day. Driving is like breathing to him. He is not in the habit of braking until the final corner." It is at times like these that experience can make all the difference, in terms of tyre choice, strategy and even in the driving. Panizzi saw the signs shown to him along the route and quickly understood what was required. He backed off to make sure of his second place finish, which was what the Peugeot bosses wanted to see. "My tyres never got up to temperature," lamented Panizzi. Having opted for the super soft rubber, Tommi had made the right choice, while Panizzi, like most of the others, had opted for the harder slicks, which would wear better but would be harder to get up to temperature. "Makinen does not rely on luck to win," underlined Jean-Pierre Nicolas. "He is not a triple world champion for nothing. He reminded us of exactly what it takes to win. Technique and driving skill alone are not enough. You need the perfect strategy and a bit of luck as well, but you have to make some of that yourself. We are still learning. It is next year that counts."

Makinen, the big cat had finally dealt with the three lion cubs. But what of the rest?

Were any of the other drivers even involved in this nail-biting San Remo? With all due respect to their talents, the answer has to be no.

Didier Auriol did try all the same as he tried to keep in the running for the championship title against Tommi Makinen. "I have never pushed it so hard on tarmac," he admitted at the end of stage nine. "If I keep up this pace, it will end in tears." Didier was on the rev limiter of his ability but his Toyota was not much help. The Corolla is not the Celica. "It was fine, going downhill or on the flat," commented Auriol. "But there was something wrong with the engine in the last few kilometres. A pain!" Finally, more serious problems with the turbo and the differential made his situation even more hopeless. He was very happy to have salvaged what he could by finishing third, which meant he was still in the hunt for the title and crown. Carlos Sainz had a touch more pace than his team mate, but ended up in a ditch on stage six. The back end slipped away from him, he hit the mountain, dived off backwards and landed fifty metres down the hill. He escaped with a few cuts on his back, but more painfully, his morale had taken a serious knock. Carlos is not in the habit of flying off the road very often, but this year Didier has had the edge, which might explain it all.

136.3

At Ford, the ephemeral and unloved Simon Jean-Joseph, did the maximum with the minimum and Colin McRae did not disappoint, or at least not when he kept it on the road. The Scotsman was the only one, apart from the terrible trio of Delecour, Panizzi and Makinen, to win a stage. But his performance came to yet another premature end after his speciality party piece, the crash. This one involved landing twenty metres off the road. In his defence, the five minutes he lost because of engine problems might have caused him to lose concentration. But once again, he failed to go the distance. He had not seen the end of a rally since Corsica.

In the Subaru camp, Richard Burns and Juha Kankkunen knew that their Pirelli tyres would not give them any advantage, to put it mildly. Indeed the whole rubber issue was giving David Richards sleepless nights. Nevertheless, Burns put up some

136.2
Gilles Panizzi was unbeatable in the dry, before making several mistakes when the going got greasy.

137.2
This time we nearly caught a glimpse of the old "Fast Freddy" again, but it came too late for the constructors' trophy.

interesting stage times. In the end however, it was the wise and steady Juha Kankkunen who came off best, despite not being too partial to the Italian tarmac. He finished up with a point for sixth place, having come in at the end of the first leg down in seventeenth spot.

137.2

There was nothing much new to report at Seat and Skoda, who were both waiting for some developments. Finally for Citroen, Philippe Bugalski was still living off his marvellous double in Catalunya and Corsica. But the months had passed and the light and agile Xsara is coming to the end of its life, while the four wheel drive opposition was not. Bug was off the pace on the first day and took a while to shake off the torpor induced by too much driving in the French championship without too much opposition. One could read something into that. It was like a handing over ceremony between colleagues, between two members of the PSA Group. It was a case of Citroen or Peugeot, as the board did not want to see two members of the same family at each other's throats. The balance swung in favour of Peugeot, who would no doubt lead rallies again and win them too.

DELECOUR GETS ON HIS BIKE. What would have happened if Francois Delecour had won the San Remo? He would have stood on the top rung of the podium, but very probably he would have then been pulled off it by an FIA court. And all that for a few kilometres in the saddle of a velocipede; a non-motorised vehicle with two wheels, considered as a reconnaissance tool. But articles 14.1.1 and 14.3 of the regulations had struck nevertheless. They forbid any reconnaissance outside those organised officially. But the article in question does not specify if this involves reconnaissance on two or four wheels, or maybe even one; after all, Formula 1 world champion Mika Hakkinen trained with a circus and can ride a unicycle and could have given the rally boys some useful hints! Shekhar Mehta, the most experienced of the FIA men wanted to exclude the Frenchman and be done with it. In the end, a two minute penalty was imposed after an appeal from Francois Delecour. Never one to miss an opportunity when he feels he is in the right, he turned up for the verdict on a bicycle. As the event was run under this appeal from Peugeot, Delecour started the rally with zero penalties. In the end, Peugeot withdrew their appeal, once Delecour was out, knowing it would have been a futile exercise anyway. However, this did not stop poor Francois from banging on about it at length in his column in the French "Rallyes Magazine." Here is just a brief extract of what he had to say: "That people are capable of thinking I did it deliberately, that I could be as Machiavellian as to go out on a stage on a bicycle just to upset the stewards and annoy the other competitors is really sordid. What amazes me is that people found the time to make a phone call to say 'we saw Delecour on a stage.' I saw Daniel Grataloup, an extremely straight and intelligent co-driver and at no time did he think of saying to me, 'watch out, we are on a stage, we could be in trouble.' Don't make me believe that by riding a bike on a stage you can find the right line. Daniel's first reaction was to stop everything. I did not have a clue what to do. Thankfully, the only thing that gives me a buzz today is driving my car. It still beats everything else."

IT SHOULD HAVE BEEN A GREAT opportunity, like a long dreamed of cruise. It turned out that he was boarding a ship of troubles as the second Focus driver, more tolerated than accepted with runs in Greece and Finland with the Puma kit car. Simon Jean-Joseph believed in Ford but the feeling was not reciprocal. Simon turned out to be just a standard bearer of a campaign aimed at selling the Focus everywhere, including France. What he could do at the wheel counted for little and let us not forget the racist remarks which could be heard flying around the Ford trucks. Simon, got into the Focus after ten months with virtually no testing. "And I am expected to put in good times," he stated, seeming depressed and disorientated. He tried and he acquitted himself reasonably well, regularly setting top ten times. In the end he just missed out on sixth place, after Malcolm Wilson told him to make sure he got to the finish. "I haven't got any reference point," he continued. "Which means that I cannot go at it from start to finish the way I am used to doing in the French championship. Sometimes I feel lost. It's a shame it has to end like this." The irony of it all was that he did deliver a point to Ford, as Aghini, who was officially sixth was not eligible for championship points. It meant that the team which had been so inconsiderate to him was finally able to put an end to a run of four rallies without points, the last one dating back to Radstrom's sixth place in Argentina. Maybe Ford should not have put all its money on one horse. Simon Jean-Joseph summed up the whole sorry incident thus: "My aim this year was to show that I was capable of performing at a high level. I don't think I looked too bad."

"PETIT BUG" CAN BE SOMETHING of a daydreamer when things are not going his way. Philippe Bugalski still had a lingering memory of his podium in the Catalunya rally, when he was up there with two multiple world champions. Then he did it again in Corsica and he was hoping to do the triple here in San Remo. He was not able to live the dream for very long, even though the plan of campaign was in place. He had done a lot of testing in Italy during the summer and both he and Puras were in full trophy mode. But it was not to last long. Puras was very unhappy the moment he sat behind the wheel of a Citroen prepared in France - don't ask why all was fine with the Spanish built car - and it went wrong right from the start of stage three with a clutch problem. He did manage to latch onto the Peugeot pack on the first day, even racking up a fastest time. Then on the greasy and dirty roads of the second day, he went into a decline, before perking up honourably for the last leg. His final effort ended in a wall, within sight of the finish. "I dinged it and then one kilometre later the back end was all over the place and I had a bigger off." The saddest part of this story is that there will be no sequel and the Xsara will become a museum piece. Sob! It is not fair and it deserved better. But one should never forget the maxim that sport is here to serve commerce and not the other way around. We must wait and see what Bug can do to bounce back. He has had offers.

138.1
Didier Auriol was the only one to match the pace of Makinen and Panizzi. Although he tried all he knew, six points now separate him from the Flying Finn in the race for the drivers' crown.

138.2 - 139.4
Seat had a less than convincing first outing on tarmac. Fed up with it all, Piero Liatti announced he was hanging up his helmet at the end of the event.

138.3 - 139.1
Tommi Makinen's mount was as efficient as ever and combined with a bold tyre choice in the last stage, it was enough to give him the win, while Freddy Loix was fourth.

138.4
Was an unstable Corolla to blame for Carlos Sainz's crash?

138.1

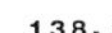

138.2

138.3

138.4

SANREMO

"The lions have their claws clipped..."

139.2 - 139.3

An astonishing performance from Marcus Gronholm. The Finn managed to keep up with his two team-mates during his third tarmac rally.

139.5

Simon Jean-Joseph set several impressive stage times, but orders from Malcolm Wilson forced him to steady his pace.

139.1

139.3

139.4

139.2

139.5

41ST SANREMO RALLY

TOP ENTRIES

1 Tommi Makinen – Risto Mannisenmaki
MITSUBISHI LANCER EV.6
2 Freddy Loix – Sven Smeets
MITSUBISHI CARISMA GT
3 Carlos Sainz – Luis Moya
TOYOTA COROLLA WRC
4 Didier Auriol – Denis Giraudet
TOYOTA COROLLA WRC
5 Richard Burns – Robert Reid
SUBARU IMPREZA WRC
6 Juha Kankkunen – Juha Repo
SUBARU IMPREZA WRC
7 Colin McRae – Nicky Grist
FORD FOCUS WRC
8 Simon Jean-Joseph – Fred Gallagher
FORD FOCUS WRC
9 Harri Rovanpera – Risto Pietilainen
SEAT CORDOBA WRC EV.2
10 Piero Liatti – Carlo Cassina
SEAT CORDOBA WRC EV.2
11 Armin Schwarz – Manfred Hiemer
SKODA OCTAVIA WRC
12 Emil Triner – Milos Hulka
SKODA OCTAVIA WRC
14 François Delecour – Daniel Grataloup
PEUGEOT 206 WRC
15 Gilles Panizzi – Herve Panizzi
PEUGEOT 206 WRC
16 Andrea Aghini – Loris Roggia
TOYOTA COROLLA WRC
18 Philippe Bugalski – Jean-Paul Chiaroni
CITROEN XSARA KIT CAR
19 Jesus Puras – Marc Marti
CITROEN XSARA KIT CAR
20 Toni Gardemeister – Paavo Lukander
SEAT CORDOBA WRC EV.2
21 Marcus Gronholm – Timo Rautiainen
PEUGEOT 206 WRC
22 Markko Martin – Toomas Kitsing
TOYOTA COROLLA WRC
24 Gianfranco Cunico – Luigi Pirollo
SUBARU IMPREZA WRC
25 Petter Solberg – Philip Mills
FORD FOCUS WRC
26 Henrik Lundgaard – Jens Anker
TOYOTA COROLLA WRC
27 Andrea Navara – Simona Fideli
FORD ESCORT WRC
28 Andrea Dallavilla – Danilo Fappani
SUBARU IMPREZA WRC
29 Luis Climent – Alex Romani
SUBARU IMPREZA WRC
30 Volkan Isik – Erkan Bodur
TOYOTA COROLLA WRC
31 Abdullah Bakashab – Michael Park
TOYOTA COROLLA WRC
32 Isolde Holderied – Catherine François
TOYOTA COROLLA WRC
34 Renato Travaglia – Flavio Zanella
PEUGEOT 306 KIT CAR
35 Adruzilo Lopes – Luis Lisboa
PEUGEOT 306 KIT CAE
36 Alister McRae – David Senior
HYUNDAI COUPE EV.2
39 Tapio Laukkanen – Kaj Lindstrom
RENAULT MEGANE MAXI
40 Kenneth Eriksson- Staffan Parmander
HYUNDAI COUPE EV.2
41 Martin Rowe – Derek Ringer
RENAULT MEGANE MAXI
44 Kris Princen – Dany Colebunders
RENAULT MEGANE MAXI
46 Gustavo Trelles – Martin Christie
MITSUBISHI LANCER EV.6
47 Hamed Al Wahaibi – Tony Sircombe
MITSUBUSHI LANCER EV.5
48 Manfred Stohl – Peter Muller
MITSUBISHI LANCER EV.5

12th leg of the 1999 world rally championships for constructors and drivers
12th leg of the constructors' «2 litre», production car drivers' and teams'world cups

Date: *11 - 13 October 1999*

Route: *1384,58 km divided into 3 legs, 18 stages on tarmac roads (384,88 km)*
1st leg : Monday 11th October, Sanremo – Sanremo, 6 stages (214,73 km)
2nd leg : Tuesday 12th October, Sanremo – Acqui terme – Sanremo, 8 stages (167,98 km)
3rd leg : Wednesday 13th October, Sanremo – Sanremo, 4 stages (111,03 km)

Starters/Finishers: *119/55*

Renault did very well in terms of the 2 litre championship, once both Hyundais had retired.

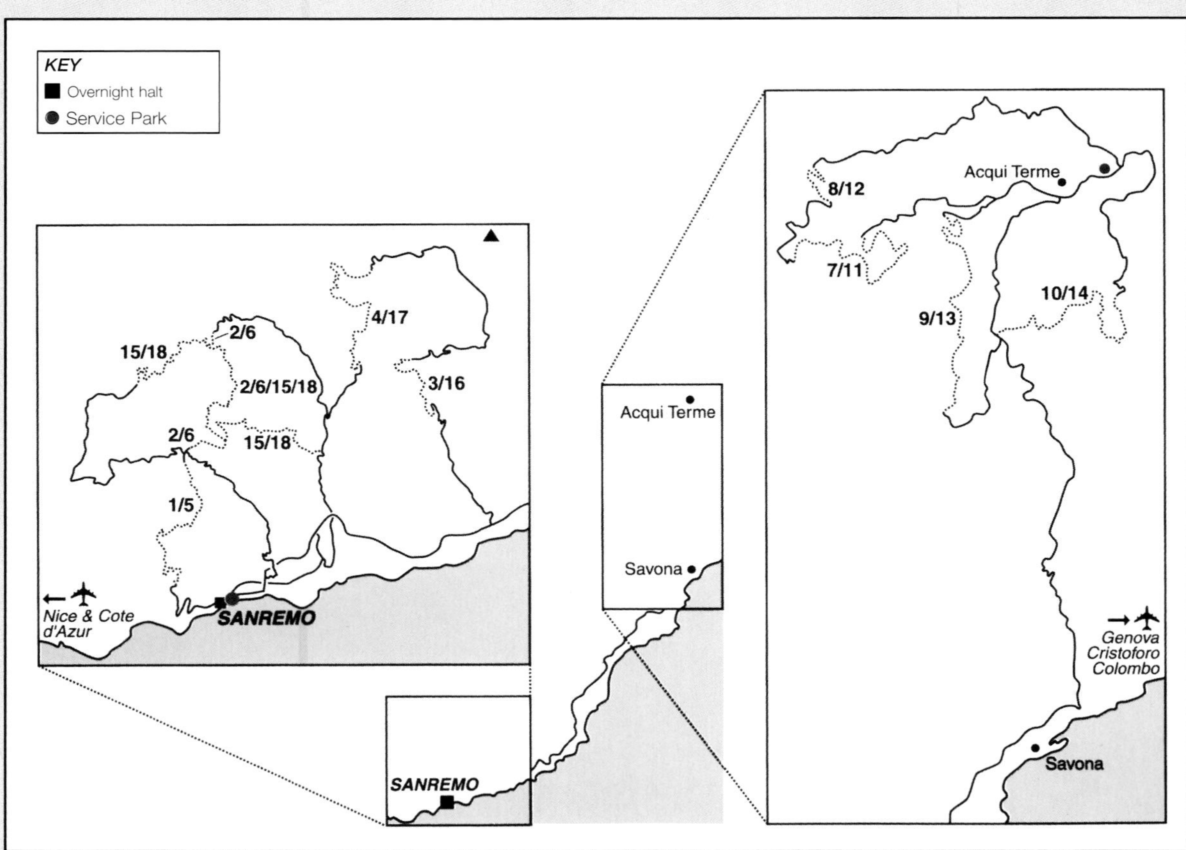

SPECIAL STAGE TIMES

SS.1 San Remolo 1 (18,50 km)
1. Panizzi 12'03"4 ; 2. Delecour 12'05"4 ; 3. Gronholm 12'08"7 ; 4. Sainz et McRae 12"11"6; Gr.N Stagni 13'01"9 ; F2 Bugalski 12'13"6

SS.2 Monte Ceppo 1(19,53 km)
1. Delecour 13'22"5 ; 2. Panizzi 13'24"8 ; 3. Puras 13'26"9 ; 4. McRae 13'31" ; 5. Bugalski 13'32"2 ; Gr.N Stagni 14'29"

SS.3 Pantasina 1 (9,28 km)
1. Panizzi 6'20"9 ; 2. Delecour et Bugalski 6'22"8 ; 4. Gronholm 6'23"6 ; 5. Auriol 6'24"2; Gr.N Al Wahaibi 6'53"9

SS.4 Colle d'Oggia 1 (20,53 km)
1. Panizzi 13'45"2 ; 2. Delecour 13'45"7 ; 3. Auriol 13'48"8 ; 4. Bugalski 13'48"4 ; 5. McRae 13'50"3 ; Gr.N Galli 14'56"6

SS.5 San Romolo 2 (18,50 km)
1. Panizzi 11'59"5 ; 2. Delecour 12'00"7 ; 3. Gronholm 12'01"5 ; 4. Sainz 12'02"2 ; 5. Auriol 12'04"1 ; Gr.N Stagni 13'01"7 ; F2 Bugalski 12'05"1

SS.6 Monte Ceppo 2 (19,53 km)
1. Delecour 13'17"7 ; 2. Gronholm 13'20"8 ; 3. Makinen 13'22"5 ; 4. Bugalski 13'22"6 ; 5. Panizzi 13'23" ; Gr.N Galli 14'15"1

SS.7 Torre del Vengore 1 (29,50 km)
1. Delecour 21'25"4 ; 2. Gronholm 21'34" ; 3. Makinen 21'37"3 ; 4. Burns 21'38"2 ; 5. Panizzi 21'41"1 ; Gr.N Galli 22'53"6 ; F2 Travaglia 22'23"3

SS.8 Loazzolo 1 (7,36 km)
1. Panizzi 4'55"1 ; 2. Delecour 4'55"6 ; 3. Gronholm 4'56"7 ; 4. Makinen 4'57"6 ; 5. Auriol 4'57"9 ; Gr.N Galli 5'14"3 ; F2 Bugalski 5'09"6

SS.9 Turpino 1 (24,45 km)
1. McRae 15'19"6 ; 2. Auriol 15'22"9 ; 3. Delecour 15'23"3 ; 4. Panizzi 15'24"5 ; 5. Makinen 14'27"7 ; Gr.N Galli 16'23" ; F2 Bugalski 15'32"2

SS.10 Ponzone 1 (22,68 km)
1. Makinen 17'04"3 ; 2. Panizzi 17'07"5 ; 3. Delecour 17'09" ; 4. Auriol 17'13"1 ; 5. Dallavilla 17'17"6 ; Gr.N Galli 18'20"4 ; F2 Lopss 17'33"9

SS.11 Torre del Vengore 2 (29,5 km)
1. Makinen 21'09"6 ; 2. Auriol 21'15" ; 3. McRae 21'17" ; 4. Panizzi 21'21"3 ; 5. Loix 21'26" ; Gr.N Galli 22'56"9 ; F2 Bugalski 22'13"9

SS.12 Loazzolo 2 (7,36 km)
1. McRae 4'52"7 ; 2. Delecour 4'52"8 ; 3. Panizzi 4'53"7 ; 4. Loix 4'54" ; 5. Gronholm 4'54"5 ; Gr.N Stagni et Stohl 5'16"6 ; F2 Bugalski 5'03"9

SS.13 Turpino 2 (24,45 km)
1. Makinen 15'21"3 ; 2. Auriol 15'23"8 ; 3. Loix 15'28"3 ; 4. Delecour 15'28"4 ; 5. Aghini 15'32"1 ; Gr.N Galli 16'29"9 ; F2 Bugalski 15'42"7

SS.14 Ponzone 2 (22,68 km)
1. Makinen 16'57" ; 2. Panizzi 17'06"5 ; 3. Auriol 17'09"5 ; 4. Gronholm 17'03"2 ; 5. Delecour 17'17"1 ; Gr.N Galli 18'31"2 ; F2 Bugalski 17'47"1

SS.15 Colle Langan 1 (40,34 km)
1. Makinen 27'51"3 ; 2. Auriol 28'02"9 ; 3. Gronholm 28'06" ; 4. Loix 28'08" ; 5. Delecour 28'14"8 ; Gr.N Galli 30'42"5 ; F2 Bugalski 28'18"

SS.16 Pantasina 2 (9,28 km)
1. Delecour 6'41"3 ; 2. Bugalski 6'42"9 ; 3. Auriol 6'43"9 ; 4. Kankkunen 6'44"3 ; 5. Panizzi 6'46"6 ; Gr.N Stohl 7'13"6

SS.17 Colle d'Oggia 2 (20,53 km)
1. Panizzi 14'24"3 ; 2. Bugalski 14'25"5 ; 3. Makinen 14'28"6 ; 4. Aghini 14'30" ; 5. Auriol 14'30"2 ; Gr.N Stohl 15'20"1

SS.18 Colle Langan 2 (40,34 km)
1. Makinen 28'14'17 ; 2. Auriol 28'21"2 ; 3. Gronholm 28'22" ; 4. Kankkunen 28'31"7 ; 5. Panizzi 28'34"5 ; Gr.N Stohl 30'27"9 ; F2 Longhi 29'37"8

RESULTS AND RETIREMENTS

	Driver/Co-Driver	Car	Gr	Total Time
1	**Tommi Makinen - Risto Mannisenmaki**	**Mitsubishi Lancer Ev.6**	**A**	**4h26m45s**
2	Gilles Panizzi - Herve Panizzi	Peugeot 206 WRC	A	4h27m03s
3	Didier Auriol - Denis Giraudet	Toyota Corolla WRC	A	4h27m27,2s
4	Freddy Loix - Sven Smeets	Mitsubishi Carisma GT	A	4h29m58,1s
5	Andrea Aghini - Loris Roggia	Toyota Corolla WRC	A	4h30m35,2s
6	Juha Kankkunen - Juha Repo	Subaru Impreza WRC	A	4h30m45,5s
7	Simon Jean-Joseph - Fred Gallagher	Ford Focus WRC	A	4h30m59,5s
8	Marcus Gronholm - Timo Rautiainen	Peugeot 206 WRC	A	4h31m25,8s
9	Gianfranco Cunico - Luigi Pirollo	Subaru Impreza WRC	A	4h32m35,2s
10	Andrea Navarra - Simona Fideli	Ford Escort WRC	A	4h34m47,3s
12	**Piero Longhi - Lucio Baggio**	**Renault Megane Maxi**	**A**	**4h37m45,1s**
15	**Volkan Isik - Erkan Bodur**	**Toyota Corolla WRC**	**A**	**4h39m38,7s**
22	**Gianluigi Galli - Guido D'Amore**	**Mitsubishi Lancer Ev.4**	**N**	**4h47m19,8s**
SS.4	Kenneth Eriksson - Staffan Parmander	Hyundai Coupe Ev.2	A	Accident
SS.6	Carlos Sainz - Luis Moya	Toyota Corolla WRC	A	Accident
SS.7	Alister McRae - David Senior	Hyundai Coupe Ev.2	A	Accident
SS.7	Richard Burns - Robert Reid	Subaru Impreza WRC	A	Transmission
SS.9	Armin Schwarz - Manfred Hiemer	Skoda Octavia WRC	A	Accident
SS.14	Colin McRae - Nicky Grist	Ford Focus WRC	A	Accident
SS.15	Piero Liatti - Carlo Cassina	Seat Cordoba WRC	A	Engine
SS.15	Toni Gardemeister - Paavo Lukander	Seat Cordoba WRC	A	Engine
SS.15	Gustavo Trelles - Christie Martin	Mitsubishi Lancer Ev.6	N	Accident
SS.16	François Delecour - Daniel Grataloup	Peugeot 206 WRC	A	Alternator
SS.18	Philippe Bugalski - Jean-Paul Chiaroni	Citroen Xsara Kit Car	A	Accident

GOSSIP

• LIATTI DIVORCE

There was no love lost between the taciturn Piero Liatti and the Seat team and it showed in the results sheets. Liatti had this to say: "The car is working better than in Catalunya and Corsica, but it is not enough. It is a long way off in fact." It looks as though nothing will stop the situation from ending up in the divorce courts. Will Liatti live to fight another day, especially after his failure with Subaru, or will he head for the rally drivers' sunshine retirement home?

• THE RETURN OF AGHINI

Andrea Aghini, known as Ago, slipped back into the routine of the good old days from a few seasons back. The winner of the 1982 San Remo "played" with the world championship regulars, a long way ahead of his usual rivals from the Italian championship.

• SCHWARZ ON THE SLIDE

Official Skoda driver Armin Schwarz has done his sums, before falling off the road that is. "When the car is working fine, we are one second per kilometre off the pace." Not a very motivating situation.

• AN END WITHOUT A FINISH

The two Hyundai drivers, Alister McRae and Kenneth Eriksson had been given firm orders: get to the finish. They both failed to deliver, ending up in a ditch. It is not always easy being a driver. That meant that Renault, with a trio of Meganes, which had travelled from Italy, England and Austria, can see a two litre title coming their way, when the company had not even planned to go for it.

• GALLI WHO?

Retirement struck both men who were fighting for the Group N title, Al Wahaibi and Trelles. So the surprise winner, for the second consecutive year was local boy Gianluigi Galli in a Mitsubishi.

• LOIX IS BACK.

He had rather disappeared from view, fallen to the lower reaches of the results sheet. Fast Freddy Loix was back on form, setting some good times on the Italian tarmac. He finished his performance with fourth place, his third of the season. Would it be enough to save his drive?

EVENT LEADERS

SS.1	Panizzi
SS.2	Delecour
SS.3 – SS.5	Panizzi
SS.6 – SS.13	Delecour
SS.14	Panizzi
SS.15	Makinen
SS.16	Delecour
SS.17	Panizzi
SS.18	Makinen

BEST PERFORMANCES

	1	2	3	4	5	6
Panizzi	6	3	1	2	4	1
Makinen	6	-	3	1	2	-
Delecour	4	6	2	1	2	1
McRae	2	1	2	1	-	
Auriol	-	5	2	2	4	2
Bugalski	-	3	1	1	-	3
Gronholm	-	2	5	2	1	-
Loix	-	-	1	2	1	2
Puras	-	-	1	-	-	-
Kankkunen	-	-	-	2	-	3
Sainz	-	-	-	2	-	1
Aghini	-	-	-	1	1	-
Burns	-	-	-	1	-	-
Dallavilla	-	-	-	-	1	-
Jean-Joseph	-	-	-	-	-	3
Travaglia	-	-	-	-	-	1
Cunico	-	-	-	-	-	1

CHAMPIONSHIP CLASSIFICATIONS

Drivers

1. Tommi Makinen	58
2. Didier Auriol	52
3. Carlos Sainz	38
3. Juha Kankkunen	38
5. Richard Burns	35

Constructors

1. Toyota	103
2. Subaru	79
3. Mitsubishi	74
4. Ford	36
5. Seat	18

Group N

1. Gustavo Trelles	69
2. Hamed Al Wahaibi	53
3. Manfred Stohl	27

Two Litres

1. Renault	101
2. Hyundai	75
3. Volkswagen	24

Team's Cup

1. Toyota Mobil Team Turkey Volkan Isik	46
2. Valencia Terra Mar Team Luis Climent	40
2. F.Dor Rally Team Frederic Dor	40

PREVIOUS WINNERS

1973	Therier - Jaubert Alpine Renault A110
1975	Waldegaard - Thorszelius Lancia Stratos
1976	Waldegaard - Thorszelius Lancia Stratos
1977	Andruet - Delferrier Fiat 131 Abarth
1978	Alen - Kivimaki Lancia Stratos
1979	Fassina - Mannini Lancia Stratos
1980	Rohrl - Geistdorfer Fiat 131 Abarth
1981	Mouton - Pons Audi Quattro
1982	Blomqvist - Cederberg Audi Quattro
1983	Alen - Kivimaki Lancia Rally 037
1984	Vatanen - Harryman Peugeot 205 T16
1985	Rohrl - Geistdorfer Audi Sport Quattro S1
1986	Alen - Kivimaki Lancia Delta S4
1987	Biasion - Siviero Lancia Delta HF 4WD
1988	Biasion - Siviero Lancia Delta Integrale
1989	Biasion - Siviero Lancia Delta Integrale
1990	Auriol - Occelli Lancia Delta Integrale
1991	Auriol - Occelli Lancia Delta Integrale
1992	Aghini - Farnocchia Lancia Delta HF Integrale
1993	Cunico - Evangelisti Ford Escort RS Cosworth
1994	Auriol - Occelli Toyota Celica Turbo 4WD
1995	Liatti - Alessandrini Subaru Impreza
1996	McRae - Ringer Subaru Impreza
1997	McRae - Grist Subaru Impreza WRC
1998	Makinen - Mannisenmaki Mitsubishi Lancer Ev.5

“So that his honour and courage could

not be called into question…”

AUSTRALIA

It was a battle of the best in the shade of the eucalyptus trees. If Kankkunen still had a chance, albeit more mathematical than real of being world champion, it was really down to a duel between Tommi Makinen and Didier Auriol for the title crown. The Frenchman was in attack mode right from the start, spraying the pebbles that pass for a road surface in West Australia. But his Toyota let him down too soon, putting him off the road. Makinen could adopt cruise mode from then on, leaving Richard Burns and Carlos Sainz to fight it out for a win which eventually went to the younger man.

At the wheel of an undriveable Corolla, Didier Auriol hit a tree. The Frenchman somehow managed to get the wreck to the next service area, but the engine had suffered enough. Despite the tireless efforts of his mechanics, it refused to fire up again. The last chance of a second world championship had just evaporated.

IT IS A BAD DREAM. It started two hours after the champagne in the room from where the press was busy telling the world that Makinen had been crowned for a fourth time. The FIA press delegate grabbed the microphone to announce that Gabriele Cadringher, the technical delegate has sniffed out something dodgy on the Mitsubishi. Some piece or other is five millimetres longer than allowed and is about to change the result. Tommi Makinen is disqualified although he still has the right to appeal. Andrew Cowan does not have to think about it for long. But wait! Wake up! Rallying is not Formula 1 and its media exposure is nowhere near as great, neither is its chicanery and that is no bad thing.

Because although Auriol went out on the first day, the suspense as to the title holder lasted until the very end of the event as Makinen had to keep it on the road to be crowned. So unlike it's more famous sporting relative in Formula 1, the rally championship was fought out between men in Australia. It was a great fight carried out with the same sense of urgency as that employed by the kangaroos which hop around in front of the cars in the Bunnings forest.

Didier Auriol knew what he had to do. If Tommi Makinen scored four more points than him, the Finn would be champion before the start of the RAC.

The Frenchman did not need a strategy. All he could do was go flat out from the word go. "I will not adjust my pace to his," he promised. "I will just try and beat him. I don't know if I can, but that's the idea: to be in front, even if it's by a few seconds, but be in front." And that is exactly what he did. The Toyota immediately proved to be quicker than the Mitsubishi. It was only by one tenth in the Langley Mickey Mouse stage, slap bang in the centre of Perth, 2.3s on York Railway, 2.2s in Muresk 1, and 4.5s in Muresk 2, where Makinen's gearbox played up. Auriol was leading, but not by much. It was good for morale if nothing else, because Makinen admitted later he was never really worried. "I was not in the slightest bit destabilised. I was calm. Last year, Didier had also been very quick in these parts. I refuse to take too many risks. These stages are not natural and they are treacherous. They are too short to make a difference. It is in the forest that it matters."

Wise Tommi would be proved right and very soon at that. Sooner than he thought. In the fifth stage, almost thirty kilometres through the eucalyptus trees, Makinen was quickest. In the sixth stage, Auriol ran wide. "Already in the previous stage, the car had become undriveable," he stated. "It was a differential problem, the same as the one we had on the shake-down, the day before the start. The car was using all the road, going right and left without me being able to do anything about it. Then the inevitable happened. I got off line on a left hander. It was too late to brake. So I aimed between the trees, but there was one too many! On Denis Giraudet's pace notes the corner read: "50 metres flat left, slight right flat, flat left right." It was one corner too many. The much modified Corolla hobbled out of the factory nursing its wounds. They have not yet lost too much time, just 25 seconds. But the mechanical mayhem is serious and irreparable. The radiator is punctured and there is plenty of twisted metal. At the Mundaring service point the mechanics sweat blood for twenty minutes, trying to straighten the Corolla by tying a strap to a truck and pulling. But it is all in vain. The starter motor refuses to fire up the engine and it is all over. Ove Andersson uncorks a good bottle as a consolation prize. That's class! Auriol looks sad: "If only I had gone off while trying too hard." His fate is no longer in his blue gloved hands. "Makinen has been very lucky for the past few seasons. Maybe his luck will change," hopes Giraudet. Why not? Short of having signed an all-risks insurance policy with destiny, Makinen could now control his fate with his left foot on the brake and slacken the pace to be sure of the title. "The moment I heard Didier was out, I began to slow down," he admitted. He would not set any fastest times after that. I would like to wrap up the title before the RAC," he had said before the start. "Things do not usually go well for me there. To be champion by driving slowly is not exciting, but that is what it will take." In short, Tommi just had to be a good boy. But don't be deceived, that is easier said than done. Driving within yourself always carries the risk of losing concentration. Twice before, Tommi had made that sort of mistake on rallies where he had found himself in a similar situation. In 1996 on the RAC and in 1998 on, yes of course, the RAC. It would be a long road to Perth. But the Mitsubishi held out and so did its driver. There were a couple of mini moments. On the ninth stage when the anti-puncture foam in his Michelins decided not to work for once after a brief encounter with a rock. Out in front, after Auriol's retirement and Makinen's decision to slow the pace, another race had begun; a race for victory. "Those who have nothing to play for in the championship, like Burns and McRae seem very determined," Makinen had noted. "I have not yet won this year and I have to put the record straight," declared Sainz. Peugeot were not over confident, but even they had their dreams. Only Kankkunen could be counted on to show some circumspection. Even if he pretended "not to have a hope," he did have an infinitesimal chance of taking the championship away from Makinen and Auriol. Mind you, that would require him to win the last two rallies with Makinen retiring on both, not to mention what Auriol would have to do or not do.

A sort of natural selection would soon decimate the field. Didier Auriol's demise was preceded by that of Juha Kankkunen, rapidly followed by Colin McRae. "There are a lot of mistakes being made," observed Tommi Makinen. "It shows to what extent our sport is run on the limit and how far you have to go to win."

Kankkunen abandoned all hope on stage five, ripping off a wheel and breaking his suspension thanks to a foolish tree crossing the road in front of him. McRae, who has made a career out of reminding us that to err is human, waited until stage twelve to throw his Ford Focus away yet again. Third, almost a minute behind the battling Sainz-Burns

"There are a lot of mistakes being made. It shows to what extent our sport

duo, Colin had nothing to lose. Except his life. In a long right corner at the end of a long straight, an innocuous bump launched Air McRae at a speed of 160 km/h. When Colin landed after his unscheduled flight, the Ford tipped over on its side, flattened a tree and flew into bits like a constellation of stars in the forest. It was certainly spectacular. "It was a big, big, big, accident," commented Nicky Grist. "It was the most frightening accident I have ever had," said Colin McRae. For the fourth time in eight starts, Colin had been responsible for his own downfall. It was not what a team boss expected from a team leader. He only has to look at the career details of guys like Kankkunen, Sainz or Auriol to see the difference. The "greats" do not crash all the time; maybe once or twice a year. Speaking of which, Carlos Sainz was now in an excellent position to finally win a rally this year. His only problem was that he was not the only one. The Peugeots of Delecour and Gronholm were no longer in the running either for victory or even in the race because of various problems. This left Burns to set his sights on the same target as Sainz. It was a great battle for the top honours. As they lined up to start the third and final leg, Burns had a slender four second lead as they prepared for the grand finale, run almost exclusively in Bunnings. There were less than a dozen cars at the finish after just under 400 stage kilometres. On stage twenty, Bunnings West, the first on the third day, Carlos went into attack mode getting to within a second. Burns was beginning to tremble. "That time did not make our life easy," admitted the Scot. "We had to push like mad because of it and to take risks which were really a bit too much." So in the next stage, Bunnings North, Burns attacked, but the Toyota faltered with a lack of pressure. It was enough to lose Sainz ten seconds and the rally. "We tried everything," he said. "But in today's rallies, the slightest problem spells disaster." Then the scene moved to Bunnings South. Sainz, the matador who does not know how to give up, set another fastest time, sticking his bandilleros with something approaching despair, so that his honour and courage could not be called into question. But Burns is too close and it is left to him to wrap up the spectator stage at Langley Park, the last of the rally. The prize giving can thus commence. The best prize goes to Makinen. Toyota pick up the constructors trophy without having won a single rally. It is some sort of consolation for Auriol and Sainz who have proved to be worth their weight in gold.

WHAT THOUGHTS GO THROUGH Tommi Makinen's mind now that he is a four times world champion. This was the first question he was asked once the deed was done and declared official. And this is what he replied: "Of a fifth title. It's as easy as that." His future seems pretty clear. After having tried the Seat Cordoba and thought about an astronomical salary, in itself a useful way of upping the bidding, Tommi signed on for more of Mitsubishi, for two years. He did not come cheap either. There was talk of eight million pounds, and then what? Talking to Autosport, the four times world champion spoke of being fed up. Fourteen rallies, with recceing and testing is a heavy programme for a very rich young family man. So he is thinking of getting out of the car for good at the end of 2001. "At the moment I am in a frame of mind to stop in two years. But maybe I will change my mind when the time comes." Tommi Makinen will only be 37 years old when that moment comes.

GARY CONNELLY IS THE INVENTIVE promoter of the Australian rally, which regularly wins the prize for the best run event. This time he came up with yet another good idea: a reverse start order. It is common knowledge that on snow or on the loose, the honour of being first on the road, which goes to the man who was quickest on the previous leg, is more of a disadvantage as the first one through has the job of a snow plough. This means that the more cunning drivers lift off just a bit in order to slide a couple of places down the order. Hardly logical in a world where speed is of the essence. Connelly therefore came up with the following system: on the first leg, the first sixteen would start in reverse order, while for the second and third legs, the first twelve would choose their start position between one and sixteen. "It's an excellent idea," commented Tommi Makinen. And so it proved to be in practice. Surely it could now be applied to other events. The only slight criticism was that this method cannot take the weather into account. The drivers make their choice well before they have a chance to know what the skies will do that day. So a lot is still left to luck. The paradox of this story is that the more traditional rallies never thought of this formula. Perhaps you have to be new to the game to think clearly.

CARLOS SAINZ KNOWS WHAT team strategy means and he has often been the beneficiary. He had therefore willingly accepted to put himself at the service of Didier Auriol. "If I can I will do it without hesitating," he promised. This was to be his final mission for Toyota, apart from helping them to the constructors' championship. Firstly, because the rallying arm of Toyota Team Europe, based in Cologne was quitting the world of rallying, as the Formula 1 project had hoovered up all the budget. Sainz was therefore obliged to leave a team he had come to regard as home. Carlos had no trouble finding another seat. He was pulling all the strings in his negotiations, hesitating over tying his future to Seat, the Spanish constructor. He also came close to Subaru despite memories of a previous stormy divorce. He finally plumped for Ford. It was a surprising choice. Because Ford is currently an English-Scottish bastion built by Malcolm Wilson around Colin McRae. But Carlos has never backed away from a challenge. He thus rejoins a driver whom he partnered at Subaru in 1994 and 1995. He also returns to Ford, for whom he drove under difficult circumstances in 1996 and 1997. These were not his two most productive periods. He won four events in 1994 and 1995, three in 1996 and 1997, without picking up a championship title.

...n on the limit and how far you have to go to win." Tommi Makinen

146.1

146.2

146.3

147.1

147.2

AUSTRALIA

"So that his honour and courage could not be called into question..."

146.1

Another fourth place for Freddy Loix and the Belgian seemed to have renewed confidence.

146.2 - 147.3

For the first time since its competition debut, the 206 WRC did not lead the rally.

146.3

On the last leg, Thomas Radstrom tried everything to hold off Gronholm's Peugeot, but it was in vain.

146.4

Throwing everything he had at the third leg, Richard Burns showed just what he could do.

147.1

Carlos Sainz's second place handed the constructors' championship to Toyota.

147.2-4-5-6

As Burns and Sainz duelled, they were the only two to be more than a match for the pace of Finland's Tommi Makinen, who lifted off to be sure of third place.

147.3

147.4

147.5

12TH RALLY AUSTRALIA

TOP ENTRIES

1 Tommi Makinen - Risto Mannisenmaki
MITSUBISHI LANCER EV.6

2 Freddy Loix - Sven Smeets
MITSUBISHI CARISMA GT

3 Carlos Sainz – Luis Moya
TOYOTA COROLLA WRC

4 Didier Auriol – Denis Giraudet
TOYOTA COROLLA WRC

5 Richard Burns – Robert Reid
SUBARU IMPREZA WRC

6 Juha Kankkunen – Juha Repo
SUBARU IMPREZA WRC

7 Colin McRae – Nicky Grist
FORD FOCUS WRC

8 Thomas Radstrom – Fred Gallagher
FORD FOCUS WRC

9 Harri Rovanpera – Risto Pietilainen
SEAT CORDOBA WRC EV.2

10 Toni Gardemeister – Paavo Lukander
SEAT CORDOBA WRC EV.2

14 François Delecour – Daniel Grataloup
PEUGEOT 206 WRC

15 Marcus Gronholm – Timo Rautiainen
PEUGEOT 206 WRC

16 Pasi Hagstrom – Tero Gardemeister
TOYOTA COROLLA WRC

17 Possum Bourne – Craig Vincent
SUBARU IMPREZA WRC

18 Neal Bates – Coral Taylor
TOYOTA COROLLA WRC

19 Yoshihiro Kataoka – Satoshi Hayashi
MITSUBISHI LANCER EV.6

20 Frederic Dor – Didier Breton
SUBARU IMPREZA WRC

21 Gustavo Trelles – Martin Christie
MITSUBISHI LANCER EV.6

22 Hamed Al Wahaibi – Tony Sircombe
MITSUBISHI LANCER EV.6

23 Toshihiro Arai – Roger Freeman
SUBARU IMPREZA

24 Ed Ordynski – Iain Stewart
MITSUBISHI LANCER EV.4

25 Michael Guest – David Green
SUBARU IMPREZA

26 Manfred Stohl – Peter Muller
MITSUBISHI LANCER EV.6

27 Uwe Nittel – Klaus Wicha
MITSUBUSHI LANCER EV.6

28 Katsuhiko Taguchi – Ron Teoh
MITSUBISHI LANCER EV.6

30 Kenneth Eriksson – Staffan Parmander
HYUNDAI COUPE EV.2

31 Tapio Laukkanen – Kaj Lindstrom
RENAULT MEGANE MAXI

32 Alister McRae – David Senior
HYUNDAI COUPE EV.2

33 Mark Higgins – Bryan Thomas
VOLKSWAGEN GOLF GTI 16V

34 Martin Rowe – Derek Ringer
RENAULT MEGANE MAXI

13th leg of the 1999 world rally championships for constructors and drivers
13th leg of the constructors' «2 litre», production car drivers' and teams'world cups

Date: *4 - 7 November 1999*

Route: *1424,23 km divided into 3 legs, 23 stages on loose surface roads (395,88 km)*
1st leg : Thursday 4th et Friday 5th November, Perth – Mundaring – Perth, 11 stages (134,99 km)
2nd leg : Saturday 6th November, Perth – Collie – Perth, 8 stages (160,87 km)
3rd leg : Sunday 7th November, Perth – Bunnings, 4 stages (100,02 km)

Starters/Finishers: *84/49*

Hyundai had to win if they wanted to take the 2 litre title in the final round of the world championship.

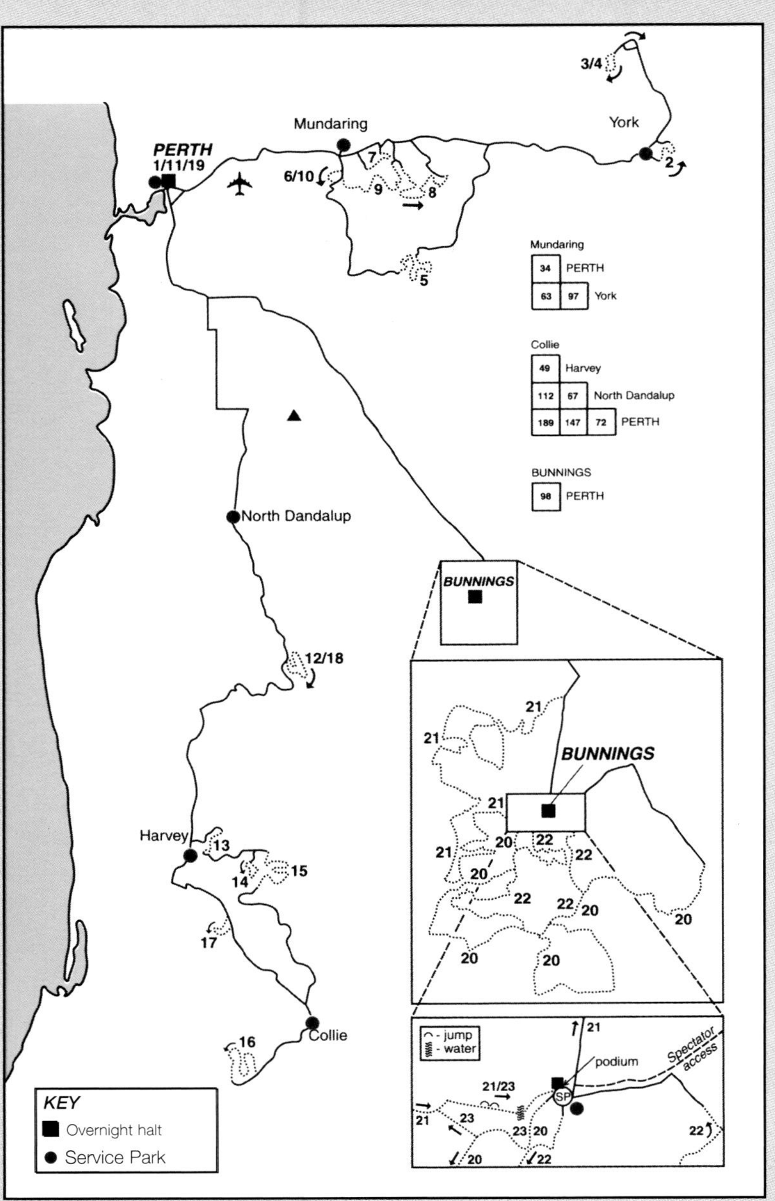

SPECIAL STAGE TIMES

SS.1 Langley Park 1 (2,20 km)
1. McRae 1'35"5 ; 2. Auriol 1'35"9 ; 3. Makinen 1'36" ; 4. Kankkunen 1'36"1 ; 5. Loix 1'36"4 ; Gr.N Taguchi 1'40"9 ; F2 Laukkanen 1'44"1

SS.2 York Railway (5,30 km)
1. Auriol 2'36"8 ; 2. Kankkunen et Rovanpera 2'38"6 ; 4. Makinen et McRae 2'39"1 ; Gr.N Trellss 2'52"4 ; F2 Eriksson 2'53"3

SS.3 Murssk 1 (6,81 km)
1. Auriol 3'28"9 ; 2. McRae 3'30"1 ; 3. Burns et Kankkunen 3'31" ; 5. Makinen 3'31"1 ; Gr.N Arai 3'47"4 ; F2 Eriksson 3'50"2

SS.4 Murssk 2 (6,81 km)
1. Auriol 3'25"3 ; 2. McRae 3'26" ; 3. Sainz 3'27"1 ; 4. Burns 3'27"4 ; 5. Kankkunen 3'28"2; Gr.N Taguchi 3'44"2 ; F2 Eriksson 3'45"8

SS.5 Beraking (28,59 km)
1. Makinen 15'54"2 ; 2. McRae 15'54"5 ; 3. Auriol 15'55"6 ; 4. Sainz 16'00"7 ; 5. Burns 16'01"9 ; Gr.N Al Wahaibi 17'11"8 ; F2 Eriksson 17'24"8

SS.6 Atkins 1 (4,42 km)
1. Burns 3'00"9 ; 2. Sainz et McRae 3'01"2 ; 4. Makinen 3'01"9 ; 5. Gardemeister 3'05"2 ; Gr.N Nittel 3'13"1 ; F2 Laukkanen 3'16"1

SS.7 Kevs (10,18 km)
1. McRae 5'48"4 ; 2. Sainz 5'49"7 ; 3. Burns 5'51"5 ; 4. Makinen 5'52"8 ; 5. Gardemeister 5'55"4 ; Gr.N Taguchi 6'15"6 ; F2 Eriksson 6'20"7

SS.8 Flynns (34,01 km)
1. Burns 20' ; 2. Sainz 20'01"8 ; 3. Makinen 20'02"2 ; 4. McRae 20'12"6 ; 5. Loix 20'28"3 ; Gr.N Taguchi 21'32"6 ; F2 Eriksson 21'33"7

SS.9 Helena (30,05 km)
1. Sainz 16'36"9 ; 2. Burns 16'41"5 ; 3. Rovanpera 16'55"6 ; 4. Gardemeister 16'59" ; 5. Loix 17'01"6 ; Gr.N Nittel 18'18"3 ; F2 Eriksson 18'06"4

SS.10 Atkins 2 (4,42 km)
1. Sainz 2'58"5 ; 2. McRae 2'59"7 ; 3. Burns 2'59"8 ; 4. Makinen 3'00"2 ; 5. Gardemeister 3'02"6 ; Gr.N Taguchi 3'12" ; F2 Eriksson 3'13"7

SS.11 Langley Park 2 (2,20 km)
1. Sainz 1'36" ; 2. McRae 1'36"4 ; 3. Gronholm 1'37"4 ; 4. Burns 1'37"5 ; 5. Radstrom et Batss 1'37"7 ; Gr.N Arai 1'40"9 ; F2 McRae 1'45"3

SS.12 Murray Pinss 1 (18,53 km)
1. Burns 10'56"2 ; 2. Makinen 10'59"2 ; 3. Sainz 11'03"9 ; 4. Gronholm 11'07"6 ; 5. Rovanpera 11'10" ; Gr.N Ordynski 11'46"9 ; F2 Laukkanen 11'38"1

SS.13 Harvey Weir (8,19 km)
1. Burns 4'47"5 ; 2. Sainz 4'52"2 ; 3. Makinen 4'55" ; 4. Rovanpera 4'55"9 ; 5. Gardemeister 4'58"9 ; Gr.N Ordynski 5'10"6 ; F2 Laukkanen 5'10"7

SS.14 Stirling Wsst (15,89 km)
1. Burns 9'37"5 ; 2. Sainz 9'39"6 ; 3. Makinen 9'43"5 ; 4. Gronholm 9'47"4 ; 5. Rovanpera 9'48"8 ; Gr.N Ordynski 10'13"5 ; F2 Laukkanen 10'15"7

SS.15 Stirling East (35,48 km)
1. Sainz 19'58" ; 2. Burns 20'05" ; 3. Makinen 20'15"8 ; 4. Rovanpera 20'36"1 ; 5. Gronholm 20'42" ; Gr.N Ordynski 21'32"8 ; F2 Laukkanen 21'21"

SS.16 Wellington Dam (45,42 km)
1. Burns 25'40"8 ; 2. Sainz 25'45"2 ; 3. Makinen 26'18"8 ; 4. Gronholm 26'25"3 ; 5. Radstrom 26'39"3 ; Gr.N Taguchi 27'48"1 ; F2 Laukkanen 27'24"5

SS.17 Brunswick (16,63 km)
1. Sainz et Burns 9'14"6 ; 3. Makinen 9'25"9 ; 4. Gronholm 9'27"3 ; 5. Loix 9'28"2 ; Gr.N Ordynski 10'03"5 ; F2 Laukkanen 9'57"2

SS.18 Murray Pinss 2 (18,53 km)
1. Sainz 10'49"2 ; 2. Burns 10'50"2 ; 3. Makinen 11'00"3 ; 4. Gronholm 11'02"7 ; 5. Loix 11'06"5; Gr.N Nittel 11'47"3 ; F2 Laukkanen 11'31"3

SS.19 Langley Park 3 (2,20 km)
1. Sainz 1'36"4 ; 2. Burns 1'36"6 ; 3. Gronholm 1'37"1 ; 4. Makinen 1'38" ; 5. Loix 1'38"6 ; Gr.N Nittel 1'41"7 ; F2 McRae 1'46"4

SS.20 Bunnings Wsst (35,29 km)
1. Sainz 17'38"6 ; 2. Burns 17'42" ; 3. Rovanpera 18'08"5 ; 4. Radstrom 18'13"2 ; 5. Gronholm 18'14"4 ; Gr.N Arai 19'19"1 ; F2 Rowe 19'18"4

SS.21 Bunnings North (36,84 km)
1. Burns 19'47"9 ; 2. Sainz 19'58"7 ; 3. Rovanpera 20'14"4 ; 4. Gronholm 20'17"8 ; 5. Makinen 20'19"5 ; Gr.N Arai 21'48"9 ; F2 Eriksson 22'02"2

SS.22 Bunnings South (25,16 km)
1. Sainz 15'09"2 ; 2. Burns 15'09"3 ; 3. Gronholm 15'23" ; 4. Rovanpera 15'31"6 ; 5. Loix 15'37"3 ; Gr.N Ordynski 16'27"9 ; F2 Eriksson 16'32"4

SS.23 Michelin TV Stage (2,73 km)
1. Sainz 1'36"1 ; 2. Burns 1'36"2 ; 3. Radstrom 1'38"1 ; 4. Gronholm 1'38"3 ; 5. Loix 1'41" ; Gr.N Nittel 1'44" ; F2 Higgins 1'47"7

RESULTS AND RETIREMENTS

	Driver/Co-Driver	Car	Gr	Total Time
1	**Richard Burns – Robert Reid**	**Subaru Impreza WRC**	**A**	**3h44m31,5s**
2	Carlos Sainz – Luis Moya	Toyota Corolla WRC	A	3h44m43,1s
3	Tommi Makinen – Risto Mannisenmaki	Mitsubishi Lancer Ev.6	A	3h49m02,9s
4	Freddy Loix – Sven Smeets	Mitsubishi Carisma GT	A	3h52m04s
5	Marcus Gronholm – Timo Rautiainen	Peugeot 206 WRC	A	3h52m33,4s
6	Harri Rovanpera – Risto Pietilainen	Seat Cordoba WRC	A	3h52m44,3s
7	Thomas Radstrom – Fred Gallagher	Ford Focus WRC	A	3h53m01,1s
8	**Toshihiro Arai – Roger Freeman**	**Subaru Impreza**	**N**	**4h05m49,8s**
9	**Kenneth Eriksson – Staffan Parmander**	**Hyundai Coupe Ev.2**	**A**	**4h05m58,4s**
10	Martin Rowe – Derek Ringer	Renault Megane Maxi	A	4h06m29,1s
SS.2	Possum Bourne – Graig Vincent	Subaru Impreza WRC	A	Driving belt
SS.5	Juha Kankkunen – Juha Repo	Subaru Impreza WRC	A	Accident
SS.6	Didier Auriol – Denis Giraudet	Toyota Corolla WRC	A	Engine
SS.7	Hamed Al Wahaibi – Tony Sircombe	Mitsubishi Lancer Ev.6	N	Accident
SS.8	Gustavo Trelles – Martin Christie	Mitsubishi Lancer Ev.6	N	Accident
SS.8	Frederic Dor – Didier Breton	Subaru Impreza WRC	A	Turbo
SS.11	François Delecour – Daniel Grataloup	Peugeot 206 WRC	A	Gearbox
SS.12	Colin McRae – Nicky Grist	Ford Focus WRC	A	Accident
SS.15	Yoshihiro Kataoka – Satoshi Hayashi	Mitsubishi Lancer Ev.6	A	Accident
SS.16	Neal Bates – Coral Taylor	Toyota Corolla WRC	A	Accident

EVENT LEADERS

SS.1	McRae
SS.2 – SS.5	Auriol
SS.6 – SS.7	McRae
SS.8	Makinen
SS.9 – SS.11	Sainz
SS.12 – SS.23	Burns

BEST PERFORMANCES

	1	2	3	4	5	6
Sainz	10	7	1	1	-	2
Burns	8	7	3	2	1	-
Auriol	3	1	1 -	-	-	
McRae	2	5	1	1	1	-
Makinen	1	1	8	5	3	2
Rovanpera	-	1	3	2	4	5
Kankkunen	-	1	1	1	1	-
Gronholm	-	-	3	7	2	4
Radstrom	-	-	1	1	2	4
Loix	-	-	-	1	6	2
Gardemeister	-	-	-	1	4	3
Bates	-	-	-	-	1	-
Delecour	-	-	-	-	-	1

GOSSIP

• DOR JAM.

Delecour and Gronholm drew the short straw when it came to the starting order. On the first leg, they lost huge amounts of time in the dust of Frederic Dor, a pleasant enough gentleman driver, slowed by a broken turbo. It was hard to swallow. But the Peugeots were never in the running for a win. Gronholm had to fight hard for fifth place and Delecour retired with a shrapnelled gearbox.

• HAGSTROM INJURED.

The Finn Pasi Hagstrom, driver of the third Toyota did not make the start. He broke a leg on the recce, when he had an unfortunate encounter with a forest vehicle. With a damaged joint he could be out for three months.

• BACK TO THE USA.

A very official rally will be organised in June in Colorado. It could soon be brought into the world championship programme.

• THIRY WITH SKODA.

Bruno Thiry carried out his first test session in the Skoda Octavia WRC which he was to drive on the RAC. He said he was pleasantly surprised by the car, apart from the lack of power at low revs.

• THE RETURN OF NITTEL.

Uwe Nittel, nicknamed minitel (because he was recruited via the minitel system) made a discrete return to the fray. The former team mate of Makinen (of course) was driving a Group N Mitsu with which he finished twelfth. Despite retiring after an accident, Gustavo Trelles took the title from Al Wahaibi.

• RENAULT ON A HIGH.

Despite a win for Kenneth Eriksson, Hyundai could not be sure of the two litre title which was slipping from their grasp. Renault had gone to the bother of entering the Englishman Rowe to limit the damage. Hyundai now had to finish first and second on the RAC which would be no easy task.

CHAMPIONSHIP CLASSIFICATIONS

Drivers

1. Tommi Makinen World Champion	62
2. Didier Auriol	52
3. Richard Burns	45
4. Carlos Sainz	44
5. Juha Kankkunen	38

Constructors

1. Toyota World Champion	109
2. Subaru	89
3. Mitsubishi	81
4. Ford	36
5. Seat	19

Group N

1. Gustavo Trelles Cup Winner	69
2. Hamed Al Wahaibi	53
3. Toshihiro Arai	29

Two Litres

1. Renault	102
2. Hyundai	88

Team's Cup

1. Toyota Mobil Team Turkey Volkan Isik	46
2. Valencia Terra Mar Team Luis Climent	40
2. F.Dor Rally Team Frederic Dor	40

PREVIOUS WINNERS

1989	Kankkunen - Piironen Toyota Celica GT-Four
1990	Kankkunen - Piironen Lancia Delta Integrale
1991	Kankkunen - Piironen Lancia Delta Integrale
1992	Auriol - Occelli Lancia Delta HF Integrale
1993	Kankkunen - Grist Toyota Celica Turbo 4WD
1994	McRae - Ringer Subaru Impreza
1995	Eriksson - Parmander Mitsubishi Lancer Ev.2
1996	Makinen - Harjanne Mitsubishi Lancer Ev.3
1997	McRae - Grist Subaru Impreza WRC
1998	Makinen - Mannisenmaki Mitsubishi Lancer Ev.5

"Those slimy autumnal tracks..."

GREAT BRITAIN

It had all been announced as a fait accomplis. Richard Burns and Colin McRae were on home turf and no one else was going to get a look in. It turned out to be half true, because Colin McRae is going through a phase of destroying every car that passes through his bare hands. But Richard the Lionheart was true to his word. He crushed the RAC, splashing his rivals with his latent talent. The Burns- Subaru-Pirelli triumvirate was almost unbeatable. It was a shame that Marcus Gronholm, who went

off the road, and Francois Delecour, who was once again let down by his gearbox, were not able to capitalise on the promise shown by the Peugeots.

152.1

152.1
The Peugeot drivers, Marcus Gronholm and Francois Delecour were the only ones to mount a challenge to the Subarus.

152.2
At his second attempt on this event, Martin Brundle was partnered by the veteran Arne Hertz, but he posted yet another retirement.

"It was a bit touch and go at times, but you have to take luck when it comes your way. This third one-two finish really makes us very happy. Richard really drove a fantastic rally."

David Richards

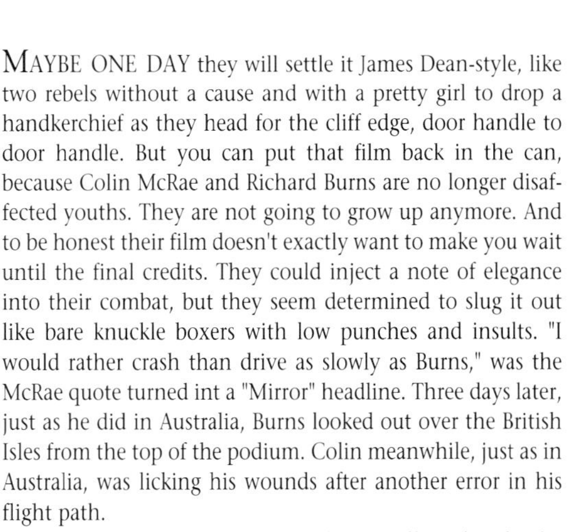

MAYBE ONE DAY they will settle it James Dean-style, like two rebels without a cause and with a pretty girl to drop a handkerchief as they head for the cliff edge, door handle to door handle. But you can put that film back in the can, because Colin McRae and Richard Burns are no longer disaffected youths. They are not going to grow up anymore. And to be honest their film doesn't exactly want to make you wait until the final credits. They could inject a note of elegance into their combat, but they seem determined to slug it out like bare knuckle boxers with low punches and insults. "I would rather crash than drive as slowly as Burns," was the McRae quote turned int a "Mirror" headline. Three days later, just as he did in Australia, Burns looked out over the British Isles from the top of the podium. Colin meanwhile, just as in Australia, was licking his wounds after another error in his flight path.

Burns had every right to feel proud and puff out his slender chest like a bullfrog, because the manner of his winning bordered on insolence. He wiped the forest roads with the opposition winning no less than twelve of the twenty two stages! It was not as easy as it looked however. Burns had the advantage of the Subaru- Pirelli combo, which proved very efficient at dealing with the slimy autumnal tracks, but he had to fight off Makinen sometimes, Kankkunen occasionally and Gronholm and Delecour almost all the time.

On the opening day and its traditional run through the parks and stately homes of England, which open their golden portals to get in some much needed cash to repair their leaky roofs, the eventual winner had opted to sit back from the action. "It is too easy to lose this rally right at the start and anyway, this is not where it is won," he explained. His team-mate, the unpredictable Juha Kankkunen was more in the mood, setting several fastest times, his cigarillo never far from his lips. "I'm having fun. I've got nothing to prove, so I am enjoying myself," was his justification. The Peugeots of Marcus Gronholm and Francois Delecour were "agile and easy" according to both of them, who soon got stuck into the fight for the lead. It was good publicity, but it would not go the distance. The most surprising aspect of this first day was how many top flight drivers dinged their cars, despite claiming they were taking it steady. It was proof that the winding park roads, as well as the spaghetti map round Cheltenham racecourse and the Silverstone circuit were tricky and treacherous. The bodywork experts in all the teams took consolation that the Mickey Mouse day would soon be a thing of the past. As from next year, the RAC would finally abandon this out-dated tradition. Kankkunen topped the time sheet at the end of it, but with only nine percent of the stage distance covered, it did not mean much.

Finally, on Monday, the circus headed for the hills and valleys of Wales, where the real battle could commence. From the start, Burns showed what he had in mind. He took the lead, which he would maintain right to the end. There was one heart-stopping moment, shortly after he had set three fastest times on the trot, which caused the carrot topped racer to think it might be all over. The Subaru was smoking; worse still it was on fire and the extinguisher had to be called into play. Could it be the turbo? Luckily no, it was a simple oil fire, caused by a tiny hole in the filter and the driver could breathe a sigh of relief. Some sharp object had outwitted the sump guard's defences, but it was easily fixed and Burns was never troubled again. Because, behind him, the errors were coming in thick and fast, forcing some of his rivals out of the event and others to the back of the order. First of all, Tommi Makinen hit a fence post, just as he did the previous year on his way to the title, demolishing the rear suspension. Then, inevitably, it was the turn of Colin McCrash, hitting a tree in a service area. "There were only three trees there and I had to hit one of them," before another off in the last stage of the day. Carlos Sainz was very embarrassed with his beginner's error. Trying to take the safe line round a hairpin, he fell in the ditch "at 5 km/h." Then Didier Auriol had a straight-on moment caused naturally, by " a bad tyre choice." Only Francois Delecour had a legitimate excuse. The gearbox, yet again the ruddy gearbox had let him down. Maybe the design of this transverse unit is to blame. Maybe its constructor, X-trac, has not done its job properly. Whatever, it is certainly Peugeot's Achilles Heel. "When we have fixed it we will win a lot of rallies," says Delecour. According to Gronholm's engineer, the mechanics changed part or all of the gearbox no less than fourteen times during a week's testing in Wales. Jean-Pierre Nicolas, who is not in the habit of disguising the truth said: "It is nearer to five actually, but even five is too many." Peugeot's hopes of winning the title in 2000 are currently in jeopardy.

On the final day, the rally moved to the less scenic industrial and coal mining area of South Wales and the battle got even tougher. Not for Richard Burns; still leading and still making it look easy. "The joy of winning overcomes any problems," he would pontificate later. Behind him there was a chorus of "Ten Green Bottles." Marcus Flying Gronholm, who reminds many people of Ari Vatanen, because of his speed on the

Renault won the 2 litre world cup, thanks to excellent work from the privateer teams using the Megane Kit Car.

stages and the speed with which he flies off them, was true to his reputation, going straight on at a forest corner. "I ended up seventy metres down a hill," he said. A BBC man who had witnessed the incident expressed what everyone was thinking. He put his arm round Gronholm, when he was back in the service area: "It's surprising to see you hear looking okay." Francois Delecour was still on track, literally and figuratively. He had his sleeves rolled up and was passing cars in rapid succession, to get the nose of the 206 into fourth spot. It was all the more impressive as that gearbox was still giving trouble. It is not easy to drive a car with a gearbox threatening to lock up and throw you into the scenery at any moment. There was only one stage left, but very few top guns were still in the running. Sainz, Auriol and Schwarz all had accidents, while Makinen and Evans suffered broken engines. Only four kilometres remaining and the forests were left behind. The final scene was played out in the relative safety of Margam park, but it was enough to do for Delecour's gearbox. The Frenchman was left to dream of what might have been. It was too unfair.

BRUNDLE BREAKS. The last time he tried was back in 1996 and his rally ended in a snowy mess with flames licking around his Escort for good measure. "I had tackled the event like a grand prix, always pushing it further and faster and the way it ended was pretty much inevitable," he recalled. Former grand prix star and now TV commentator, could not let the RAC escape him this way. It is not his style. So he tried again this year. "I miss not driving full time," he admitted. Given his media appeal, it was not too hard for Brundle to get his hands on a decent car. In the end it was Toyota who lent him a car; a full works Corolla, which shared its parking bay with the similar mounts of Didier Auriol and Carlos Sainz. It was in return for a favour. "Carlos drove my Toyota GT One (a Le Mans car) last year in Barcelona and he promised, as did Didier, to help me get the most out of the Corolla." The approach was clearly a professional one, which was only to be expected. "I want to finish and if possible in the top forty." Martin could remember having got pretty near the top ten on some of the stages, the first time he tried. For much of the event he met his target, running in the top thirty to forty. But in the dusk on the second day, Martin once again stepped a bit too hard on the loud pedal, mabe suffering from a touch of over-confidence. The result was a smashed in front end and a fatally wounded radiator. The Corolla limped into Builth Wells but got no further. "It is not a problem of speed. I've got that. Rushing round Casino Square in Monaco at 200 km/h teaches you a few things. But in rallying, staying on the road is not as simple as it sounds. The common factor is finding the limit. In rallying, just like in F1, you are always looking for it. Then the hard part is not going over it."

RENAULT CROWNED. How can you be beaten when you have no opposition? Somehow, Hyundai, who entrusted its preparation to the English company MSD, managed it nevertheless. Hyundai was the only manufacturer chasing after the two litre world championship, but it finished behind Renault who just happened to be there. Renault were on 105 points, Hyundai with 98. Only a one-two finish for the Japanese and all the Renaults retiring could change the story of the championship. Thus Renault added its name to that of Peugeot, who had won in the past back in 1995, but without really chasing after this title. All the same, Renault did make sporadic attempts to support the efforts of the teams and importers who dabbled with the Megane.

On the RAC, it was actually Mark Higgins' VW which took the top honours. Tappio Laukkanen led for much of the event, but his car did not re-start after a service point, not for any mechanical reason, but because the team got it wrong. The mechanics had put fuel in the tank in an attempt to coax a recalcitrant fuel pump back into life, but as this is forbidden in the regulations, Renault UK took the decision to withdraw, rather than face exclusion and the negative publicity that could generate. They were not prepared to mess up their title for a false victory.

Next year, there is every chance that the two litre class will disappear from the calendar. FIA would like to see at least four marques involved, but they are dreaming. Even Hyundai wants to switch to four wheel drive. The success of one category has effectively killed off another one. But it is not important. The growth of classes within classes for publicity benefits has always tended to diminish the importance of the main event.

BETWEEN CHAMPIONS. It was like an end of term school outing to reward bright students. The RAC is often a rally reward for national champions who have worked well on their own home patches. This little step up to the big time is a useful move to mark their cards with team managers. Most notable in this group were Tappio Laukkanen, the Finn who won the British championship and the Pole, Krzystof Holowczyc who won the Polish title.

154.1

154.2

154.3

GREAT BRITAIN

"Those slimy autumnal tracks..."

154.1 - 155.2

Set-up difficulties on the Lancer meant that Tommi Makinen was never able to challenge for the lead.

154.2

The Panizzi brothers were on a fact finding mission and they were the only Peugeot crew to finish.

154.3

At the wheel of a Skoda Octavia, Bruno Thiry celebrated his return to the world championship by beating his team-mate and finishing fourth.

155.1

In the absence of his main rivals, the Teams' Cup stayed firmly in the hands of Luis Climent.

155.3

Sparkling form - 12 stage wins - Richard Burns won "his rally" for the second year running.

155.4-5

On the penultimate stage, both Toyotas retired. Didier had an accident and Carlos broke his suspension. Despite winning the constructors' championship in Australia, the TTE team members were extremely disappointed at the way they left the world rally stage.

155.1

155.2

155.3

155.5

55TH RALLY OF GREAT BRITAIN

14th leg of the 1999 world rally championships for constructors and drivers
14th leg of the constructors' "2 litre", production car drivers' and teams'world cups

Date: *21 - 23 November 1999*

Route: *1815,48 km divided into 3 legs, 22 stages on loose surface roads (389,39 km)*
1st leg : Sunday 21st November, Cheltenham - Silverstone - Cheltenham, 7 stages (35,61 km)
2nd leg : Monday 22nd November, Cheltenham - Builth - Cheltenham, 8 stages (156,71 km)
3rd leg : Tuesday 23rd November, Cheltenham - Silverstone - Cheltenham, 7 stages (197,07 km)

Starters/Finishers: *160/90*

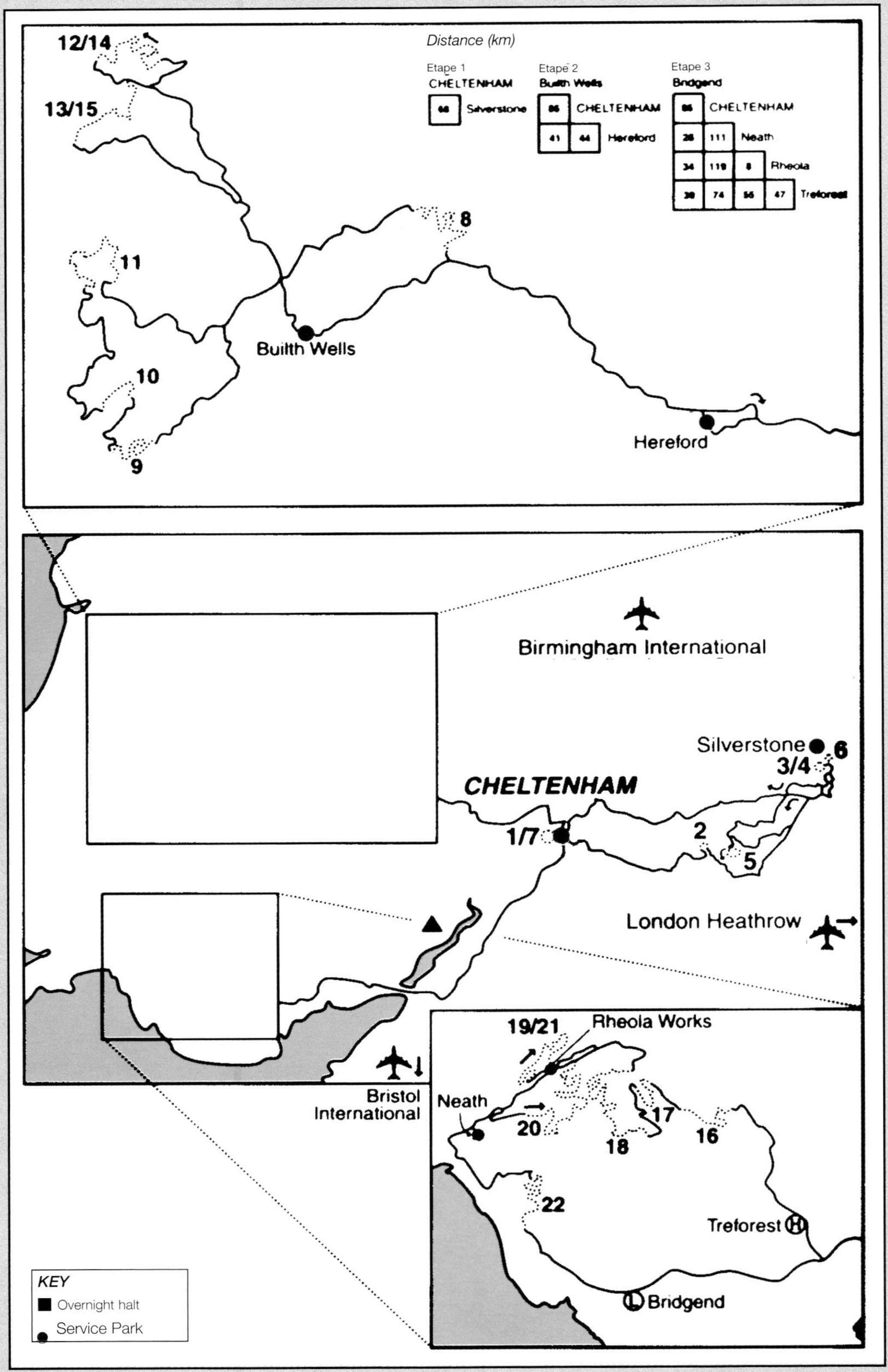

TOP ENTRIES

1 Tommi Makinen – Risto Mannisenmaki
MITSUBISHI LANCER EV.6

2 Freddy Loix - Sven Smeets
MITSUBISHI CARISMA GT

3 Carlos Sainz – Luis Moya
TOYOTA COROLLA WRC

4 Didier Auriol – Denis Giraudet
TOYOTA COROLLA WRC

5 Richard Burns – Robert Reid
SUBARU IMPREZA WRC

6 Juha Kankkunen – Juha Repo
SUBARU IMPREZA WRC

7 Colin McRae – Nicky Grist
FORD FOCUS WRC

8 Thomas Radstrom – Gunnar Barth
FORD FOCUS WRC

9 Harri Rovanpera – Risto Pietilainen
SEAT CORDOBA WRC EV.2

10 Toni Gardemeister – Paavo Lukander
SEAT CORDOBA WRC EV.2

11 Armin Schwarz – Manfred Hiemer
SKODA OCTAVIA WRC

12 Bruno Thiry – Stephane Prevot
SKODA OCTAVIA WRC

14 François Delecour – Daniel Grataloup
PEUGEOT 206 WRC

15 Marcus Gronholm – Timo Rautiainen
PEUGEOT 206 WRC

16 Gwyndaf Evans – Howard Davies
SEAT CORDOBA WRC

17 Markko Martin – Toomas Kitsing
TOYOTA COROLLA WRC

18 Luis Climent – Alex Romani
SUBARU IMPREZA WRC

19 Krzysztof Holowczyc – Jean-Marc Fortin
SUBARU IMPREZA

20 Petter Solberg – Phil Mills
FORD FOCUS WRC

21 Jesus Puras – Marc Marti
TOYOTA COROLLA WRC

22 Gilles Panizzi – Herve Panizzi
PEUGEOT 206 WRC

23 Tapio Laukkanen – Kaj Lindstrom
RENAULT MEGANE MAXI

24 Alister McRae – David Senior
HYUNDAI COUPE EV.2

25 Mark Higgins – Bryan Thomas
VOLKSWAGEN GOLF GTI 16V

26 Kenneth Eriksson – Staffan Parmander
HYUNDAI COUPE EV.2

27 Martin Rowe – Derek Ringer
RENAULT MEGANE MAXI

29 Manfred Stohl – Peter Müller
MITSUBISHI LANCER EV.6

32 Jarmo Kytoletho – Arto Kapanen
VAUXHALL ASTRA KIT CAR

33 Abdullah Bakhashab – Michael Park
TOYOTA COROLLA WRC

42 Matthias Kahle – Dieter Schneppenheim
TOYOTA COROLLA WRC

45 Martin Brundle – Arne Hertz
TOYOTA COROLLA WRC

49 Mark Fisher – Kevin Gormley
SUBARU IMPREZA WRC

63 Pernilla Walfridsson – Ulrika Mattsson
MITSUBISHI LANCER EV.6

SPECIAL STAGE TIMES

SS.1 Cheltenham 1 (1,91 km)

1. Gronholm/Makinen 1'47"4 ; 3. Delecour 1'47"5; 4. Burns 1'47"6 ; 5. Sainz 1'48" ; Gr.N Easson 1'55"; F2 McRae 1'57"9

SS.2 Cornbury (4,17 km)

1. Kankkunen 2'51"8 ; 2. Solberg 2'55"1 ; 3. Gardemeister 2'55"2 ; 4. Delecour 2'55"7 ; 5. Martin 2'56" ; Gr.N Stacey 3'06"7; F2 Higgins 3'14"1

SS.3 Silverstone 1 (10,02 km)

1. Kankkunen 7'31"1 ; 2. Delecour 7'33"4 ; 3. Gronholm 7'33"9 ; 4. Burns 7'34"6 ; 5. Auriol 7'37"8 ; Gr.N Stohl 8'01"3; F2 McRae 8'00"3

SS.4 Silverstone 2 (10,02 km)

1. Kankkunen 7'30"9 ; 2.Burns 7'33"1 ; 3. Delecour 7'33"7 ; 4. Auriol 7'33"8 ; 5. Gronholm 7'35"5 ; Gr.N Stohl 7'57"7; F2 Kytoletho 7'54"1

SS.5 Blenheim (5,62 km)

1. Gronholm 3'56"6 ; 2. Burns 3'57"6 ; 3. McRae 3'58"2 ; 4. Delecour 3'58"3 ; 5. Sainz/Kankkunen 3'58"6 ; Gr.N Stohl 4'21"8 ; F2 Laukkanen 4'24"3

SS.6 Super Spéciale (1,96 km)

1. Burns 1'30"3 ; 2. Makinen 1'30"4 ; 3. Gronholm 1'30"7 ; 4. Thiry 1'30"8 ; 5. Sainz/McRae 1'31"1 ; Gr.N Tuthill 1'37"5; F2 Kytoletho 1'36"9

SS.7 Cheltenham 2 (1,91 km)

1. Makinen 1'43"1 ; 2. Burns/Delecour 1'44" ; 4. Gronholm 1'44"4 ; 5. Sainz 1'45" ; Gr.N D.Higgins 1'54"1; F2 Eriksson 1'51"3

SS.8 Radnor (23,69 km)

1. Burns 11'55"9 ; 2. Kankkunen 12'04"5 ; 3. McRae 12'09"4 ; 4. Gronholm 12'09"8 ; 5. Rovanpera 12'13"9 ; Gr.N Stohl 12'59"3; F2 Laukkanen 13'07"7

SS.9 Crychan (16,89 km)

1. Burns 9'46"7 ; 2. Gronholm 9'52"4 ; 3. Sainz 9'55"6 ; 4. Kankkunen 9'57"8 ; 5. Auriol 9'58"1 ; Gr.N Stohl 10'46'6; F2 Laukkanen 10'41"

SS.10 Esgair Dafydd (8,64 km)

1. Burns 5'18"8 ; 2. Kankkunen 5'20"3 ; 3. Gronholm 5'22" ; 4. Auriol 5'22"3 ; 5. Sainz 5'23"6 ; Gr.N Stohl 5'45"7; F2 Higgins 5'48"2

SS.11 Tywi (22,65 km)

1. Gronholm 14'13"3 ; 2. Kankkunen 14'25"3 ; 3. Burns 14'29"7 ; 4. Evans 14'30"7 ; 5. Rovanpera 14'34"3 ; Gr.N D.Higgins 15'30"7; F2 Higgins 15'18"4

SS.12 Sweet Lamb 1 (25,70 km)

1. Burns 15'56" ; 2. Makinen 16'03"1; 3. Kankkunen 16'03"9 ; 4. Delecour 16'19"3 ; 5. Gronholm 16'19"5 ; Gr.N D.Higgins 18'05"6; F2 Laukkanen 17'55"3

SS.13 Myherin 1 (16,72 km)

1.Burns 10'01" ; 2. McRae 10'04"4 ; 3. Gronholm 10'08"4 ; 4. Kankkunen 10'11"1 ; 5. Delecour 10'14"6 ; Gr.N D.Higgins 11'49"6; F2 Higgins 11'06"5

SS.14 Sweet Lamb 2 (25,70 km)

1. Burns 16'33"3 ; 2. Makinen 16'34"5 ; 3. Kankkunen 16'39" ; 4. McRae 16'39"4 ; 5. Gronholm 16'42"3 ; Gr.N D.Higgins 19'11"3; F2 Laukkanen 18'17"

SS.15 Myherin 2 (16,72 km)

1. Kankkunen 10'27"4 ; 2. Burns 10'30"8 ; 3. Delecour 10'32" ; 4. Gronholm 10'32"3 ; 5. Sainz 10'38"2 ; Gr.N/F2 11'17"2 (Temps forfaitaire)

SS.16 St Gwynno (13,67 km)

1. Sainz 6'49"2 ; 2. Delecour 6'52"3 ; 3. Burns 6'53" ; 4. Gronholm 6'54"1 ; 5. Kankkunen 6'54"3 ; Gr.N Wood 7'41"1 ; F2 Laukkanen 7'16"9

SS.17 Tyle (10,55 km)

1. Burns 5'48"5 ; 2. Gronholm 5'51"4 ; 3. Sainz 5'53"1 ; 4. Delecour 5'53"4 ; 5. Kankkunen 5'54"5 ; Gr.N Ferreyros 6'31"7 ; F2 Laukkanen 6'18"2

SS.18 Rhondda (35,82 km)

1. Burns 20'01"2 ; 2. Kankkunen 20'16"2 ; 3. Gronholm 20'17"8 ; 4. Sainz 20'22"7 ; 5. Delecour 20'36"6 ; Gr.N Tuthill 22'37"5 ; F2 Rowe 21'47"5

SS.19 Rheola 1 (31,47 km)

1. Burns 17'54"2 ; 2. Makinen 18'01"3 ; 3. Delecour 18'03"1 ; 4. Sainz 18'03"6 ; 5. Kankkunen 18'07"1 ; Gr.N Morgan 19'34"4 ; F2 Higgins 19'20"4

SS.20 Resolfen (46,45 km)

1. Burns 25'47" ; 2. Delecour 25'49"5 ; 3. Sainz 25'51"9 ; 4. Rovanpera 26'03"8 ; 5. Kankkunen 26'04"2 ; Gr.N Tuthill 28'26"6 ; F2 Higgins 27'48"

SS.21 Rheola 2 (31,47 km)

1. Kankkunen 18'09"3 ; 2. Delecour 18'21"1 ; 3. Radstrom 18'25" ; 4. Rovanpera 18'25"5 ; 5. Burns 18'28"5 ; Gr.N Ferreyros 19'57"1 ; F2 Higgins 19'34"5

SS.22 Margam (27,64 km)

1. Burns 17'09"8 ; 2. Kankkunen 17'15"9 ; 3. Rovanpera 17'33"8 ; 4. Loix 17'47"7 ; 5. Panizzi 17'57" ; Gr.N Ferreyros 19'44"4 ; F2 Rowe 18'51"4

RESULTS AND RETIREMENTS

	Driver/Co-Driver	Car	Gr	Total Time
1	**Richard Burns - Robert Reid**	**Subaru Impreza WRC**	**A**	**3h53m44,2s**
2	Juha Kankkunen - Juha Repo	Subaru Impreza WRC	A	3h55m31,5s
3	Harri Rovanpera - Risto Pietilainen	Seat Cordoba WRC	A	3h58m39,5s
4	Bruno Thiry - Stephane Prevot	Skoda Octavia WRC	A	4h02m11,7s
5	Freddy Loix - Sven Smeets	Mitsubishi Carisma GT	A	4h03m19,5s
6	Thomas Radstrom - Gunnar Barth	Ford Focus WRC	A	4h03m47,5s
7	Gilles Panizzi - Herve Panizzi	Peugeot 206 WRC	A	4h04m17,8s
8	Markko Martin - Toomas Kitsing	Toyota Corolla WRC	A	4h05m21,5s
9	Petter Solberg - Phil Mills	Ford Focus WRC	A	4h06m54s
10	Matthias Kahle - Dieter Schneppenheim	Toyota Corolla WRC	A	4h08m48,2s
12	**Luis Climent - Alex Romani**	**Subaru Impreza WRC**	**A**	**4h11m57,8s**
15	**Mark Higgins - Bryan Thomas**	**Volkswagen Golf Kit Car**	**A**	**4h15m37s**
22	**Ramon Ferreyros - Gonzalo Saenz**	**Mitsubishi Lancer Ev.5**	**N**	**4h22m27,5s**
SS.11	Alister McRae - David Senior	Hyundai Coupe Ev.2	A	Accident
SS.12	Toni Gardemeister - Paavo Lukander	Seat Cordoba WRC	A	Clutch
SS.13	Martin Brundle - Arne Hertz	Toyota Corolla WRC	A	Accident
SS.15	Colin McRae - Nicky Grist	Ford Focus WRC	A	Accident
SS.19	Armin Schwarz - Manfred Hiemer	Skoda Octavia WRC	A	Accident
SS.19	Marcus Gronholm - Timo Rautiainen	Peugeot 206 WRC	A	Accident
SS.19	Tommi Makinen - Risto Mannisenmaki	Mitsubishi Lancer Ev.6	A	Engine
SS.21	Didier Auriol - Denis Giraudet	Toyota Corolla WRC	A	Accident
SS.21	Carlos Sainz - Luis Moya	Toyota Corolla WRC	A	Suspension
SS.22	François Delecour - Daniel Grataloup	Peugeot 206 WRC	A	Gearbox

GOSSIP

• PANIZZI IS LEARNING

"We could not put him under less pressure," explained his boss Jean-Pierre Nicolas. Gilles Panizzi was under simple orders, to get used to driving on the loose at whatever pace he chose. To be honest, Gilles was not very comfortable, even though he came close to scoring points, thanks to the high number of retirements.

• THIRY IS BACK

Sacked by Subaru, Bruno Thiry had not turned a wheel on the world championship trail since the Tour of Corsica. His comeback, at the wheel of the bulky Skoda was stupefying. When Thiry puts his mind to it, anything is possible. Fourth place owed everything to his talent.

• ROVANPERA AT LAST

Maybe it was the thought of losing his Seat seat which fired him up. Whatever the reason, Rovanpera was finally back on form and at last he managed to get on the podium

• IT'S PERU

In the absence of Uruguay's Gustavo Trelles and Hamed Said Al-Wahaibi from Oman, the exotic mood continued in Group N, with victory going to Ramon Ferreyros from Peru. Truly rallying is a global sport!

• RICHARDS GETS RICH

David Richards, co-owner of the Prodrive business which prepares the Subarus sold 49 percent of his company. It is reckoned he will use the funding to return to Formula 1.

• LESSONS

The English pull most of the strings in rallying these days, but they should not be so free with their criticism of the organisational shortcomings of the Monte, Corsica, Argentina or Portugal. The second part of the second leg of the rally witnessed the biggest traffic jam in the history of the sport, which meant that only ten competitors managed to get to stage fifteen.

EVENT LEADERS

SS.1	Makinen
	Gronholm
SS.2 - SS.7	Kankkunen
SS.8 - SS.22	Burns

BEST PERFORMANCES

	1	2	3	4	5	6
Burns	12	4	2	2	1	-
Kankkunen	5	4	2	2	5	2
Gronholm	3	2	5	4	3	-
Makinen	2	4	-	-	-	2
Sainz	1	-	3	2	6	2
Delecour	-	4	4	5	2	1
McRae	-	1	2	1	1	4
Solberg	-	1	-	-	-	1
Rovanpera	-	-	1	2	2	3
Gardemeister	-	-	1	-	-	2
Radstrom	-	-	1	-	-	-
Auriol	-	-	-	2	2	3
Thiry	-	-	-	1	-	1

CHAMPIONSHIP CLASSIFICATIONS

Drivers	
1. Tommi Makinen	**62**
2. Richard Burns	55
3. Didier Auriol	52
4. Juha Kankkunen	44
4. Carlos Sainz	44
Constructors	
1. Toyota	**109**
2. Subaru	105
3. Mitsubishi	83
4. Ford	37
5. Seat	23
Group N	
1. Gustavo Trelles	**69**
2. Hamed Al Wahaibi	53
3. Toshihiro Arai	29
Two Litres	
1. Renault	**105**
2. Hyundai	98
Team's Cup	
1. Valencia Terra Mar Team Luis Climent	**50**
2. Toyota Mobil Team Turkey Volkan Isik	46
3. F.Dor Rally Team Frederic Dor	40

PREVIOUS WINNERS

1974	Makinen - Liddon Ford Escort RS 1600
1975	Makinen - Liddon Ford Escort RS
1976	Clark - Pegg Ford Escort RS
1977	Waldegaard - Thorszelius Ford Escort RS
1978	Mikkola - Hertz Ford Escort RS
1979	Mikkola - Hertz Ford Escort RS
1980	Toivonen - White Talbot Sunbeam Lotus
1981	Mikkola - Hertz Audi Quattro
1982	Mikkola - Hertz Audi Quattro
1983	Blomqvist - Cederberg Audi Quattro
1984	Vatanen - Harryman Peugeot 205 T16
1985	Toivonen - Wilson Lancia Delta S4
1986	Salonen - Harjanne Peugeot 205 T16
1987	Kankkunen - Piironen Lancia Delta HF
1988	Alen - Kivimaki Lancia Delta Integrale
1989	Airikkala - McNamee Mitsubishi Galant VR4
1990	Sainz - Moya Toyota Celica GT-Four
1991	Kankkunen - Piironen Lanica Delta Integrale
1992	Sainz - Moya Toyota Celica Turbo 4WD
1993	Kankkunen - Piironen Toyota Celica Turbo 4WD
1994	McRae - Ringer Subaru Impreza
1995	McRae - Ringer Subaru Impreza
1996	Schwarz - Giraudet Toyota Celica GT-Four
1997	McRae - Grist Subaru Impreza WRC
1998	Burns - Reid Mitsubishi Carisma GT

1999 World Championship for Drivers

	DRIVERS	Monte-Carlo	Swedish	Safari	Portugal	Catalunya	France	Argentina	Greece	New Zealand	Finland	China	Italy	Australia	Great Britain	TOTAL
1	Tommi Makinen	10	10	0	2	4	3	3	4	10	2	0	10	4	0	62
2	Richard Burns	0	2	0	3	2	0	6	10	0	6	6	0	10	10	55
3	Didier Auriol	4	3	6	4	0	5	4	0	3	3	10	4	0	0	52
4	Juha Kankkunen	6	1	0	0	1	1	10	0	6	10	3	1	0	6	44
	Carlos Sainz	6	6	4	6	0	5	2	6	1	4	4	0	0	0	44
6	Colin McRae	0	0	10	10	0	3	0	0	0	0	0	0	0	0	23
7	Philippe Bugalski	0	0	0	0	10	10	0	0	0	0	0	0	0	0	20
8	Freddy Loix	0	0	0	0	3	0	0	3	0	0	0	3	3	2	14
9	Harri Rovanpera	0	0	1	0	0	0	0	0	0	2	2	0	1	4	10
10	Jesus Puras	0	0	0	0	0	6	0	0	0	0	0	0	0	0	6
	Gilles Panizzi	0	0	0	0	0	0	0	0	0	0	0	6	0	0	6
	Toni Gardemeister	0	0	0	0	0	0	0	0	0	4	2	0	0	0	6
	Thomas Radstrom	0	4	0	0	0	0	1	0	0	0	0	0	0	1	6
	Bruno Thiry	2	0	0	1	0	0	0	0	0	0	0	0	0	3	6
15	Marcus Gronholm	0	0	0	0	0	0	0	0	0	3	0	0	2	0	5
16	François Delecour	3	0	0	0	0	0	0	0	0	0	0	0	0	0	3
	Ian Duncan	0	0	3	0	0	0	0	0	0	0	0	0	0	0	3
17	Andrea Aghini	0	0	0	0	0	0	0	0	0	0	0	2	0	0	2
	Markko Martin	0	0	0	0	0	0	0	2	0	0	0	0	0	0	2
	Possum Bourne	0	0	0	0	0	0	0	0	2	0	0	0	0	0	2
	Petter Solberg	0	0	2	0	0	0	0	0	0	0	0	0	0	0	2

1999 World Championship for Manufacturers

	MANUFACTURERS	Monte-Carlo	Swedish	Safari	Portugal	Catalunya	France	Argentina	Greece	New Zealand	Finland	China	Italy	Australia	Great Britain	TOTAL
1	TOYOTA	4	9	10	10	10	18	6	6	5	7	14	4	6	0	109
2	SUBARU	7	3	0	3	5	2	16	10	6	16	9	2	10	16	105
3	MITSUBISHI	10	10	0	2	10	6	3	7	11	2	0	13	7	2	83
4	FORD	0	4	13	11	0	6	1	0	0	0	0	1	0	1	37
5	SEAT	5	0	2	0	1	0	0	0	4	4	2	0	1	4	23

REGULATIONS : DRIVERS' CHAMPIONSHIP : All results count. 1 st 10 point, 2 nd 6 point, 3rd 4 points, 4th 3 points, 5th 2 points, 6th 1 point
MANUFACTURERS' CHAMPIONSHIP : To be eligible, the constructors who have registered with FIA, must take part in all the events with a minimum of two cars. The first two cars score the points according to their finishing position. All results are taken into consideration. Points scale is the same as for the drivers.

1999 Production Car Championship for Drivers (Group N)

	DRIVERS	Monte-Carlo	Swedish	Safari	Portugal	Catalunya	France	Argentina	Greece	New Zealand	Finland	China	Italy	Australia	Great Britain	TOTAL
1	Gustavo Trelles	8	1	0	8	5	13	13	0	13	0	8	0	0	(0)	69
2	Hamed Al Wahaibi	0	0	13	0	13	5	0	13	8	0	0	1	0	(0)	53
3	Toshihiro Arai	0	0	0	0	0	0	0	0	3	0	13	0	13	(0)	29
4	Manfred Stohl	0	3	3	0	0	0	0	0	0	5	0	8	0	(0)	27
5	Ramon Ferreyros	0	0	0	3	0	0	0	8	0	0	0	0	(0)	13	24
6	Katsuhiko Taguchi	0	0	0	0	0	0	0	0	5	0	5	0	3	(0)	13
7	Jorge Recalde	0	0	0	0	0	0	8	0	0	0	0	0	0	(0)	8
	Luis Climent	0	0	8	0	0	0	0	0	0	0	0	0	0	(0)	8
	Ed Ordynski	0	0	0	0	0	0	0	0	0	0	0	0	8	(0)	8

REGULATIONS : The classification is based on the total number of rallies minus one. At least one rally outsideEurope has to be entered. Points scored as follows ; 1 st 10, 2nd 6, 3rd 4, 4th 3, 5th 2, 6th 1. The points are added with those scored in the different capacity classes (up to 1300cc ; 1301 – 2000cc, over 2000cc) on the following scale : 1st 3 points, 2nd 2 points, 3rd 1 point. Class points are only attributed to drivers finishing in the top six of the production car classification.

1999 Manufacturers Rally World Cup for 2-Litre car

	MANUFACTURERS	Monte-Carlo	Swedish	Safari	Portugal	Catalunya	France	Argentina	Greece	New Zealand	Finland	China	Italy	Australia	Great Britain	TOTAL
1	RENAULT	16	(3)	(0)	(7)	10	16	10	10	(4)	16	(0)	16	8	(6)	102
2	HYUNDAI	(0)	(0)	10	15	(0)	(0)	(0)	13	16	4	16	(0)	13	7	95

REGULATIONS : in order to score points, the constructor must take part in at least 10 rallies of which two must be outside Europe. The 8 best results count for the final classification. The two best placed cars score points : Scale of points : as for the drivers.

1999 FIA Team's Cup

	TEAMS	Monte-Carlo	Swedish	Safari	Portugal	Catalunya	France	Argentina	Greece	New Zealand	Finland	China	Italy	Australia	Great Britain	TOTAL
1	VALENCIA TERRA MAR TEAM	0	(0)	4	6	10	10	(0)	10	(0)	(0)	(0)	(0)	(0)	10	50
2	TOYOTA MOBIL TEAM TURKEY	0	0	(0)	10	6	(0)	(0)	(0)	(0)	10	10	10	(0)	(0)	46
3	F.DOR RALLY TEAM	0	(0)	10	4	(0)	(0)	10	4	6	6	(0)	(0)	(0)	(0)	40
4	TEAM MITSUBISHI OMAN	0	0	6	0	3	0	(0)	(0)	10	(0)	(0)	(0)	(0)	(0)	19
5	TOYOTA TEAM SAUDI ARABIA	0	0	0	0	4	(0)	(0)	6	(0)	(0)	(0)	6	(0)	(0)	16
6	WINFIELD WORLD R.T.	0	0	0	0	2	0	(0)	(0)	(0)	(0)	6	(0)	(0)	(0)	8

REGULATIONS : To be eligible to score points each team must take part in 7 Cup rallies with at least one outside Europe, with a maximum of 2 cars (Group A or Group N) per team. Only the best placed car can score points according to its position relative to the other cup competitors, on the same scale of points as the FIA world rally championship.

World Championship for Manufacturers

1973 Alpine-Renault
1974 Lancia
1975 Lancia
1976 Lancia
1977 Fiat
1978 Fiat
1979 Ford
1980 Fiat
1981 Talbot
1982 Audi
1983 Lancia
1984 Audi
1985 Peugeot
1986 Peugeot
1987 Lancia
1988 Lancia
1989 Lancia
1990 Lancia
1991 Lancia
1992 Lancia
1993 Toyota
1994 Toyota
1995 Subaru
1996 Subaru
1997 Subaru
1998 Mitsubishi
1999 Toyota

World Championship for Drivers

1977 Sandro Munari (I)
1978 Markku Alen (SF)
1979 Bjorn Waldegaard (S)
1980 Walter Rohrl (D)
1981 Ari Vatanen (SF)
1982 Walter Rohrl (D)
1983 Hannu Mikkola (SF)
1984 Stig Blomqvist (S)
1985 Timo Salonen (SF)
1986 Juha Kankkunen (SF)
1987 Juha Kankkunen (SF)
1988 Miki Biasion (I)
1989 Miki Biasion (I)
1990 Carlos Sainz (E)
1991 Juha Kankkunen (SF)
1992 Carlos Sainz (E)
1993 Juha Kankkunen (SF)
1994 Didier Auriol (F)
1995 Colin McRae (GB)
1996 Tommi Makinen (SF)
1997 Tommi Makinen (SF)
1998 Tommi Makinen (SF)
1999 Tommi Makinen (SF)

1977-1978 : FIA Cup for Drivers

Group N Cup Winners

1987 Alex Fiorio (I)
1988 Pascal Gaban (B)
1989 Alain Oreille (F)
1990 Alain Oreille (F)
1991 Grégoire de Mevius (B)
1992 Grégoire de Mevius (B)
1993 Alex Fassina (I)
1994 Jesus Puras (E)
1995 Rui Madeira (P)
1996 Gustavo Trelles (ROU)
1997 Gustavo Trelles (ROU)
1998 Gustavo Trelles (ROU)
1999 Gustavo Trelles (ROU)

Manufacturers of 2-Litre Cars Cup Winners

1993 General Motors Europe
1994 Skoda
1995 Peugeot
1996 Seat
1997 Seat
1998 Seat
1999 Renault

1995-1996 : World Championship for Manufacturers 2-Litre

Team's Cup

1998 H.F. Grifone
1999 Valencia Terra Mar - Luis Climent

Drivers who have won World Championship Rallies from 1973 to 1999

DRIVER	NO. of wins	RALLIES
Andrea Aghini (I)	1	1992 I
Pentti Airikkala (SF)	1	1989 GB
Markku Alen (SF)	**20**	1975 P 1976 SF 1977 P **1978** P-SF-I 1979 SF 1980 SF 1981 P 1983 F-I 1984 F 1986 I-USA 1987 P-GR-SF 1988 S-SF-GB
Alain Ambrosino (F)	1	1988 CI
Ove Andersson (S)	1	1975 EAK
Jean-Claude Andruet (F)	3	1973 MC 1974 F 1977 I
Didier Auriol (F)	**19**	1988 F 1989 F 1990 MC-F-I 1991 I 1992 MC-F-GR-RA-SF-AUS 1993 MC **1994** F-RA-I 1995 F 1998 E 1999 C
Fulvio Bacchelli (I)	1	1977 NZ
Bernard Beguin (F)	1	1987 F
Miki Biasion (I)	**17**	1986 RA 1987 MC-RA-I **1988** P-EAK-GR-USA-I **1989** MC-P-EAK-GR-I 1990 P-RA 1993 GR
Stig Blomqvist (S)	**11**	1973 S 1977 S 1979 S 1982 S-I 1983 GB **1984** S-GR-NZ-RA-CI
Walter Boyce (CDN)	1	1973 USA
Philippe Bugalski	2	1999 E-F
Richard Burns (GB)	5	1998 EAK-GB 1999 GR-AUS-GB
Ingvar Carlsson (S)	2	1989 S-NZ
Roger Clark (GB)	1	1976 GB
Gianfranco Cunico (I)	1	1993 I
Bernard Darniche (F)	7	1973 MA 1975 F 1977 F 1978 F 1979 MC-F 1981 F
François Delecour (F)	4	1993 P-F-E 1994 MC
Ian Duncan (EAK)	1	1994 EAK
Per Eklund (S)	1	1976 S
Mikael Ericsson (S)	2	1989 RA-SF
Kenneth Eriksson (S)	6	1987 CI 1991 S 1995 S-AUS 1997 S-NZ
Tony Fassina (I)	1	1979 I
Guy Frequelin (F)	1	1981 RA
Sepp Haider (A)	1	1988 NZ
Kyosti Hamalainen (SF)	1	1977 SF
Mats Jonsson (S)	2	1992 S 1993 S
Harry Kallstom (S)	1	1976 GR
Juha Kankkunen (SF)	**23**	1985 EAK-CI **1986** S-GR-NZ **1987** USA-GB 1989 AUS 1990 AUS **1991** EAK-GR-SF-AUS-GB 1992 P **1993** EAK-RA-SF-AUS-GB 1994 P 1999 RA-SF
Anders Kullang (S)	1	1980 S
Piero Liatti (I)	1	1997 MC
Colin McRae (GB)	**18**	1993 NZ 1994 NZ-GB **1995** NZ-GB 1996 GR-I-E 1997 EAK-F-I-AUS-GB 1998 P-F-GR 1999 EAK-P
Timo Makinen (SF)	4	1973 SF-GB 1974 GB 1975 GB
Tommi Makinen (SF)	**19**	1994 SF **1996** S-EAK-RA-SF-AUS **1997** P-E-RA-SF **1998** S-RA-SF-I-AUS **1999** MC-S-NZ-I
Shekhar Mehta (EAK)	5	1973 EAK 1979 EAK 1980 EAK 1981 EAK 1982 EAK
Hannu Mikkola (SF)	**18**	1974 SF 1975 MA-SF 1978 GB 1979 P-NZ-GB-CI 1981 S-GB 1982 SF-GB **1983** S-P-RA-SF 1984 P 1987 EAK
Joaquim Moutinho (P)	1	1986 P
Michele Mouton (F)	4	1981 I 1982 P-GR-BR
Sandro Munari (I)	**7**	1974 I-CDN 1975 MC 1976 MC-P-F **1977** MC
Jean-Pierre Nicolas	5	1973 F 1976 MA 1978 MC-EAK-CI
Alain Oreille (F)	1	1989 CI
Rafaelle Pinto (P)	1	1974 P
Jean Ragnotti (F)	3	1981 MC 1982 F 1985 F
Jorge Recalde (RA)	1	1988 RA
Walter Rohrl (D)	**14**	1975 GR 1978 GR-CDN **1980** MC-P-RA-I **1982** MC-CI 1983 MC-GR-NZ 1984 MC 1985 I
Bruno Saby (F)	2	1986 F 1988 MC-NZ
Carlos Sainz (E)	**22**	**1990** GR-NZ-SF-GB 1991 MC-P-F-NZ-RA **1992** EAK-NZ-E-GB 1994 GR 1995 MC-P-E 1996 RI 1997 GR-RI 1998 MC-NZ
Timo Salonen (SF)	**11**	1977 CDN 1980 NZ 1981 CI **1985** P-GR-NZ-RA-SF 1986 SF-GB 1987 S
Armin Schwarz (D)	1	1991 E
Kenjiro Shinozuka (J)	2	1991 CI 1992 CI
Joginder Singh (EAK)	2	1974 EAK 1976 EAK
Patrick Tauziac (F)	1	1990 CI
Jean-Luc Therier (F)	5	1973 P-GR-I 1974 USA 1980 F
Henri Toivonen (SF)	3	1980 GB 1985 GB 1986 MC
Ari Vatanen (SF)	**10**	1980 GR **1981** GR-BR-SF 1983 EAK 1984 SF-I-GB 1985 MC-S
Bjorn Waldegaard (S)	**16**	1975 S-I 1976 I 1977 EAK-GR-GB 1978 S **1979** GR-CDN 1980 CI 1982 NZ 1983 CI 1984 EAK 1986 EAK-CI 1990 EAK
Achim Warmbold (D)	2	1973 PL-A
Franz Wittmann (A)	1	1987 NZ

A: Austria - AUS: Australia - BR: Brasil - C: China - CDN: Canada - CI: Ivory Coast - E: Spain - EAK : Kenya - F: France - GB: Great Britain - GR: Greece - I: Italy - MA: Marocco MC: Monte-Carlo - NZ: New Zealand - P: Portugal - PL: Poland - RA: Argentina - RI: Indonesia - S: Sweden - SF: Finland - USA : United States of America